Incentives to Work

BAUM

Incentives to Work

**DAVID
MACAROV**

 Jossey-Bass Inc., Publishers
615 Montgomery Street • San Francisco • 1970

INCENTIVES TO WORK
David Macarov

Copyright © 1970 by Jossey-Bass, Inc., Publishers

Copyright under Pan American and
Universal Copyright Conventions

Jossey-Bass, Inc., Publishers
615 Montgomery Street
San Francisco, California 94111

Library of Congress Catalog Card Number 71-110629

Standard Book Number SBN 87589-054-7

Manufactured in the United States of America
Composed and printed by York Composition Company, Inc.
Bound by Chas. H. Bohn & Co., Inc., New York

JACKET DESIGN BY WILLI BAUM, SAN FRANCISCO

FIRST EDITION

Code 7005

THE JOSSEY-BASS BEHAVIORAL SCIENCE SERIES

General Editors

WILLIAM E. HENRY
University of Chicago

NEVITT SANFORD
Wright Institute, Berkeley

Special Adviser in Social Welfare

MARTIN B. LOEB
University of Wisconsin

Preface

The paradox of poverty amidst affluence and of abject need despite constantly improved and broadened social welfare programs is both the starting point and the subject matter of *Incentives to Work*. The paradox was sharpened for me on my return to the United States after some years of living abroad, and the impetus to seek the reason for the incongruity was strengthened by my studies of social policy while at Brandeis University.

Thirty-five million Americans were poor in 1964. Not only were they poor in reference to some esoteric definition—they did not have 22 cents per meal, the amount fixed by the Department of Labor as necessary for the barest subsistence during a temporary emergency period—but obviously the wealth of the country was not being shared with them, nor were welfare payments large enough to lift them out of poverty. The reason for this imbalance is openly and explicitly stated by public and officials alike: If unearned income approaches too close to salaries, people will stop working.

It does not seem to matter that only five million of the poor are working, and only one-half of them work year-round and full-time; or that the great majority of the remainder cannot work because of age, disability, or youth; or that they are discouraged from working as a matter of public policy so they can stay home and take care of their children; or that they cannot find work despite sincere efforts. These facts have no bearing on the attitudes that shape the programs.

So deeply ingrained is this fear of a work disincentive that some of the programs to reduce or eliminate poverty are described in other terms—children's allowances, family allowances, demogrants—and attempt to make payments to the nonpoor as well as the poor, despite the added costs. Yet, the extent to which unearned income does reduce incentive to work, under what circumstances, and among which people have been but little investigated. It seems strange that such a pervasive and influential belief, upon which the entire social welfare system and large parts of the economic and social system are based, has been so little examined. Perhaps the difficulties of incentive research and the expense of mounting long-term experiments account for part of the lack. In addition, however, there seems to be an underlying social need to believe that unearned income will destroy the incentive to work, and hence an unwillingness to examine the question.

Incentives to Work is an attempt to pull together the scattered research and insights which bear upon work incentives and to offer some guidelines for further investigation. It would be naive to believe that research, as such, changes public policy. However, if public policy regarding the poor stands in the way of possibilities for change, perhaps the findings contained in this book can offer some guidance to the perplexed.

Incentives to Work was made possible by a special research fellowship from the Department of Health, Education, and Welfare, and I express my gratitude to the department and specifically to Milton Wittman, who suggested that I apply for the fellowship. Many people have shared with me their thoughts and suggestions concerning incentive research, and I truly regret that space does not permit me to thank each of them by name. However, I do express my appreciation to Robert Morris, Wyatt C. Jones, and Morris S. Schwartz, each of whom contributed substantially to the content of this book. If there is a first among equals, Charles I. Schottland must lead all the others to whom I owe thanks because my interest in income maintenance programs generally, and the guaranteed minimum income specifically, was awakened and nurtured in discussions with him. Each one of these persons has helped to make my book better, but none of them is responsible for its errors, defects, or failings. That responsibility is solely mine.

I record my gratitude to Arthur Michaels and Paul Abrahamson, who made available to me the ideal summer place for reading, thinking, and writing.

It is customary to thank one's wife and children for suffering through dissertation deprivation with thoughtfulness and courage. I would be less than honest if I did not acknowledge that the expressed impatience to return to our home in Jerusalem voiced by my wife, Frieda, and by my children, Varda, Yehudit, Raanan, and Annette, overcame the procrastinating tendencies to which I am more than prone and contributed greatly to the completion of the manuscript. Withal, they were understanding, kind, and helpful, for which I am grateful.

DAVID MACAROV

Jerusalem
January 1970

Contents

Incentives
to Work

Prologue

The existence of a persisting core of poor people within the most affluent nation in the world has been acknowledged by the government of the United States as an anachronism and a challenge. Through its legislative and executive organs, the government has announced its intention to eradicate poverty. Among the methods which have been proposed is that of guaranteeing an annual minimum income to everyone, either through the expansion of existing programs, or the use of new programs.

Each proposal contains certain problems—of paying money to those who are not in need, or not paying enough to those who are in need; of encouraging undesirable side effects; of requiring more staff, or of being suddenly overstaffed; of linking services too closely to payments, or not closely enough. No problem is more ubiquitous, however, than that of the presumed effect of an annual

minimum income on incentive to work. Throughout the planning
of each program, the fear of a work disincentive is always present,
if not given primacy. Work incentives, in turn, are seen as linked
to the aggregate economy, to certain sectors of the economy, to the
self-images and mental health of those whose incentives would
presumably be affected, and, indeed, to the basic ideology of the
nation.

There seems to be general agreement that the guarantee
of a subsistence-level income would severely and adversely affect
the work incentives of all those whose income is presently below,
or at the level of, such a guarantee. In addition, there seems to be
some fear, if not belief, that persons receiving an income guarantee
would then be so satisfied with it and with their life conditions
that they would have no incentive to work at all, even for salaries
higher than their guarantee. The idea of a group of employable
persons being assured their living even if they do not work seems
to arouse fear in some quarters—fear for the productivity of the
economy, for the moral fiber of the recipients, and for the historical
authenticity of the American experience. Coupled with this fear
is a passionate anger, out of all proportion to the number of people
concerned or to the probable effect of a guaranteed income on the
economy. This anger is expressed through articles bearing titles
such as "Paying People Not to Work"; in polemic letters to editors;
in radio talk programs; in Congressional hearings; and in other
discussions of the poverty problem.

Indeed, the proposals made by President Nixon in August
1969 for changes in the welfare system were specifically based upon
a fear that America might become "a welfare state that undermines the incentive of the working man." As a consequence of this
fear, the proposed basic allowance for a family of four is $1,600,
which is approximately one-half of the amount estimated as
needed for subsistence by such a family, based upon the Department of Labor's 1964 temporary and emergency food budget.

Opinions that a subsistence income guarantee would have
little or mixed effects, or would even result in positive work incentives, have few proponents. Yet, only isolated studies of the
question exist, and no experiments have been completed which
would test the actual effects of unearned income under the con-

ditions that would presumably prevail with an income guarantee at an actual subsistence level.

At this writing, the University of Wisconsin's Institute on Research on Poverty—in conjunction with Mathematica, a New Jersey research organization—has undertaken an experimental study in which several variants of a negative tax scheme will be administered on a sample basis over a three-year period (Watts, 1968). As useful as the results of such experiments will undoubtedly be, they will not answer all of the questions concerning the long-term effects of non-time-limited unearned income that prohibits the receipt of earned income (or uses it as an offset) and is paid as of right through impersonal means.

Consequently, this book is an examination of the evidence currently available on the effect of unearned income on incentives to work, and an exploration of some of the social-psychological reasons that account for the intensity of feeling with which the presumed disincentive effect of a subsistence income guarantee is viewed by the general public. The framework within which this study is cast is that of the proposed guaranteed minimum income, at a level which provides a subsistence existence, and the population which it examines comprises the people who would be affected by such a guarantee.

Chapter One examines the concept of a guaranteed minimum income, and notes the concern with an incentive effect which such a proposal elicits. Chapter Two examines methods of drawing the poverty line and the impact that views of poverty have on such methods, and identifies the operational definition of poverty used in this study. Using this criterion of poverty, Chapter Three delineates, insofar as the data permit, who and where the poor are. As a preliminary to examining the work incentives of the poor, Chapter Four discusses the American work ethic generally, and Chapter Five explores the assumption that the poor do not share, or do not share fully, in this work ethic because of the existence of a culture or subculture of poverty.

Turning to the actual evidence concerning incentives and disincentives, Chapter Six discusses some of the problems which beset all research, but are accentuated when dealing with questions

of poverty and incentive. Chapter Seven outlines the findings
which can be derived from studies of incentive generally, and the
next three chapters analyze the evidence within existing programs
of AFDC and General Assistance, of disability payments, and of
unemployment insurance respectively.

Chapter Eleven is in the nature of an exploration, examining
the effect of a disincentive factor if one were to arise as a result
of an income guarantee. Chapter Twelve points out some of the
research needed on work incentives; the problems involved in
doing such research; and some factors which need to be considered.
The Thirteenth and final chapter is, as final chapters are wont to
be, a summing up and drawing of conclusions.

Since no research is bias-free, the researcher owes it to himself to try to understand his own biases, and to try to guard against
letting them influence his findings. He also owes it to his audience to
acknowledge his bias before them, so that they can be guided in
reading his study; and, in addition, to share with them the change
in his beliefs that resulted from engaging in the study.

Consequently, let me acknowledge that I believe passion-
ately that poverty—life below a level of subsistence, let alone
decency—can and should be completely eliminated in the United
States, no matter what the cost or the obstacles. Further, thirty years
of experience with insurance-type programs, categorical programs,
counseling programs, training programs, and other such devices
indicate to me that the only way to eradicate poverty is to give
money to the people who need it—on no other basis and for no
other reason than that they need it. I happen to believe that such
a program would have very positive results for the economy, for
the social structure, and for specific problems such as slums or
mental illness. This is not, however, of the essence: I believe that
poverty should be eliminated simply because it should not exist.

This study was begun with the intention of examining the
evidence concerning the effect of unearned income on incentives
to work within the framework of a guaranteed minimum income,
regardless of the author's bias. However, as the study progressed,
the professional literature, the experimental findings, as well as
public expressions were examined, it became clear that the "facts"
were only a part of the total picture, and perhaps a minor part;

the "feelings" (which are also facts)' were surprising in their intensity and in their irrationality, but mostly in the malevolence which they directed toward the poor. Consequently, it became a subtheme of this study to seek for an explanation for such attitudes toward the poor, and especially toward their assumed disinclination to work.

1

Guaranteed
Minimum Income

*P*overty and governmental efforts
to prevent its existence and to alleviate its effects are coeval with
the establishment of America. Some of the original colonies, like
Georgia, were first settled by debtors taken from English prisons,
to whom the threat of poverty was a well-remembered and ever-
present danger. Other colonies required groups of would-be immigrants to guarantee that their members would not become public
charges. Thus, the first group of Jews who wanted to settle in New
Amsterdam were required to give the so-called Stuyvesant Pledge
that they would take care of their own. These early beginnings of

the American fear of people who may prove to be unproductive and become a burden on others have been depicted, albeit facetiously, thus (Hansen, 1952):

> Whenever a vessel anchored in the James River and a few score weary and emaciated gentlemen, worn out by three months upon the Atlantic, stumbled up the bank, the veterans who had survived nature's vigorous "seasoning" looked at one another in despair and asked, "Who is to feed them? Who is to teach them to fight the Indians and grow tobacco, or clear the marshy land and build a home in the malaria-infested swamps? These immigrants certainly are a problem [p. 493]."

Some colonies established what today would be called "income maintenance programs" on a categorical basis, as when Plymouth ruled in 1636 that any soldier injured in defense of the colony "shall be maintained competently by the Colony during his life."

It seems that in their efforts to deal with poverty the colonists were basically imbued with the spirit of the Elizabethan Poor Law and the Law of Charitable Uses of 1603, which they brought with them. These laws assigned to government only the most residual social welfare functions. Later, the "life, liberty, and pursuit of happiness" clause of the Declaration of Independence and the "general welfare" clause of the Constitution were also not intended to put the government into the social welfare business.

Nevertheless, the establishment of a governmental system of free, universal, and compulsory education was a step of enormous significance for social welfare, as were homestead grants, mechanics lien laws, homestead exemptions from bankruptcy, income-tax deductions for dependents and for philanthropic contributions, farm supports, and legislation supporting union activity. In the arena of more direct action, "outdoor relief" from government sources and "indoor relief" maintained and operated by towns date from the middle of the seventeenth century, whereas the first full-time paid welfare workers in America date back to the employment of Special Relief Agents by the government during the Civil War.

Although these steps were taken, social welfare activities on the part of the government were usually obscured both in fact and in the public mind by the activity of private voluntary agencies.

The paid agents of the Charity Organization Societies, the crusading reformers like Dorothea Dix, and later, in the 1930s, the members of the four professional social work organizations (plus the two-thirds of the profession who were not members of any of these associations) caused social welfare to be generally equated in the public mind with voluntary associations and trained social workers, whereas governmental activities were seen as supplementing private voluntary efforts through the routine work of civil service employees.

With the advent of the Depression, however, governmental participation in social welfare was the only possible appropriate reaction to the magnitude of the problem, and the Social Security Act of 1935 was one of the first results. The provisions of that Act established the basic structure and philosophy of governmental social welfare activities in the United States until today. The Social Security Act established insurance-type programs in which benefits are paid out in response to a specific situation (for example, retirement, unemployment) and are funded through payroll taxes, and categorical programs in which benefits are paid out from general revenues in the event of demonstrated need (by dependent children, the blind, the disabled, and the aged). In addition, there is the residual category of general assistance, which is intended to aid anyone who falls through the net of the other services.

After more than thirty years of operation of these and other income-maintenance programs, with extensions and improvements constantly made to them, it is estimated that almost one-fifth of the American people live below a poverty line which is based upon a Department of Labor "temporary and emergency" food budget. The recognition of this fact and public concern about it are a recent and dramatic development on the American social welfare scene.

It is interesting to speculate about the causes of the current concern with poverty. One possibility is that America is concerned about wiping out the obvious blemish of poverty on the image which it seeks to project, a concern spurred on by the continued existence of communist nations; their competition with the United States for the allegiance, loyalty, and support of the so-called newly developing, nonaligned, or neutralist nations; and their sometimes startling and unexpected scientific and military successes, coupled with the examples of poverty in the United States which they use as illustrations of the failure and inherent defects of the American system. Another possibility is that the increasing affluence of America has both highlighted the existence of poverty as a contrast, and made it appear that the economic capacity to eradicate that condition is at hand. Harrington's explosive book—*The Other America* (1963)—certainly stimulated national discussion of this aspect of the problem of poverty. A third possibility is that the civil rights movement, campus revolts, and antiwar activities add up to a consciousness of social unrest, of which poverty is felt to be a part or a cause; or to which poor people are felt to be potentially attracted.

It is also possible that responsiveness to poverty stems from a heightened awareness of man's responsibility to man, brought about by consciousness of the possibility of widespread annihilation of human life, if not total extinction, by use of super weapons. Finally, concern with poverty may have stemmed from its use as a political issue—a concern which conceivably would have centered on child-abuse, family break-up, mental health, or automation if these had been made campaign issues or slogans at the proper time. For example, although the writings of Galbraith were influential in getting President Kennedy to think about organizing a poverty program, it was the very discussion and initiation of the program which focused national attention on poverty.

The extent to which any, all, or a combination of these factors might be responsible for the current concern with poverty is not clear, but that there is such a concern is obvious. In this connection, the plans being undertaken, studied, or urged upon the government of the United States loom large. Among other things, these plans include widening coverage and increasing benefits in some existing welfare programs; the establishment of new programs, or new categories in old programs; and the creation of new administrative units to deal with aspects of the poverty problem. Among the widened-coverage proposals are those for increasing payments and benefits under Social Security (or OASDHI); blanketing in certain uncovered groups; establishing federal monetary standards for state/federal assistance programs;

and modifying experience ratings under the Unemployment Insurance rulings. New programs being proposed include families' and children's allowances, and fatherless family insurance. New categories in existing programs include considering unemployment as an acceptable reason for need by families with dependent children (AFDC-UP), and changing the definition of permanent disability under the Aid to the Permanently and Totally Disabled Act. New administrative units to deal directly with the problem of poverty include the Office of Economic Opportunity; and to deal with certain aspects of poverty, the Department of Housing and Urban Development. In addition to these proposals and changes, the concept of a guaranteed minimum income for all has been discussed at many levels, and at the present moment a special task force is engaging in a two-year study of this proposal at the request of the President.

Simply stated, the concept of a guaranteed minimum income is the establishment of an income floor below which no one would be permitted to fall. In looking for the historical roots of this idea, a distinction must be made between the concept of equality—which is an equal sharing of what is available—and that of a minimum guarantee. Equal sharing may result in less than the desired minimum, whereas establishment of a minimum does not necessarily imply equal sharing. Tribal societies, utopian communities, and modern kibbutzim may all assure members an equal share of resources, without being able to guarantee that the share will be adequate by any predetermined standard. An income guarantee, on the other hand, although it lessens the inequality of income distribution, has not been proposed as a method for completely equalizing income distribution.

One of the earliest attempts to guarantee workers a minimum income, after the break-up of the feudal system made such income a governmental problem, occurred in England in 1795. There the justices and some clergymen of Berkshire, meeting in Speenhamland, grappled with the problem of widespread destitution among workers. The war in Europe, two successive years of drought, and the failure of the cloth industry had impoverished industrial and agricultural workers alike. In order to protect workers against low wages and high costs of living, a wage supplement was guaranteed by the government whenever salaries dropped below a "floor," which was linked to the cost of bread and the size of the family. It was estimated that such an income guarantee would cost the government one-tenth the cost of maintaining a family which had been permitted to become completely destitute. The experiment proved disastrous; for recognizing that the government would bridge whatever gap existed between salaries and prices, and given large-scale unemployment which meant a "sellers' market" in jobs, employers promptly dropped their wage levels so that their labor costs were simply subsidized by the government. Since there were no provisions for compensatory price cuts, the difference became a subsidy from the government to the employers, with little gain and indeed much loss to the workers, as even employers who had previously paid more than the "floor" lowered their salary scales. As the Webbs (Webb and Webb, 1911) described it, the subsidy acted as "A sort of 'bounty' to those trades and those employers not paying full subsistence wages, and led to a constant extension of the system. What was happening was an ousting of the self-supporting by the parasitic industries [p. 90]."

The high hopes of the Speenhamland experiment foundered, not on the laziness of the workers, but on the avarice of the employers. Two factors seem to have contributed to the failure of the plan. The requirement that one be a worker in order to qualify for a salary supplement made holding a job a condition of eligibility, and thus made it possible for employers not only to withhold salaries, but in so doing also to withhold the supplements, thereby permitting them to dictate the terms of the job, including salary. This provision, which seems to be more implicit than explicit in the plan, might have resulted from the absence of any belief or feeling that nonworkers were entitled to any kind of income. Again, the limitation of supplements to those who worked might have been based upon a fear of a work disincentive if nonworkers were given income; or, it might have been simply due to lack of anticipation of the results of the act as drawn. A second factor leading to the failure of the Speenhamland experiment was a failure to recognize the difference between measures designed to aid the underpaid—which presupposed widespread employment and limited unemployment—and measures designed to cope with widespread unemployment. The Speenhamland experiment attempted to apply a wage-supplement plan in a period of mass unemployment.

Another proposal having to do with guaranteeing incomes came from an Austrian engineer, Josef Popper-Luykens, who in 1912 suggested a guaranteed income linked to a proposal for universal national service. After young people performed their service, they would be qualified for an income guarantee for the rest of their lives. A somewhat similar plan was proposed in 1932 by Prestonie Martin, a faculty wife at Rollins College. This plan has been described as:

> A National Livelihood Plan under which everyone eighteen to twenty-six years old would serve a term of work, as boys now do military service. These "Commons" would raise and process food, and make clothes and all other necessities of life for the government, which would hand them out to everyone free of charge. Food and other regularly needed products would be delivered to every door by a huge parcel post system. After serving their terms of work, the Commons would then become "Capitals," free either to loaf and live on the goods produced by the Commons or to produce luxuries for money that could be spent on the luxuries produced by other Capitals [Bird, 1967, p. 74].

In 1934 Huey Long began a bid for the Presidency of the United States with his "Share the Wealth" program, which promised an annual income of $5,000, a $30-per-month old age pension, a homestead, radio, and car to each citizen. It is an interesting fact that over thirty years after Long's plan was advanced, with the subsequent rise in the cost of living, none of the current plans, as noted below, proposes an income floor as high as Long proposed. At approximately the same time, Francis E. Townsend attracted a relatively large following, and enough political power to be a serious factor in a number of election contests, with a plan which called for $200 per month for those over sixty (as contrasted with the age of sixty-five, which was later incorporated into the Social Security Act); the plan would have been financed by a federal sales tax.

In 1942, Schumpeter proposed the eradication of poverty in America by a scheme which combined elements of an income guarantee and a plan for equalization of income distribution. Although this plan entailed a radical change in the American economic system, Schumpeter (1942) nevertheless contended that "In the United States . . . there need not lurk, behind modern programs of social betterment, that fundamental dilemma . . . between economic progress and immediate increase of the real income of the masses [p. 384]." Almost simultaneously, Rhys Williams (1943)' put forth a similar plan for Great Britain.

Other proposals, similar to but not identical with those for a guaranteed annual income, include those for a guaranteed annual wage, being put forth for certain employees by the United Auto Workers; employment guarantees, with the government as the employer of last resort; and a recent proposal that a tax be levied to give each Negro a monthly payment for ten years to recompense the injustices done to their ancestors in the past. These do not propose to guarantee an income to all citizens, workers or nonworkers, colored or white, but are nevertheless part of the same philosophic stream as are income guarantee proposals.

Three specific proposals in recent years, each with its own emphasis, have been influential in focusing attention on the idea of a guaranteed minimum income:

Milton Friedman proposed, in a 1962 book, a reverse income tax to replace all other forms of social welfare, and to make up a part of the poverty gap. Perhaps Professor Friedman's position as an economic advisor to then Presidential candidate Barry Goldwater gave his proposal weight and brought it to the attention of a wider and more influential public than would otherwise have been possible. Certainly, support from the so-called conservative camp was a novelty that seemed to give such a proposal at least the hope of realization through bipartisan support.

In 1962 Robert Theobald published *Free Men and Free Markets* in mimeographed form, followed by extensive excerpts published in *The Nation* in mid-1963, and publication of the book late in the same year. In 1965, a soft-cover version of the book appeared. These various modes and dates of publication may have brought the essential ideas, which were a Basic Economic Security Plan and Committed Spending, to the attention of a wider audience than would have been possible otherwise. In any case, Theobald wrote from the opposite end of the politico-economic spectrum from Friedman, calling for income guarantees as an ultraliberal step.

In July 1964, Edward E. Schwartz, in what seemed to be basically an attack on the means test, proposed a Family Security Benefit. Since this article was originally published in the journal of the National Association of Social Workers, it might have primarily influenced still another audience—social welfare professionals, and others interested in and charged with determination of social welfare policies. The extent to which Theobald and Friedman were influenced by, or even knew about, Rhys Williams' proposal is not clear, but Schwartz acknowledges his debt to her book.

Since the Friedman, Theobald, and Schwartz publications, a number of books, anthologies, and articles have been published on the subject of poverty generally, and on either implicit or explicit proposals for a guaranteed annual income. In general, the programs put forth can be categorized along at least three dimensions, which are not mutually exclusive.

Some programs are designed to eradicate all poverty under a predetermined level of income, whereas others use poverty as the basic criterion for benefits, aiming to eliminate only a part of the condition and leaving the remainder to be overcome by other income-producing methods, or not at all. Of the first type are programs which set a poverty level and propose to pay everyone under that level enough money to reach it. Programs which acknowledge a poverty level, and then propose to pay 14 per cent of the normal income tax exemptions, or 50 per cent of the gap, or use a sliding scale of exemptions, are of the second type.

A second difference is between those proposals which would use present mechanisms and programs, suitably amended, to guarantee a minimum income to all, and those which would use a new program or programs for the same end. The former involves changes in the insurance-type programs to extend coverage, increase benefits, reduce waiting times and vesting times, standardize payments, establish higher minimums, possibly increase taxes and raise the taxable bases, use general revenues, and blanket in those who are uncovered; and changes in the grant programs to extend coverage, increase benefits, establish minimums, standardize payments, and liberalize eligibility requirements. Proposed new programs, on the other hand, include demogrants, children's allowances, families' allowances, and a reverse income tax.

A third difference is between those programs which are intended to supplement existing programs, and those which are proposed as substitutes for all present income-maintenance mechanisms. Lampman (1965) makes proposals which would not, of themselves, eradicate poverty, but assume that they will supplement and complement existing programs while reducing their magnitude. Friedman, on the other hand, proposes a reverse income tax as a replacement for all existing social welfare programs, and is reported to have indicated his fear that his proposal will be used to add a program, rather than to substitute for old ones.

In addition to these differences in proposals, there are also policy issues involved in changed or new income-maintenance programs. These include the questions of services versus payments; payments as of legal right or through administrative ruling; and the psychological effect of contributory programs versus noncontributory programs. Underlying all of the existing and proposed income-maintenance programs, however, lies the assumption that receipt of unearned income in amounts large enough to guarantee subsistence will result in disincentive to work.

Theobald, alone, bases his proposal on a vision of an automated economy in which there will not be sufficient work for everyone, or even for the majority of the employable population, and his plan is designed to break the link between work and income. In effect, Theobald assumes a work disincentive caused by a guaranteed income, and welcomes it. All of the other proposals likewise assume a disincentive effect, but fear it.

Thus, Schwartz proposes a sliding scale for his Family Security Benefits as a "work incentive feature." Friedman defends his proposal by saying that it does not eliminate incentive entirely. Lady Rhys Williams would limit benefits to the employed, unemployable, and unemployed who are willing to accept suitable employment. Lampman rejects one proposal on the basis that "A good many of the presently working poor and even some of the non-poor . . . [might] work less than they do now and rest on the income guarantee," and defends another variation as closing the income gap "without destroying incentives of the low-income earners." However, this variation is also rejected by Lampman (1965) because, among other reasons, it would entail tax rates on the rich which "would be severe disincentives to work, save, and invest [p. 9]" on their part. Tobin (1966) says, " 'Human nature' . . . is a reason to give the subsidies in a way that does not destroy but indeed reinforces the incentive of the recipients to work and to increase the economic value of their work [p. 33]."

In every case, whether desired or feared, there is an assumption that unearned income will invariably create disincentive to work. So widespread is this assumption that it underlies many discussions of income-maintenance plans, and the interpretation of most of the research which has been done on actual and proposed plans. In fact, it has been held to be "A major concern to those who are charged with the formulation of policies and programs. . . . The issue is one of keeping a delicate balance between compensation for losses in capacities and insurance against economic consequences of such losses on the one hand, without rewarding negative motivations toward work on the other [Nagi, 1967]."

This concern with incentive seems to involve four aspects. One fear is that people who are working for wages equal to or less than the guaranteed income would stop working; or, if they are unemployed or out of the labor force, that they would not seek work. In other words, the assumption is that it would take sums larger than the guarantee to induce such people to work. The second, and sometimes concomitant concern, is that people who are assured their subsistence without working will be so content with that situation that they will refuse to work, even if offered more money than the guaranteed income. This viewpoint assumes that a guarantee of subsistence would satisfy recipients to the point that they would drop out of the labor market and become a permanently dependent subsidized underclass, content with their condition. In other words, even sums larger than the guarantee would not induce them to work. The third position is that people receiving unearned income which nevertheless leaves them poor would work only to the point of achieving subsistence, but would do no more than that. In short, the assumption is that their wants would not extend beyond achieving a subsistence existence. Finally, there is the most extreme view that people receiving unearned income which nevertheless leaves them below the poverty line will not work, even to achieve a subsistence level, as long as they receive *any* unearned income; that is, unearned income destroys work incentives as such.

These various views of, or feelings about, the work incentives of the poor are not always differentiated or articulated by those who deal with the question of the effect of unearned income, but inasmuch as their final effects would be quite different, such a division seems called for.

Since one of the most pervasive concerns of those who deal with or think about income-maintenance programs is the effect of such programs on incentive to work, the major focus of this study is on the evidence which exists, or which needs to be sought, on the extent to which people would change their work patterns as a consequence of such a guarantee. As a first step in this direction, it is necessary to determine who would be affected by such guarantees, and such determination is, in turn, dependent upon the level at which incomes would be guaranteed or, in current language, at which the poverty line would be drawn. It is to this issue that the next chapter is addressed.

2

Drawing the Poverty Line

*P*overty may be defined or measured in a number of ways. Machlup (1965), for example, suggests five standards for measurement: (1) a fixed consumption standard; (2) a fixed place (lowest decile or quintile) of the income distribution; (3) a proportion of the average median income; (4) a fixed standard rising annually; and (5) a fixed standard rising periodically as necessary.

Others have made different suggestions, such as style of life, gap between aspirations and achievements, or international comparisons. All such methods of measurement seem to be categorizable into poverty as defined in relative, normative, and absolute terms. Although these definitions, like all definitions, rest ultimately upon subjective criteria, these are the categories which will be used in this chapter.

Relative poverty is based upon a comparison of two or more situations, either by the persons involved or by others. Such comparisons may be based upon statistics, styles of life, reference groups, or self-feelings. From a statistical point of view, a definition of relative poverty may be arrived at by comparing one fraction of the income distribution among the population with another. For example, the lowest quintile (or any other fraction) of the income distribution in the United States can be defined as poverty-stricken in relation to the rest of the population. Such comparison may be useful for factual purposes, as in pointing out that since the early 1940s there has been no significant change in the shares of personal income going to the poorest fifth and the richest fifth in the United States (Epstein, 1963); or the definition may be used as a *reductio ad absurdum,* in the sense that Goldwater is quoted as saying that attempts to eliminate poverty are as futile as "Greyhounds chasing a mechanical hare. You will never catch up. There will always be a lowest one third or one fifth," and therefore poverty cannot be eliminated (Dirks, 1965, p. 10).

The statistical definition of poverty is also used to compare fractions in other countries—the upper middle class in India, or the respectable working class in Sweden—with poor Americans, with the result that the poorest Americans can be shown to be living in comparative affluence. This comparison is further sharpened when the units used are not just money income, but include nutrition, housing, health, and possessions.

The statistical definition is also useful in indicating the gaps between various strata in the income distribution; the increase or decrease in such gaps, and their rates of change; and the changes in sizes of the various parts of the distribution. Smolenskin (1965) essays a statistical definition, based on budgets and the gross national product, and arrives at the conclusion that the minimum-comfort budgets per capita have generally been around one-half of real gross national product per capita.

Another method of viewing poverty relatively is to compare life styles. The importance of patterns of consumption in determining the social status of individuals was pointed out in detail long ago by Veblen (1918)', who held that while utility of consumption was indicative of one life style, conspicuous consumption was a determinant of another status in society. Flowing from this conception is the style of life criterion which defines poverty according to the existence of indoor toilets, density of dwelling occupancy, amount of education, or existence of socio-psychological problems. Such definitions work both ways: A person with sufficient income who wastes it on non-style-of-life items (for example, get-rich-quick plans)' and thereby lives in squalor may be defined as poor; whereas one with insufficient income who somehow maintains appearances may be defined as nonpoor.

However, consumption patterns are only one part of the style of life criterion. There are, in addition, income considerations. Amount of income is an obvious criterion for poverty, but, less obviously, both regularity and source of income may also be indicators of poverty. Income which is acquired only sporadically and at uncertain intervals, even though averaging respectable amounts, may mark someone as poor. An artist or any other creative person who makes only occasional sales; a forest guide or ski instructor, whose services are used only seasonally; or farmers living from crop to crop may all be viewed as living in poverty by those whose incomes are regular and dependable.

The importance of source of income has been pointed out by the Lynds (1937)', Warner (1949)', and others. One criterion for being a member of the upper class may consequently be that the wealth connected with this designation be inherited rather than earned. Conversely, income—even partial income—from welfare sources is believed by a number of observers to be enough to designate a family as poor (S. M. Miller, 1965)'. In the same way, although children who are supported by their parents to adulthood are not considered to be poor because of this source of support, parents who are completely supported by their children are often so considered. In the same vein, the type of work—that is, the source of income—is one of the most commonly used indicators of socioeconomic status. Thus, although the lifetime earnings of a skilled electrician and of a high school teacher are substantially the same (H. P. Miller, 1964), the latter is generally considered to be of higher status.

Finally, a consideration which has to do with life styles is the distinction made between the respectable and the unrespectable, or the deserving and the undeserving, poor. Those who have been reduced to penury by circumstances presumably beyond their control—accident, disability, widowhood, illness, or even business reverses—may be distinguished in the mind of others from those whose poverty is their "own fault"—drunkenness, laziness, gambling, lack of initiative, lack of persistence, being victimized by others, and even remaining with the wrong or an unsuitable mate. The same style of living might even be visualized as poverty in one case and as better than deserved in another.

Again, relative poverty may be determined by the reference group or groups used as comparisons. The concept of relative deprivation, of which relative poverty (or the hypothesis of relative income) is one aspect, was derived by Stouffer (1949) in his study of American soldiers.[1] Noting that Negro soldiers from the northern parts of the United States did not seem to feel more deprived on contact with the stronger forms of discrimination which they met on being stationed in the South, Stouffer and his associates attributed this to the fact that the colored soldiers were viewing their own positions in relation to colored civilians in the south, for whom discrimination was a much more onerous matter, rather than in relation to their own previous situations. Similarly, the morale of soldiers overseas did not seem to be related to their condition as compared with that of soldiers still in the States (which presumably would have resulted in low morale), but rather with the condition of other overseas soldiers—distance from large cities, from the fighting front, and so on. From this was derived the theory that deprivation is relative, a function of the reference group being used.

In the same way, poverty appears to be relative, depending upon which other groups or individuals are used for comparison. Both Herzberg's (Herzberg et al., 1959) and Lawler's (1967)

[1] See also Merton and Kitt, 1950.

studies indicated that satisfaction with salary may be contingent upon the salaries of others doing substantially the same work, or with the same amount of seniority or responsibility. The money amount of salary has been found to be important to some people only insofar as it implies recognition, acceptance, and approval from salient reference groups. Vroom (1964) holds that "Satisfaction stemming from the receipt of wages is dependent, not on the absolute amount of these wages, but on the relationship between that amount and some standard of comparison used by the individual. The standard may be an adaptation level derived from wages received at previous times or a conception of the amount of wages received by other people [p. 151]."

The question of which groups are important to individuals or to selected categories of individuals is a matter for empirical research under various circumstances. However, the general question as to whether members of a given socioeconomic stratum compare themselves to the stratum closest to or farthest from them is subject more to conjecture than to evidence. Galbraith (1958), for example, feels that "Envy almost certainly operates efficiently only as regards nearby neighbors [p. 75]," whereas Orshansky (1965) says merely that "When the boon of prosperity is more general, the taste of poverty is more bitter [p. 42]." Lerner (1957), too, holds that "The poverty at the bottom of the pyramid was the harder to bear because of the lush living not only at the top (this has been true throughout history) but even in the middle-income groups [p. 337]."

Focus on poverty as a national problem did not appear until about 1962, and at that time 30 per cent of the population had family incomes of $8,000 or over; whereas in 1929 only 8 per cent had such incomes (in equivalent dollars); and in 1947 16 per cent did (H. P. Miller, 1964). Consequently, it is possible that the visibility of affluence among the middle and upper classes (or the mythology of such affluence spread by movies, TV, advertisements, and so on) created as great or greater feelings of comparative disadvantage among the poorest than did the modest and perhaps less visible advantages enjoyed by the not-quite-so-poor. In both cases, however, reference to others was assumed to have created feelings of disadvantage.

Reference to other groups may be not only in terms of comparative incomes or life-styles, but may also include the size of the gap between groups and the speed with which the gap is increasing or decreasing. In this connection H. P. Miller (1965)' comments, "The poor will not be satisfied with a given level of living year after year when the levels of those around them are going up at the rate of about 2.5 per cent per year [p. 94]." An economic growth rate which raises the income or standard of living of the entire population, but which raises that of the poorest at a slower rate or to a lesser degree, actually increases the amount of relative poverty that exists. Such changes include both absolute costs—that is, the current cost of subsistence foodstuffs compared to previous times—and changes in expectations—that is, refrigerators rather than ice-boxes, and flush toilets rather than privies.

Finally, insofar as reference groups determine relative poverty, it would be a mistake to think of those groups which are presently in existence as the only salient reference groups. Thelen (1954)' points out that reference groups may include: (1)' The effective group—the actual group of people one meets with in a given place, interacts with, tests ideas upon, appraises oneself by, and learns from. (2) The representative group to which one subscribes in extragroup settings, whose views one consciously puts forth and to whose instructions one responds. (3)' The abstracted or "relic" group—a faceless group whose people, roles, and actions have dropped out of memory, but whose coercive beliefs remain. The values of this group have been internalized. (4) The "hangover" group—previous groups, like families, from which unresolved conflicts, anxieties, and cravings continue to exist and affect current group participation. (5)' The fantasied, or constructed, group—the imagined group which supports, applauds, and appreciates the individual, often in a way that actual groups do not.

It is obvious from this description of possible reference groups (which is not exhaustive)' that some of the reference groups which influence feelings exist in the present, others continue to exert influence although they no longer exist in reality, whereas others are hoped-for or fantasied future groups. One may therefore be in poverty in reference to the past, the present, or the future.

Thus, relative poverty is a subjective definition, and as such contains elements of the self-image of the person doing the defining. Self-image, in turn, is largely, if not entirely, a function of perceived other-images—the person viewing himself as he thinks others view him. Consequently, there are elements of a self-fulfilling prophecy in self-feelings and categorizations of the poor: Persons who feel that they are poor act like poor people are expected to act, and are then treated like poor people, confirming their images of themselves; and, conversely, people who are treated as poor come to view themselves as such, act accordingly, and thus confirm the correctness of the treatment received. Consequently, one measure of relative poverty is the extent to which people are treated as poor. The existence of such differential treatment of the poor has been documented in terms of their contacts with merchants, with loan sharks, with the police, with school authorities, and others.

Since it is not comfortable to be treated as poor, or to think of oneself as poverty-stricken, several devices may be utilized to avoid such unpleasantness. One of these is to define oneself as middle-class, as do many people who are defined by others as lower-class. Another method of defining oneself out of poverty is to consider the existing situation as temporary, with ultimate middle-class membership, at least, assured. Such self-definitions may be found among students; young people at the beginning of their careers; the formerly nonpoor who are simply "temporarily down on their luck"; those who are "just waiting for their ship to come in"; those whose "real lives" will begin when they hit the numbers, win the sweepstakes, or are left money by an unknown benefactor; and many others whose current earnings and style of life otherwise qualify them for the designation of poor. There is also the possibility, which Kaplan (1960) holds is increasing with growing amounts of leisure, of defining oneself in terms other than occupation and income, but rather in relation to spare-time occupation and hobby, as the plumber who thinks of himself as a golfer, a musician, a skier, or a grower of roses.

However, there are people who are unable to define themselves out of poverty—who feel themselves to be poor and accept the designation because their incomes, of whatever amount, do not match their needs, wants, or, perhaps most important, their expectations. As a Welfare Administration publication (Winston, n. d.) puts it: "In an affluent society . . . where the majority of people take for granted the necessities of life and even many nonessentials . . . the deprived see evidence on every hand that a better life is attainable, and denial of opportunities creates restlessness in some, apathy and loss of motivation in others [p. 1]."

Theobald (1966) holds that this recognition of poverty is what is radically new about the situation today: "Up until now, the vast majority of the poor in America have never really *felt poor*, for they believed that they were going to be all right. Today, we have a poor class who know they are poor and who know they are going to stay poor [p. 3]."

In summary, poverty can be defined relative to statistics, style of life, reference groups, or self-images. It is also possible, however, to view poverty in normative terms. Normative poverty consists of seeing poverty as a condition which does exist, must exist, should exist, or, paradoxically, as not existing at all. For example, for some segments of the population, poverty is *expected* to exist and is therefore not seen as a problem or defined as poverty. Dependents, for example—such as children, the mentally retarded, the physically disabled, and the very old—are not expected to possess very much in terms of either income or assets, and their problem is not seen as one of poverty, but as one of a temporary or permanent disabling condition. Similarly, insofar as certain groups in society are expected to be more or less poor, their situations are not defined as poverty by those holding this expectation. In fact, certain groups are considered to expect and to deserve very little. When they have that which is assumed they expect and deserve, they are not considered poor. Groups as diverse as migrant workers, colored people, interns of various sorts, priests and members of certain religious orders, new immigrants, and youngsters are all subject to this norm which denies their situation the status of a problem and their condition the designation of poverty, by positing it as the expected nature of society.

There is a certain social utility in this type of thinking, which serves to minimize the poverty aspect of societal problems in favor of other explanations. Thus family structure, individual or multiple pathologies, ghetto conditions, and racial discrimination are seen as the problems afflicting certain sections of the population, with poverty held to be the result, rather than the root cause—or one of the causes—of the other conditions. Given these conditions, poverty is to be expected, and is no longer seen as a problem to be solved. This view of poverty-as-expected is exemplified in the manner in which certain portions of the population are denied income maintenance and other services: "Underlying much of the failure to provide equal service to Negro farmers in the South has been the preconception . . . that Negro farmers have limited needs, capabilities, and aspirations [Fuller, 1965, p. 395]."

In a slightly different vein, poverty might be viewed not only as expected, but as inevitable. Such a view may have Biblical or religious roots, including sayings: "The poor ye shall always have with you"; behaviors: "You shall not pervert justice to favor the poor"; and structures: The interest-free loan funds, the charitable orders, the collection plate, and so on. Also, poverty may be considered inevitable because of its historical existence and current ubiquitousness. It may be attributed to the inherent nature of man—original sin, the devil's handiwork, thanatos, entropy, inertia, the dependency of the infant, anomie, alienation, distance from the primal herd, or any other designation which can be used to indicate that men are not born or equipped only for work or to pursue financial success. Regardless of the basic reason assigned, the very fact that poverty has existed so widely and for so long may be taken as evidence of its inevitability.

Another source for the view of poverty as inevitable is that image of society which sees it as necessarily in or seeking balance. In sociological terms, this is the view of society as a social system which is, by definition, in equilibrium or constantly seeking equilibrium; this is an a priori assumption in Parsons' (Parsons and Shils, 1962) theory of social action, and of those who accept or use his conceptual scheme. Poverty, in this context, may be viewed as a "boundary-maintaining" mechanism. The wealthy sections of society may be conceived, no matter how hazily, as balanced by the poorer sections. In somewhat different terms, this is the same as a view of life as dependent upon luck—some are up, and some are down; or sometimes one is up, and at other times one is down. In either case, the "zero-sum game" requires a loser for every winner; for there to be people who are "up," there need to be people who are "down," and since there will always be people who are more "up" than others, some "downness"' (read poverty) is inevitable.

Although poverty may be seen as expected and inevitable within society as a whole, the majority of people are not poor. Those who are therefore deviate from the societal norm. Consequently, one way of viewing poverty is as a form of deviance. Since society casts people into roles and then expects the behaviors which are consonant with or normative for those roles, behavior which deviates from those roles is, by definition, deviant. Deviance is not, however, merely role-dissonant behavior, but behavior which is reprehensible, since it violates the norm. H. S. Becker (1963) holds that although those involved in scientific research assume deviance to occur because "Some characteristic of the person who commits it makes it necessary or inevitable that he should," "[Laymen] believe that the person who commits a deviant act . . . does so 'purposely' [pp. 3, 25]." Consequently, poor people are seen as somehow, obscurely, responsible for their own situation and thereby deserving of punishment for wilfully violating the norms of society. In this light, the two crucial images which are said to exist in the American mind are relevant: "One is that of the self-reliant craftsman . . . the man who could make something of the American resources. . . . The second has been an image . . . of a vast continent to be discovered, explored, cleared, built up, populated, energized [Lerner, 1957, pp. 50–51]." Since the poor person is obviously not the self-reliant craftsman who has built, or is building, America, he does not fit the role of the American stereotype, and in (purposely) deviating from this norm, he deserves censure.

In addition, the supposed correlation of poverty with mental illness, crime, disease, and immorality has equated the deviance of these and like behaviors with the situation of poverty. In one study, for example, the population of a town denied the existence of poverty in the town, despite the receipt of AFDC funds by some townspeople. When questioned concerning their denial, they explained that they conceived of the poor as immoral people, and they denied the existence of poverty in their town since none of the AFDC recipients were thought to be immoral (Kimmel, 1966).

Further, the disproportionate number of poor nonwhites

causes the deviant status of being nonwhite in a white culture (which is seen as deviance by many whites and nonwhites alike) to become attached to poverty as such. In other words, being poor and being nonwhite become synonymous for many purposes, and the deviance of one is associated with the other.

Another indication of the manner in which poverty is considered deviance—that is, purposeful behavior—is the extent to which the poor are exhorted to conform to middle-class standards of dress, conduct, speech, thrift, and other such virtues, including "Some greater sense of self-involvement in overcoming their personal and social afflictions [*New York Times,* November 9, 1965, quoted in Goodman, 1966]." At the same time, the poor, like any deviants, are considered unsuitable for normal company and are kept at arm's length; hence the difficulty of having effective and significant participation of the poor in social welfare programs, despite legal requirements to that end. This is in line with Mannheim's observation that every ruling class faces the dilemma of how and to what extent it will admit to leadership those lacking in the proper social background (Lipset and Bendix, 1959). One solution to this dilemma is to define them as deviant, and thus not suited for leadership. Goldwater's statement that "Most people who have no skill have no education for the same reason—low intelligence or low ambition [Dirks, 1965, p. 10]," can be understood in this light.

As mentioned above, deviance is not just non-normal behavior; it is both purposeful and reprehensible, and therefore deserving of punishment. The way in which poverty is dealt with— vagrancy laws, deportation of needy aliens, imprisonment of children with neither charge nor conviction (Polier, 1965)', termination of parental rights, midnight raids, interminable waits, and indifferent-to-insulting workers—is in itself evidence of the extent to which poverty is considered deviance.

It is also possible to view poverty not as deviance, but as pathology, with somewhat different consequences. Whereas deviance is generally considered a voluntary act, under control of the deviant and performed purposely, pathology is considered an involuntary aberration, a sickness. In this conception of poverty, the poor are helpless victims of forces—internal or external—which they cannot control. They are thus to be pitied and treated, rather than condemned and punished. The treatment consists of education, job-training, better housing, and massive doses of counseling—individually and in groups. Just as punishment is the consequence of deviance, paternalism is the outcome of pathology.

Pathology also has other connotations. Concern with the possibility of transmittal to the younger generation is expressed, and contamination of the nonpoor is feared. Consequently, preventive programs like Head Start and Upward Bound are prescribed for the young, to inoculate them against their parents' poverty; and for adults, isolation wards, in the form of low-cost mass housing, are provided. A regime of limited activities is indicated for the sick patient—sustaining recreation such as reading good books and partaking in discussion groups, rather than debilitating pastimes like reading comic books and watching television; the wholesome atmosphere of settlement houses or neighborhood centers, rather than windy street corners or noisy discotheques; cheap, if cancer-inducing cigarettes, rather than healthier but prosperous-looking cigars.

Thus, when the poor are considered pathological, they are not seen as responsible persons, and consequently decisions must be made and actions taken on their behalf and in their places, rather than giving them the rights of self-determination afforded others. In general, defining the poor as pathological makes it not only possible but also necessary to interfere in their lives, since patients are not expected to know what is good for them, and society has not only the right but also the responsibility to cure the pathological, even against their wills and even if the cure is both painful and uncertain. However, when society—rather than the poor—is seen as sick, with poverty as the symptom, then the treatment consists of seeking changes in the economic and social system as a whole—more egalitarianism, more opportunities, more humanism, and less exploitation, discrimination, and anonymity. The view of poverty as an illness causes these changes to be sought.

It is not necessarily true, however, that poverty is seen as an illness within or of society. It may be seen as simply dysfunctional for society, regardless of its nature or cause. The term *dysfunctional* includes a gamut of meanings from undesirable to dangerous. In this sense, poverty may be seen as denying the foundations of the socioeconomic system and threatening its continued growth and reputation. The very existence of poverty may be taken as evidence of the malfunctioning of the economy, especially an economy in direct competition with another type for the loyalty of new nations. In addition to being seen as evidence of malfunction, poverty may be seen as the cause of malfunction; the resources of various kinds which must be used to limit or eradicate poverty may be seen as more usefully employed in other areas, such as scientific research, foreign aid, or higher education. It has been estimated, for example, that in some cities a quarter of the annual funds are devoted to taking care of the fire, police, and health problems created by the slums—monies that might be more functional for the total society if used for preventive rather than rehabilitative purposes.

Poverty may be seen as dysfunctional for those afflicted by it, since the incidence of mental illness, family problems, physical illness, and other disorders is higher among the poor; or, poverty— like any dysfunction—may be seen as dangerous, as it impedes the smooth functioning of the total economic and social system, and may become an increasing impediment as the total economy grows and changes.

Whether poverty is seen as expected, inevitable, deviance, pathology, or dysfunction, it may nevertheless be considered to be necessary, or even desirable. For example, when poverty is defined as the gap between desire and fulfillment, then it can be seen as the necessary cornerstone to the economy of the industrialized portion of the world. The so-called insatiability of human wants, whether or not "artificially" maintained by advertising and stimulated by built-in obsolescence, is the basis of the greatest material affluence that the world has ever seen. Complete satisfaction of wants would totally disrupt the economic system of the industrialized parts of the world. In addition, a world in which all wants are satisfied is inconceivable to economists and psychologists alike, and the gap between aspirations and attainments is necessary for an understandable world. In this sense, complete absence of poverty would be a disaster. What the size of the gap between wants and achievement should be, and whether it should be the same—absolutely and proportionately—for all members of society is a normative question, but based upon the norm that views poverty, in some degree, as necessary.

In a more direct economic sense, insofar as poverty or the fear of poverty is considered the whiplash which drives men to work, its existence, or possible existence, is seen as a necessary spur to effort, if not ambition. This is the basis of the entire incentive mystique—that poverty is necessary to assure that the world's work gets done. So long as men are needed to do low-paid jobs, the fear of poverty even worse than that which they know may be the only pressure that can get them to do such work. This use of the threat of poverty permeates some existing social welfare programs; exhaustion of benefits, limitations on amounts of payments, denials based on ability to work—all are intended to offer the alternatives of making the necessary effort or suffering poverty.

Other, noneconomic, reasons support the view that poverty is necessary. Believers in a class struggle may see the experience of poverty as a necessary conditioning experience for revolutionary fervor. Moralists may need the poor to use as horrible examples. The financially successful who are unsure of the worth of their struggle may use the poor for self-assurance. Persons with pangs of conscience about their own methods of remaining out of poverty may use the visible victims of poverty to convince themselves that the end justifies the means. Thus, to some people, and perhaps to some socioeconomic systems, poverty has a distinct utility. In fact, the desirability of poverty may be postulated as a character-building experience. "From rags to riches," and "From log-cabin to president" were not espoused as descriptions in American folklore as much as they were intended as prescriptions. The rags and the log-cabin were intended to symbolize character, just as starting at the bottom of a business (even one's father-in-law's business) was considered character training, as well as business training for the future executive.

The individual usually considers such character-building poverty desirable in the past tense, or else for others. However, there are those who consider continuing poverty as a desirable state for themselves: members of religious orders who take vows of poverty; individual monks, hermits, prophets, and priests; certain groups of hippies and beatniks, for whom poverty is a symbol of spiritual freedom; utopian communal societies; and eccentrics, including certain artists, hoboes, beachcombers, and the like.

There are also those who view poverty as desirable because of the opportunities which it affords them, including the opportunity to practice direct charity, as enjoyed by most religions. For example, although the highest form of charity in Jewish life, according to the writings of Maimonides, is to create the kind of situation in which charity is unnecessary, there are nevertheless observant Jews in Israel who resist efforts to eradicate begging through social welfare agencies and through federated fund-raising, seeing these efforts as destroying their opportunities to gain merit in Heaven by giving directly to the needy. The same situation holds for Hindus in India. In the United States, the continued existence of "Fresh Air Funds," "The Hundred Neediest Cases," and similar appeals testifies to the strength of this need personally to fulfill religious and humanitarian injunctions concerning charity, and therefore to the need for the poor to make such giving possible.

Then there are those who depend upon poverty for a living—all those who dispense services and funds to the poor. This is not to say that those who deal with the poor do so to perpetuate poverty, or that they consciously or even unconsciously see poverty as desirable. On the other hand, it has been pointed out that the Iron Law of Welfare sees to it that those who need most get least; and this situation is attributable not to the poor, but to those who make, interpret, and administer policies. It was because of this feeling that a Congressional committee insisted, in the formative days of Social Security, that Aid to the Blind be in cash and not in services, since in the former case the money would go to the blind, but in the latter case, to social workers. In the same vein, a poignant sentence from an editorial in the official journal of the National Association of Social Workers (*Social Work,* 1965), concerning a reverse income tax plan to replace existing relief agencies, speaks for itself: "These approaches—to ignore or to reorganize public welfare as we know it out of existence—fail to take one matter into consideration. What is to become of the public welfare network itself, with its thousands of employees, rich accumulation of experience, and commitments to social improvement [p. 2]?" One is tempted to add, "We *need* the poor, so that we can go on helping them." Others, such as small-loan operators ("mouse men" in the terminology of the poor)`, credit jewelry and appliance houses, slumlords, pawnshops, and credit grocers—to mention only the legitimate section, who make up a definable proportion of the economy, pay taxes, buy licenses, and hire employees—need poor people as the clients and the customers of choice. Finally, some politicians use poverty as a tool. If there were no more voters whose support can be garnered through small favors and attentions because of their poverty, the method and process of politics would undergo considerable change.

It is also possible to view the poor both as exploiters and the exploited of society. To those who see society as a system from which one is entitled to withdraw only as much as one has contributed, the poor—despite the meager amount that they withdraw —have contributed even less. Thus, the attitude that the poor are deliberately exploiting society usually has moral overtones, a sense of outrage that such exploitation is permitted. Stories of beggars who drive Cadillacs, welfare recipients who own mansions, and unwed mothers who continue to have babies to receive larger welfare checks are used as proof of the exploitative activities of the poor.

Conversely, it is also possible to view the poor as subjects of exploitation, kept in their positions by those who perform or abet the exploitation. That the poor pay more for almost everything they buy has been well documented (Caplovitz, 1963); and in addition, they receive poorer medical care, lower-quality education, and are used for the fringe jobs of society. There is also an incidental exploitation in the jobs which have been created and the projects which have been mounted because of the existence of, and current concern about, the poor. It was not completely facetious when, after the creation of the Office of Economic Opportunity, a Washington wag commented, "Poverty is where the money is!"

The poor may be viewed not only as the exploited or the exploiters, but also the result of exploitation. This view, which is not confined to classical Marxists, holds that any society based upon a profit system and using hired labor must eventually seek to maximize profits by exploiting labor, and that subsequent rewards for high production doom those of low productive capacity, for whatever reason, to the bottom of the economic ladder. Current arguments that an unemployment rate of less than 4 per cent will create inflation, and is therefore to be avoided, are of this genre (Minsky, 1965). In this general view, poverty is a normative condition in an exploitative society.

It is also possible to view poverty as a game. Goffman (1959) has discussed the difference between the roles that people play, and the roles that they play at, the latter being a deliberate "put-on" for purposes of the role player. Such a "put-on" or spoof may be an attempt to minimize the difficulties of one's real role by pretending that the role is not inherent, but of choice. Berne (1964) has carried this further in his discussion of games that people play, and one can infer from both Berne and Goffman that one is *always* engaged in playing a game. In a somewhat different sense, Long (1966) has described the community as an ecology of games, each with its rules, boundaries, and roles.

In a similar way, poverty may be seen as one of the games which make up the social ecology. Just as there is the executive game, the housewife's game, or the public relations game in which rules, boundaries, and roles are observed, and which serve not only to structure life for the participants, but to also grant them role distance in the sense that "It's only a game," so poverty may be seen as one of the social games. The players are the poor versus the Establishment, the latter usually represented by social welfare workers, attendance teachers, juvenile delinquency officers, the police, housing authority officials, representatives of voluntary agencies, and survey takers. The goal of the poor is to get as many benefits as they can (or, sometimes, all those to which they may be entitled), whereas the goal of the Establishment is to keep the poor in the dark about their entitlements, to give them as few benefits as possible, and to find methods of penalizing the opposing players (such as ruling them ineligible for "other causes").

Accounts of applicants in welfare agencies or clients being dealt with by workers often make it clear that one side, at least, sees the procedure as a battle of wits, even if literally deadly serious. Thus there develops, as in any sport, the jargon of the game—good welly workers and bad welly workers, cases, nonrecurring grants, supervisors, the Resources Man, the Welfare, the Black Book, the Supplementation, and other phrases intelligible only to the players and some avid spectators. Beating the game then may become an end in itself, with actual financial results more important as symbolic scores than as resources.

The players in the welly game understand each others' roles as players, an understanding which may serve to inhibit deeper probing or communication. When roles are cast aside or when the rules of the game are broken, outside umpires may be called in. This is what happened in Newburgh, New York, in 1961, when the city manager promulgated a thirteen-point code of welfare regulations, which established new conditions for relief eligibility (Steiner, 1966). And this is happening in many places where clients are organizing, carrying out public protests, locking themselves in welfare offices, and in general no longer abiding by the rules of the game. The outside umpire then becomes the courts, the legislature, organs of government, or the press. Games which get out of hand are dangerous to players and spectators alike, as the "riot game" proves, but as long as the welfare game is played by the rules, it offers safety for players and society.

Safety is also available in denial of the existence of poverty altogether, or in refusal to see its evidence. Just as individuals avoid anxiety by rationalizing, denying, or narcotizing, so society uses the same devices. Coser (1965), for example, has called attention to the "invisibility" of the poor, arising from society's unwillingness to "see" the poor, who offend their sensibilities.

A further device by which society protects itself against acknowledging the existence of, or blame for, poverty, is the process known as scapegoating. The origin of the term and meaning of scapegoat is found in the Old Testament, when the high priest placed upon a goat the sins of the people, and sent it off into the wilderness. The element of projection was clearly present, even though the goat was not believed to have literally committed the sins for which the people felt guilty. The meaning of projecting one's own sins upon another and then accusing him of them has been explicated in much greater detail since that time. The more one shares or admires the projected traits, the more reprehensible they become in the scapegoat.[2] The common accusation that poor

[2] For an excellent description of the phenomenon of scapegoating, see Heap, 1966.

people are lazy, and really do not want to work—or, in the more elegant parlance of economists, that they choose a different leisure/work combination—together with characterizations of the poor as "immoral" and "promiscuous," among other things, takes on other meanings when seen in this light.

A further characteristic of scapegoating is that one turns on the scapegoat when group or societal considerations inhibit expression of one's own feelings. In the absence of other remedies, the scapegoat becomes a necessary device, siphoning off more violent forms of aggression against the restraints on expression or behavior. Consequently, it is possible to see poverty as serving society by performing the scapegoat role. To the extent that men would like to cease work or to work less, and to the extent that this is not regarded as socially permissible, the attribution of laziness to others, who can then be figuratively sent into the desert of ghettos and slums, may be used to siphon off aggressions which would otherwise be used to change the socioeconomic system, for better or for worse. Or, in Burke's (1965, pp. 286ff) terms, one can see poverty as promoting social cohesion through the mechanism of "victimage," which is seen as both "natural" and "normal."

If the analogy to scapegoating holds, then the more moral indignation expressed against the poor, the more envy there exists of their assumed laziness, immorality, and freedom from the demands of work. Gallup is reported to have said (Perlis, 1963), "I believe that there is a deep-seated conviction on the part of most people that they are not themselves spending their leisure time wisely, and this feeling often takes on something of the character of a guilt complex." Consequently, a society in which absolute horror at the idea of a guaranteed minimum income is expressed and in which the poor are made scapegoats might be nearer to accepting radical changes in its own work ethic than appears from its protestations. In any case, the idea of scapegoating is a very useful one for explaining the continued existence of poverty in America today and the ineffectiveness of measures adopted to combat it, and will be referred to a number of times throughout the remainder of this book.

The manner in which poverty is viewed by individuals or by groups determines where they would prefer the poverty line to be drawn. Those who see the poor as helpless advocate income sufficient to purchase the conditions they cannot otherwise achieve —in housing, health, education, and so on. Those who see the poor as exploited may want a poverty line high enough to serve as reparations; whereas those who see them as exploiters may want the line kept at subsistence, at best. Those who see poverty as necessary for the well-being of the economy want to peg the line somewhere below subsistence to assure work incentives; but those who equate poverty with original sin might oppose any sort of income guarantee, and therefore any poverty line.

The manner in which poverty is viewed by individuals and by groups determines where they prefer to draw the poverty line, as it also determines their attitudes toward methods proposed to deal, or not to deal, with poverty. For example, those who see poverty as deviance oppose any income for the poor without a quid pro quo on their part, such as undergoing treatment, participating in courses, changing their style of life, or creating a different family structure. When poverty is seen as pathology, then granting of income may be coupled with withdrawal of rights—rights to have more children, to participate in community affairs, or to spend the money without restraint. Similarly, those who see poverty as dysfunctional may be willing to invest heavily in its ultimate eradication, whereas those who see it as a game are content to try to make the rules more fair.

It is possible for one individual or group to hold several of these views simultaneously; and since no one group controls public policy regarding poverty, such policy emerges as a compromise between contending views. Thus, it is possible to have programs that are broad in scope, but ineffective as eradicators of poverty, and punitive in administration—such as national legislation which denies funds to dependent children in the hope that it will force their parents to work; or programs which are humane in execution, narrow in scope, and of doubtful efficacy as antipoverty measures—such as Upward Bound.

However, in devising income-maintenance programs for the poor, relative and normative definitions are rarely used. Only definitions of poverty in absolute terms offer the kind of stable, factual base from which policy can be determined. Absolute poverty is a definition of poverty based upon a standard considered to be necessary or desirable; but the methods of arriving at an absolute standard of poverty are themselves subjective, and include a number of conceptual and substantive problems. As Orshansky (1965a)' points out: "There is no generally accepted standard of adequacy for essentials of living except food. Even for food, social conscience and custom dictate that there be not only sufficient quantity but sufficient variety to meet recommended nutritional goals and conform to customary eating patterns. Calories alone will not be enough [pp. 45–46]."

Nevertheless, the Department of Agriculture has prepared suggested food budgets for more than thirty years, translating the criteria of nutritional adequacy as set forth by the National Research Council into quantities and types of food compatible with the preferences of United States families. These "low cost" budgets have been used for many years by welfare agencies as a standard, even if grants have not always been sufficient to meet the standard. More recently, the Department of Labor has begun issuing an "economy" food plan, intended only for temporary or emergency use, which averages out to 22 cents per meal per person in a four-person family. These budgets provide the basis for deciding upon a poverty line at a fixed consumption standard, by determining the proportion which food costs make up in a total budget, and multiplying the "low cost" or "economy" food budgets by the appropriate factor.

The most careful work in this method of drawing the poverty line has been done by Orshansky for the Social Security Administration. She has taken into consideration the differentials involved in the food budgets—and therefore in the total budgets— of males and females, farm and nonfarm residents, heads of families and unrelated individuals, ages, and size of families (Orshansky, 1965a). She has determined the poverty line for these various categories both according to the "low cost" and "economy" food budgets. Table 1 indicates the poverty line for these various categories as derived by the Social Security Administration.

In addition to the variables it has already taken into account, the Social Security Administration points out that there are others which might make substantial differences in the real amounts of

Table 1

Weighted Average of Poverty Income Criteria for Families of Different Composition, "Economy" Level—1964[a]

Number of family members	Nonfarm			Farm		
	Total	Male head	Female head	Total	Male head	Female head
1 (under age 65)	$1,580	$1,650	$1,525	$ 960	$ 990	$ 920
1 (aged 65 or over)	1,470	1,480	1,465	885	890	880
2 (under age 65)	2,050	2,065	1,975	1,240	1,240	1,180
2 (aged 65 or over)	1,850	1,855	1,845	1,110	1,110	1,120
3	2,440	2,455	2,350	1,410	1,410	1,395
4	3,130	3,130	3,115	1,925	1,925	1,865
5	3,685	3,685	3,660	2,210	2,210	2,220
6	4,135	4,135	4,110	2,495	2,500	2,530
7 or more	5,090	5,100	5,000	3,065	3,055	2,985

[a] From Orshansky (1965a), p. 52.

poverty that exist—the regional differences in cost of living, for example. In addition, the higher prices paid for food and other items by the poor, the amount of out-of-home eating required by some jobs, and the special needs of babies, persons on diets, and other idiosyncratic differences need to be measured. Nevertheless, the Social Security Administration's poverty line is the best that is available so far, and is widely used.

However, not everyone dealing with poverty agrees with the line thus drawn. Theobald (1963, p. 157), in urging a Basic Economic Security grant of $500 per year to needy children and $1,000 per year to needy adults, advances this comparatively low figure on the basis of administrative simplicity, with rapid rises envisioned as the basic proposal proves its feasibility. The President's Council of Economic Advisors, in a 1964 report, used a cash income of less than $3,000 in 1962 as a poverty line for families of two or more persons (H. P. Miller, 1964). Keyserling has defined as poverty-stricken individuals with an income of less than $2,000 and families with an income of less than $4,000 (in 1960 dollars)', and has termed "deprived" those without $4,000 and $6,000 respectively (Ferman et al., 1965). Ornati (1964) defines minimum subsistence as $2,500, minimum adequacy as $3,500, and minimum comfort as $5,500.

In addition to giving rise to such questions concerning the suitability of amounts, definitions of absolute poverty do not always express or illustrate differences within categories, for example, the difference between an income of $2,950 for a nonfarm family of four and having no cash income at all. This is both a qualitative difference to the families involved, and a difference in the ease with which the poverty could be eradicated in each case—by a grant of $50 in one case, but $3,000 in the other. Miller points out in this connection that "It was much easier to reduce the incidence of poverty by one percentage point when one-third of the families were below the poverty line than it is at present when fewer than one-fifth are at that level." Moreover, this is not just a statistical artifact, but a reflection of the human condition: "As we get closer to the very bottom of the income distribution, we are dealing increasingly with the hard-core poor [H. P. Miller, 1964, p. 89]." R. A. Gordon (1965) also points out that determination of the level of poverty, even in absolute terms, is a subjective matter, influenced by the fact that "As incomes generally rise, our standard of a bare minimum of existence is likely to rise less rapidly than our standard of, say, a minimum of decency [p. 7]." In addition, a proportional increase in everyone's mean income probably means more to the poor than it does to the rich.

In the face of these problems in drawing the poverty line, Orshansky's suggestions take on greater operational significance. Yet, despite her carefulness in distinguishing between types of individuals and families, the older undifferentiated criterion for poverty ($1,500 for individuals and $3,000 for families) continues to be used in some cases, whereas in others, a certain flattening of her distinctions sometimes takes place. Orshansky (1965a) says clearly that "The present analysis *pivots about* a standard of roughly $3,130 for a family of *four* persons, and $1,540 for an unrelated individual [p. 54; emphasis added]," but these figures are rounded off to $3,000 and $1,500 in some cases, and the size of the family is disregarded in others. The poverty level thus continues to be spoken of as an income of less than $3,000 for a family and $1,500 for an individual, without the differentiations emphasized by Orshansky. A further flattening occurs when income figures are given which define families to include individuals living alone, thereby eradicating the discernible differences in poverty levels between unrelated individuals and heads of families.

Since they are the most precise, the SSA figures will be used in the remainder of this book, supplemented when necessary by other sources.

3

Occupations
of the Poor

$\mathcal{T}$he hypothesis that a work disincentive factor would arise from a guarantee of a minimum income would seem, at first glance, to be straightforward: *People who are working for the same, or less than, the amount they would receive as a guarantee even if not working will stop working.* Thus, the effect of a guaranteed income on incentive to work need be sought only among the *working* poor; that is, investigation into the parameters and demography of this group need extend no further than to those who are employed at such low wages, or for such intermittent periods, that their incomes are the same or less than the proposed guarantee.

However, there are also other groups whose work incentives might conceivably be affected by an income guarantee, such as the income stratum directly above that of poverty, and—paradoxical as it may seem—the wealthy. There are also groups—such as the aged, the young, mothers of young children, and the disabled—which, according to articulated public policy, are neither required nor expected to work, and, in fact, it is considered desirable that they do not; however the effect of work disincentives on them is nevertheless taken into account. Finally, even more paradoxically, the effect of work disincentives on those who cannot find work—the unemployed—must be taken into consideration. The features of such groups, as well as the rationale for considering them, are examined below.

In 1964, the employed poor consisted of 3,633,000 heads of families, of whom 2,020,000 were year-round full-time workers; and 1,464,000 unrelated individuals, of whom 573,000 worked at full-time jobs from fifty to fifty-two weeks.[1] Of the 3,633,000 heads of poor families, 2,530,000 were white, and 1,103,000 were nonwhite; of the 1,464,000 unrelated individuals, 1,123,000 were white and 341,000 nonwhite.

In descending numerical order, in terms of the number of jobs held, the poor were employed as follows: *894,000 were laborers,* which included farm laborers, garage laborers, car washers and greasers, gardeners, warehousemen, and stevedores.[2] *882,000 were operatives and kindred workers,* which included, among others, apprentices at semiskilled trades; auto parking attendants; metal filers, grinders, and polishers; fruit and vegetable graders and packers, outside of factories; laundry and dry cleaning operatives; mine laborers; oilers and greasers; and textile spinners. A further breakdown of the category of laundry and dry cleaning operatives

---

[1] All of the figures concerning the employed poor in this chapter are from M. Orshansky, 1966, pp. 3–38, unless otherwise noted. Insofar as possible, other citations are based upon 1964 data, to achieve comparability with the SSA poverty index. When other years are used, this is indicated.

[2] See *1960 Census of Population Classified Index of Occupations and Industries,* United States Department of Commerce, Washington, 1960.

indicates that this grouping includes bundlers, bundle wrappers, clothes shakers, collar starchers, dampeners, folders, handymen, and machine fillers, among others.

614,000 were farmers and farm managers, the former including both owners and tenant farmers. *587,000 were service workers,* other than household, including attendants in hospitals and other institutions; bootblacks; chambermaids and maids in commercial and public institutions; charwomen and cleaners; janitors; porters; and waiters and waitresses. *478,000 were professional, technical, and kindred workers,* which included actors, dancers, musicians, and other entertainers; funeral directors and embalmers; religious workers; recreation workers; and teachers. *465,000 were private household workers,* including baby sitters, laundresses, and housekeepers. *410,000 were craftsmen and foremen,* which included brickmasons, stonemasons, and tile setters; cement finishers; repairmen; construction and maintenance painters; paperhangers; pipe fitters, and shoe repairmen. *405,000 were managers, officials, and proprietors* (excluding farms)', including buyers and shippers of farm products; railroad conductors; credit men; floor men in stores; and officials of lodges, societies, and so on. *362,000 were clerical and sales workers,* including baggagemen; bill collectors; messengers; office boys; and stock clerks.

The occupations of the poor are indicated in some detail in Table 2. Although the information available in this table is illuminating, many more data need to be gathered to make possible even educated guesses concerning the probable effect of a guaranteed income on the work patterns of those below that guarantee. For example, listing the actual jobs in which the poor are engaged, rather than simply their general occupations, might allow one to distinguish between the social statuses involved, the possibilities of work satisfactions from the work itself or from participation in work groups, and the opportunity for upward mobility. These factors, in turn, need to be linked to age, educational levels, and time on same job in order to begin understanding possible aspiration levels and their reality; promotion possibilities; and vesting of seniority rights.

Unfortunately, such information and cross-tabulations are not available, and that which is available from different sources

Table 2

OCCUPATIONS OF THE EMPLOYED POOR, 1964
(in thousands)[a]

	Family Heads						Unrelated Individuals						Total	
	Wh. Male Head of Fam.	Nonwh. Male Head of Fam.	Wh. Fem. Head of Fam.	Nonwh. Fem. Head of Fam.	Tot. Head of Fam.	% Head of Fam. by Occ.	Wh. Unrel. Male	Nonwh. Unrel. Male	Wh. Unrel. Fem.	Nonwh. Unrel. Fem.	Tot. Unrel. Ind.	% Unrel. by Occ.	Tot. Fam. Head and Unrel. Ind.	% of Tot. by Occ.
Professional and Technical	84	12	11	0	107	.03	137	7	214	13	371	.25	478	.09
Farmers and Farm Managers	470	79	16	4	569	.16	34	1	10	0	45	.03	614	.12
Managers, Officials, and Proprietors	300	26	15	5	346	.09	27	4	25	3	59	.04	405	.08
Clerical and Sales	120	16	68	11	215	.06	30	9	104	4	147	.10	362	.07
Craftsmen and Foremen	296	74	2	1	373	.10	29	6	2	0	37	.03	410	.08
Operatives	486	200	49	31	766	.21	18	25	55	18	116	.08	882	.18
Private Household Workers	0	3	32	118	153	.04	9	3	168	132	312	.21	465	.09
Other Service Workers	102	92	83	81	358	.10	30	12	164	23	229	.16	587	.11
Laborers	385	335	11	15	746	.21	65	76	2	5	148	.10	894	.18
Total	2,243	837	287	266	3,633	1.00	379	143	744	198	1,464	1.00	5,097	1.00

[a] Orshansky (1966), p. 5.

is rarely comparable. Consequently, extrapolations from demographic data into the realm of behaviors and attitudes must be
viewed as very tentative, and amenable to many changes as the
result of empirical investigations. Nevertheless, with these cautions
in mind, the SSA tabulations, and even some less refined data,
can throw some light on the whereabouts of the poor. For example,
Table 3 indicates the number and percentage of the employed
poor family heads who were full-time year-round workers in 1964
(comparable data for unrelated individuals are not available), and
Table 4 indicates the number and proportion of the members of
various occupational categories who were poor in 1964, according
to Consumer Income statistics.

Similarly, Table 5 indicates the median income of all family
heads in 1964 (the date of the SSA income figures)', and the
median income of those working year-round full-time; note that
the latter are the median incomes of the entire employed population,
and not just for those in poverty. Also, this source uses eleven
classifications of occupations, whereas the previous source uses nine.

Despite the lack of comparability between the SSA figures
and the Consumer Income figures given previously, certain factors
concerning the location of the poor can be ascertained, even if
dimly:

One of the two largest single categories of the employed
poor is that of laborers (18 per cent) and, conversely, 20 per cent
of all laborers are poor. In 1959, the latest date for which such
figures are available, the two largest groups of male laborers by
far in the lowest ($1 to $999)' stratum were construction laborers
and those in wholesale and retail trade (farm laborers are not
listed separately in the report being quoted [H. P. Miller, 1966])'.
The median salary for full-time year-round family heads who are
laborers is $5,785; but since the farm laborers and foremen are
given separately for this purpose, and their median salaries under
the same conditions are $2,802, a high proportion of farm laborers
is probably contained among the impoverished laborers. In addition,
it has been estimated that there are over one million agricultural
migrants in the United States (men, women, and children)'. In
1962, the average migrant agricultural worker earned $1,123
(Callahan, 1965)'. Incidentally, it is not possible to correlate the

Table 3

NUMBER OF POOR FAMILY HEADS WHO WORKED FULL-TIME AND YEAR-ROUND IN 1964, BY OCCUPATIONS

(in thousands)[a]

	Male Head of Family Full-time Year-round Worker	Female Head of Family Full-time Year-round Worker	Per Cent	Male Head of Family Less Than Full-time Year-round Worker	Female Head of Family Less Than Full-time Year-round Worker	Per Cent
Professional and Technical	71	3	.69	25	8	.31
Farmers and Farm Managers	441	9	.79	108	11	.21
Managers, Officials, and Proprietors	268	8	.79	58	12	.21
Clerical and Sales	81	23	.49	55	56	.51
Craftsmen and Foremen	156	0	.42	214	3	.58
Operatives	353	24	.49	333	56	.51
Private Household Workers	0	56	.37	3	94	.63
Other Service Workers	120	62	.51	74	102	.49
Laborers	350	3	.47	370	23	.53
Total	1,840	188	.56	1,240	365	.44

[a] Orshansky (1966), p. 8.

47

Table 4

PROPORTION OF POOR EMPLOYED PEOPLE, BY OCCUPATIONS, 1964
(in thousands)[a]

Occupation	Number Employed	Number of Poor	Percentage of Poor
Professional and Technical	8,834	478	.05
Farmers and Farm Managers	2,203	614	.28
Managers, Officials, and Proprietors	7,361	405	.06
Clerical and Sales	14,742	362	.02
Craftsmen and Foremen	8,680	410	.05
Operatives	12,850	882	.07
Private Household Workers	1,924	465	.24
Other Service Workers	6,496	587	.09
Laborers	4,530	894	.20
Total	67,620	5,097	.08

[a] Total numbers from *Current Population Reports* (1965b), pp. 41–42; number of poor from Orshansky (1966).

number of people living on farms with farm laborers, and/or with farm owners and tenants. In 1964, five out of eight farm residents were employed solely or primarily in nonagricultural work; while one-third of the persons whose employment was primarily or entirely in agriculture did not live on a farm (*Current Population Reports,* 1965a). The great majority of poor laborers are obviously male (95 per cent), about equally divided between whites and non-whites, and mostly heads of families (89 per cent).

The second largest category of the employed poor is that of operatives and kindred workers (18 per cent). Of those in this category, 84 per cent are family heads. In terms of the number of family heads who are full-time year-round workers, this group resembles the laborers, with 49 per cent so engaged. Median salary ($6,892), however, is somewhat higher than laborers', and consequently only 7 per cent of persons employed in this category are poor. An examination of the specific jobs included in this category would indicate that the median tends to be lifted by the highly

Table 5

MEDIAN SALARIES OF HEADS OF FAMILIES
IN VARIOUS OCCUPATIONAL CATEGORIES, 1964[a]

Categories	Total	Full-time Year-round Workers
Professional, technical, and kindred workers	$9,977	$10,469
Farmers and farm managers	3,329	3,601
Managers, officials, and proprietors (except farm)	9,289	9,600
Clerical and kindred workers	7,163	7,442
Sales workers	8,170	8,648
Craftsmen, foremen, and kindred workers	7,670	7,923
Operatives and kindred workers	6,542	6,892
Private household workers	2,367	—[b]
Service workers (except private household)	5,525	6,162
Farm laborers and foremen	2,423	2,802
Laborers (except farm and mine)	5,086	5,785
Total employed population	7,272	7,735

[a] *Current Population Reports* (1965b), p. 29.
[b] Base less than 150,000; amount not available.

unionized and highly skilled jobs included in this category—such as mine workers, tractor drivers, and photographic process workers.

However, there are jobs in this category that are distinguished from those of laborers only by more elegant job descriptions, rather than by real differences in income: auto service attendant rather than garage laborer; apprentice carpenter rather than carpenter's helper, and the like. Similarly, a handyman in a laundry is classified as an operative, whereas a truck driver's helper or a warehouseman is a laborer. Consequently, low salaries for the less skilled workers are commonplace, whether they are termed operatives or laborers.

A case in point is that of laundry and dry cleaning operatives, who are included in the operatives and kindred workers category. In 1963, more than half the nonsupervisory laundry and cleaning workers were paid less than $1.25 per hour; about 40,000 of these workers earned less than 75 cents an hour; and the hundred lowest-paid employees, according to a survey, all of whom were in large establishments with annual sales of $250,000 or more, were paid less than 35 cents per hour. From 1951 to 1963, although federal minimum wages rose 50 cents an hour, bundle wrappers in Memphis laundries received increases of only 11 cents an hour— from 47 cents to 58 cents an hour (Ferman, 1965). The two largest groups of the lowest-paid operatives in 1959 (laundry workers were not listed separately) were bus, truck, and taxi drivers; deliverymen; and auto service and parking attendants (H. P. Miller, 1966).

In terms of the numbers engaged in an occupation, the third largest number of the poor were farmers and farm managers (12 per cent), and 28 per cent of all farmers and farm managers were poor—the largest proportion of any occupation. This category includes tenant farmers or, in more colloquial language, sharecroppers, but does not include hired farm laborers, who are included under laborers, as noted above. One statistical detail is pertinent here: as long as an individual stays on a farm, although he is looking for work elsewhere, he is usually not listed as unemployed unless he did "no work at all" during the week of the survey. Consequently, it seems likely that the number of the "employed poor" who live on farms, and whose incentive to work might be affected by an income guarantee, is somewhat overstated, and that at least a proportion of these would be considered unemployed if they lived in an urban area. It should also be noted that the SSA poverty line is lower for farm families and individuals because of the assumption that they supply some of their own necessities. Thus, the poor on farms tend to be almost twice as poor as nonfarm people in terms of money income.

Of the 614,000 farm owners and managers in poverty, 569,000 are heads of families, and 79 per cent of them are full-time year-round workers. The median salary for farm owners and managers is $3,601, but, as noted above, this must be viewed against the lower poverty line for farm families. The number of unrelated individuals who are farm owners or managers is relatively small (45,000, or 7 per cent) when compared with the heads of families in the same category (569,000). (This category is not mentioned in the 1959 breakdown by jobs.)

From point of view of size, the next largest group of poor people are those engaged in service occupations, from which household workers have been extracted here for purposes of separate discussion below. A total of 587,000, or 11 per cent, of the poor are service workers, and 9 per cent of all service workers are poor. Family heads (61 per cent) are fairly evenly divided between male and female, white and nonwhite, with some weighting toward males. Among unrelated individuals, however, over 70 per cent are white females. Without further breakdown of the numbers in each job involved, it is difficult to account for the latter fact, except by observation of the apparent high incidence of white females, in contradistinction to nonwhites, as waitresses, ushers, and hairdressers, which type of job apparently outweighs the nonwhites engaged as hospital attendants, practical nurses, charwomen, cleaners, chambermaids, and maids outside of private households.

In any case, the fact that 64 per cent of poor service workers are white seems to contradict the generally held feeling that such jobs are held mostly by nonwhites. Some of this feeling may be accounted for by the fact that "service workers" are not as clearly defined in the public mind as they are in the Occupational Index. On the other hand, this category contains three of the types of jobs that contain some of the worst-paid workers in America—restaurant, hotel, and hospital employees.

In 1963 there were over 1.5 million nonsupervisory workers in restaurants and other food-service enterprises. Nearly one-fourth of these workers—300,000—were paid less than 75 cents an hour. The majority of all restaurant employees do not receive tips—cooks, helpers, busboys, dish washers, and so on; and only about one-third of restaurant employees are waiters or waitresses.

Hotels employed 489,000 nonsupervisory workers in 1963, 34,000 of whom were paid less than 50 cents per hour. Hospitals employed about 700,000 nonsupervisory nonprofessional personnel in the same year; many of the actual jobs, and therefore salaries,

were the same as those in restaurants and hotels—kitchen help,
dish washers, porters, and maids (Ferman, 1965).

With the exception of farmers and farm laborers (whose
poverty line is considerably lower than others') and of laborers,
service workers had the lowest median incomes, both in terms of
the total group, and in terms of full-time year-round workers, than
any group besides domestic service workers. On the other hand,
this group also contained some highly skilled and well-organized
categories: barbers, elevator operators, hairdressers, firemen, guards,
marshals, policemen, detectives, and sheriffs.

The category of professional, technical, and kindred workers
contains some of the highest-paid positions in the American
economy: physicians and surgeons, accountants and auditors,
college presidents, public relations men, entertainers, and so on.
Consequently, the median salary for full-time year-round workers in
this category is $10,469, the highest of any category. One-fifth
of all families in the United States received incomes above $10,000
in 1961 (Barlow et al., 1966), and their aggregate income was about
two-fifths of all personal income in the United States at that time. Obviously, with such a large number of incomes above the median, there
must be an equally large number below it; this number is 478,000, or
9 per cent of the poor. However, only 5 per cent of all persons
in this category were poor, the smallest proportion of any occupational category.

In contrast to farm owners and managers, more than
three times as many poor people in this category are unrelated
individuals than family heads. One possible reason for this is
that this category contains the kind of jobs which many people
leave on marriage, and re-enter when again single—teachers,
nurses, social workers, and so on. The number of poor people in
this category might be accounted for, in part, by three reasons:

First, there are jobs which traditionally require years of
official or unofficial apprenticeship, deliberately depressed wages,
or long periods of failure which may or may not ultimately result
in success. Interns, medical residents, student nurses, and recently
graduated lawyers working as law clerks might be seen as those
serving apprenticeships at salaries that are held low, almost as a
training discipline. Writers, musicians, and entertainers may live

on marginal salaries for years, confident that they will eventually achieve success. Young professionals in private practice may go heavily into debt for years, while keeping up appearances with practically no income, in anticipation of the gradual build-up of their clientele, practice, and income.

Another reason for low salaries in this category is the inclusion of jobs which are professional and technical only by virtue of such inclusion. For example, considering funeral directors as professionals dates back to the demand of funeral directors to be left out of the coverage of the original Social Security Act, in order to be officially classified as professionals—a request that was granted for political considerations. Insofar as thousands of rural, small—in some cases, backwoods—establishments are concerned, both their designation and their incomes affect the distribution.

Finally, there are jobs which—despite illustrious success stories—are traditionally ill-paid, albeit professional; for example, clergymen and music teachers. Some denominations or sects can pay functionaries only minimum salaries, and others require a degree of poverty of their clergy. Stories of poor widows eking out an existence by teaching piano are firmly embedded in American folklore. In fact, in the male category, the largest concentration in the lowest-income stratum in 1959 consisted of teachers and clergymen (H. P. Miller, 1966).

The heavy concentration of unrelated individuals in this category also has implications in terms of the salaries paid. Since the poverty level for nonfarm individuals under age 65 is $1,580, the 371,000 unrelated persons who are in poverty indicate that classification as a professional or technical worker is no guarantee of reasonably good salaries. In fact, as will be noted below, there are slightly more individuals with annual income of less than $1,580 in the professional and technical category than there are in the area of domestic help.

The number of poor employed as private household workers (465,000; 9 per cent) is almost equal to the number employed as professional and technical workers. This category, as could be expected, is composed mostly of females (97 per cent). About three-quarters of this category are unrelated individuals, and of the one-quarter family heads, only about one-half are year-round full-time workers. The median salary for all private household workers is $2,367, but this includes part-time workers, since not enough full-time workers were included in the sample to make a determination. Again, not enough detailed information concerning holders of various jobs is available to allow firm conclusions to be drawn, but it should be noted that baby-sitters are included in this category, which might help to account for the large number of low-salaried persons included. It is also interesting that, despite the public image of domestic workers, 57 per cent of the unrelated individuals in this category of poverty are white, as are 45 per cent of all such workers. Twenty-four per cent of all private household workers are classified as poor.

The two groups consisting of managers, officials, and proprietors, and of craftsmen and foremen each account for 8 per cent of the employed poor. Interesting is the fact that both of these poverty groups contain a high preponderance of family heads (85 per cent and 91 per cent, respectively), but among managers, officials, and proprietors, 79 per cent are family heads who are full-time year-round workers, whereas among the craftsmen and foremen, only 49 per cent of the poor family heads work year-round and full-time. The preponderance of family heads in these groups might indicate income levels that are sufficient for unrelated individuals, but insufficient for families. Six per cent of managers, officials, and proprietors are poor; and 5 per cent of craftsmen and foremen.

Of the entire nine categories, managers, officials, and proprietors have the second highest median salaries ($9,289), after professional and technical workers, whereas craftsmen and foremen rank fourth ($7,670), after sales workers.

Only 7 per cent of the poor are in clerical and sales jobs, and 94 per cent of these workers are white. Of these, about one-third are male heads of families, and one-third are unrelated females. Only 2 per cent of persons in this category are poor.

A special look should be taken at the self-employed among the poor. In 1960, there were 5,700,000 workers covered by OASDI whose earnings came exclusively from self-employment. However, since this number does not include those with incomes less than $400 (since they are not covered by OASDI), the total number should have been even larger. Of the number covered by OASDI, 52.9 per cent had earnings of less than $3,000 (Trafton, 1964). (Again, this does not mean that they were all poor according to the SSA criterion.)' Of those whose incomes came only from self-employment 42 per cent were engaged in agriculture, forestry, or fisheries; 12 per cent in services; 10 per cent in contract construction; 8 per cent in wholesale and retail trade; 7 per cent in finance, insurance, and real estate; 2 per cent in mining and manufacturing; and 23 per cent were unclassified. Although the proportion of the poor in each industry is not ascertainable from these figures, it is nevertheless worth noting that in 1959 about four in every five workers with taxable income from self-employment worked in agriculture, wholesale and retail trade, and the service industries. For the most part, the self-employed are small farmers, small businessmen, independent craftsmen, service workers, and operatives.

To summarize some of the salient facts about the employed poor:

By almost any definition or criterion, farmers—and particularly farm laborers—make up an important part of the poverty group. More farmers are poor than workers in any other occupation, and they are poor despite the lower level of poverty which is applied to them. They are almost all heads of families, and are poor despite working full-time and year-round. The large majority are white.

Laborers are not much better off than farmers. They also tend to be predominantly heads of families, but are not able to work full-time and year-round to the same extent. One out of five laborers in America is in poverty, regardless of race.

Operatives make up the third large group in poverty, and they share many of the characteristics of the other two groups— mostly heads of families, one-half of whom are poor despite year-round full-time work. There are, however, many operatives who are not poor.

Although one out of four private household workers are poor, and these are almost all females, two-thirds of whom are non-white, this group makes up less than 10 per cent of the poor, or one-half the number of either operatives or laborers.

Three economic groupings, in addition to the employed

poor, must be taken into account in assessing the effect of an income guarantee. The first of these is the group called by Orshansky the "near-poor." The second group is the economic stratum just above the poor and the near-poor; and the third is the group of the wealthy.

The so-called near-poor are those who are poor according to the "low-cost" criterion, but not by the "economy" criterion. It will be recalled that the Department of Agriculture prepared food budget figures on a low-cost basis for some years before the Department of Labor prepared its economy budget, which was lower and intended for temporary and emergency use only. Using the higher "low-cost" figures as a base, Orshansky has prepared the same type of analysis of this group for the Social Security Administration as she did of the "economy" budget-based group.

For comparative purposes, a single nonfarm individual under 65 needs $1,580 (often rounded to $1,500) under the economy criterion, and $1,885 (often rounded to $1,800) under the low-cost criterion; a nonfarm family of four needs $3,130 (often rounded to $3,000) under the former criterion, and $4,005 (often rounded to $4,000) under the latter.

The near-poor are of interest in this study because it is possible, and for some purposes may be desirable, to determine the poverty line as based upon a food budget not intended as temporary and emergency. In addition, there is the possibility that people making somewhat more than the income guarantee would be willing to forgo some income in order to cease working. Since there is, as yet, no evidence as to whether this would in fact happen, or to what extent, and up to what income levels, the size of the near-poor stratum and its occupational divisions, as given in Table 6, are presented as the group within which such a phenomenon could conceivably occur, if the guaranteed minimum income were to be based on the "economy" figures.

If the poverty line were drawn to include the near-poor—or, in other words, if the income guarantee were to be at the "low cost" level—then the stratum which might be induced to stop work for a somewhat lower income would be that which is just above the poverty line. Again, since it is not known how much income one would need to be immune to such temptation, the possible magni-

Table 6

NUMBER OF EMPLOYED PEOPLE WITH INCOMES ABOVE POVERTY
LEVEL BUT BELOW NEAR-POVERTY LEVEL,
BY OCCUPATIONS, 1964 (in thousands)[a]

Occupation	Number
Professional and Technical	180
Farmers and Farm Managers	215
Managers, Officials, and Proprietors	232
Clerical and Sales	287
Craftsmen and Foremen	400
Operatives	608
Private Household Workers	49
Other Service Workers	368
Laborers	341
Total	2,680

[a] Orshansky (1966), p. 5.

tude of the stratum can be deduced from Table 7, which indicates the income levels in the United States in 1964. If the income guarantee were to be at the $3,000 line, then 11.8 per cent of the total employed population would be subject to the guarantee (leaving out the weightings of the Social Security Administration's criterion according to age, residence, and so on), and the stratum which makes up to $500 more than that consists of 3.4 per cent. Were the guarantee to be set at the $4,000 line, 18.9 per cent of the total employed population would be subject to the guarantee, with the next highest stratum, making up to $1,000 more than that, consisting of 8.3 per cent of the employed (*Current Population Reports,* 1965b).

Finally, there is some expressed fear that a guaranteed income paid to the poor will indirectly affect the wealthy in terms of their work incentives. This argument holds that the cost of such an income guarantee will necessitate more taxes, which might affect the wealthy by putting them in higher income tax brackets,

Table 7

PROPORTION OF FAMILY HEADS, EMPLOYED FAMILY HEADS,
AND FAMILY HEADS EMPLOYED FULL-TIME
(50 TO 52 WEEKS), 1964
(percentages)ª

	Total	Total Employed	Total Worked Full-time
Under $1,000	3.2	2.3	1.8
$ 1,000 to $ 1,499	3.0	1.8	1.3
$ 1,500 to $ 1,999	3.3	1.9	1.5
$ 2,000 to $ 2,499	4.1	2.8	2.3
$ 2,500 to $ 2,999	4.0	3.0	2.7
$ 3,000 to $ 3,499	4.3	3.4	3.1
$ 3,500 to $ 3,999	4.1	3.7	3.5
$ 4,000 to $ 4,999	8.6	8.3	8.2
$ 5,000 to $ 5,999	9.9	10.4	10.7
$ 6,000 to $ 6,999	9.9	10.8	11.2
$ 7,000 to $ 7,999	9.3	10.3	10.8
$ 8,000 to $ 8,999	7.6	8.5	8.8
$ 9,000 to $ 9,999	6.3	7.1	7.4
$10,000 to $11,999	9.4	10.6	11.2
$12,000 to $14,999	6.8	7.8	8.2
$15,000 to $24,999	5.2	6.0	6.2
$25,000 and over	1.1	1.2	1.3
Total	100.0	100.0	100.0

ª *Current Population Reports* (1965b), p. 31.

to the point where additional gross income will result in so little
net income that they will elect to do less work, rather than to
invest much effort for meager additional results. Without examining the amount of income which accrues to the wealthy from
salary, as opposed to investments, speculation, and the like; and
without examining the amount of income which is earned by

corporations, rather than by individuals, and whether corporations refrain from expanding their operations because of taxes; and without examining the rationale for tax increases which are proposed from time to time by various agencies and officials of the government as a means of keeping the economy healthy and productive—it is worth noting that despite the widespread mythology that the wealthy are guided in great part by tax considerations, Barlow and his associates (Barlow et al., 1966) found that

> Only one-eighth of the sample [of the wealthy] said that they have actually curtailed their work effort because of the progressive income tax. . . . Those facing the highest marginal taxes reported work disincentives only a little more frequently than did those facing the lowest rates. . . . The implication of these findings is that the loss of annual output due to work disincentives caused by the progressive income tax is of negligible proportions. . . . There are several grounds for our reluctance to believe that so significant a fraction as one-eighth of the high-income group really worked less because of income taxes . . . it can be estimated that one-sixteenth, not one-eighth, of the high-income group had suffered a tax disincentive [pp. 3, 141].

In short, work disincentives among the wealthy due to taxes are negligible.

In addition to the near-poor, those just above the poverty line, and the wealthy—on all of whom an income guarantee might have some effect—there are also those who are outside the labor force. Logically, their incentive is not at issue since they are not potential workers, but nevertheless there is a widespread concern about the effect on work incentives of those who, insofar as formal public policy is concerned, cannot or should not work.

For example, the retirement provisions of the OASDHI program are explicitly provided to make it possible for persons who have a work record to retire at a specified age; and implicitly are intended to encourage such retirement in the interests of high production and full employment. Yet, retirement is blamed for many social and individual ills, and there seems to be some desire to allow people to retire, but to assure that they keep working anyhow. Thus, a former Secretary of Health, Education, and Welfare testified before a Congressional committee that one of the problems with which his Department was grappling was a way of permitting and encouraging the retired to continue working during their retirement.

Similarly, although the intent of the original ADC program was to make it possible for mothers of young children to remain at home and give them care, the success of the program is increasingly measured by how many mothers can be induced to leave home and go to work, even if this requires providing day care centers for their children and training courses for the mothers. In the same way, programs dealing with the disabled—the Vocational Rehabilitation Administration and Workmen's Compensation programs—are not primarily concerned with supporting or helping the disabled in their condition, but rather with returning them to the labor market. Thus, the VRA justifies its program in terms of the tax dollars paid by those returned to work, and officials of Workmen's Compensation have been vociferous in holding that if the disabled receive as much compensation as they had previously received as salaries, they would not be motivated to work, and therefore would not undertake rehabilitation.[3]

Finally, although considering the incentive to work among those who are actively seeking work and cannot find it would seem not to be pertinent, yet the fact that at least some of them will find employment if they keep looking makes it desirable that they be motivated to keep looking, and hence the unemployed are also of interest in this study.

Attitudes toward unemployment and the roles played by incentive or disincentive factors in each of the groups mentioned above will be examined in later chapters. The next chapter examines work motivations generally.

[3] See Maisonpierre, 1965.

4

Motivation
to Work

*A*lthough the motivation to work is only one among myriads of human motivations, the professional literature about work motivation alone is enormous. As early as the eighteenth century Adam Smith devoted part of his monumental treatise, *The Wealth of Nations,* to "The Causes of the Improvement in the Productive Powers of Labour," and in 1869 Galton was attempting to explain occupational inheritance in terms of natural ability. A great part of Marx's work in the nineteenth century was concerned with the relationship of man and work, and entire schools of academic discipline and professional

61

activity have since evolved around "scientific management" and "human relations in industry."

In some such cases, work is defined as physical activity; in others, as income-producing employment; in still others, as socially prescribed behavior; and in many cases these meanings are used interchangeably. A somewhat different approach is used in the present book: the various approaches to work motivation are categorized as those which derive from instinct theory; those which see work as the necessary means for satisfying material needs; and those which see work as satisfying social needs. It should be obvious that these three approaches interrelate—instinctual and material needs find expression in socially mediated forms; social needs may have the strength and pervasiveness associated with instincts, and so on. Consequently, the division made here is purely for heuristic purposes.

As a formal theoretical system, the instinct school of human behavior has been largely discredited, since the proliferation of supposed instincts to match each isolated behavior robbed the theory of whatever descriptive aspects it contained and precluded the development of further descriptive and prescriptive functions. Nevertheless, the fact that a theory of instincts existed and was widely accepted resulted in thought patterns and social structures predicated on such instincts, which persist even though the formal theory is no longer of great importance. In addition, although a coherent theory of instincts is no longer offered as an explanation of all human behavior, the assumption of the existence of instincts is not thereby necessarily denied. Veblen, for example, argued that workmanship was an important instinct in human nature, and although the satisfactions of good workmanship—creativity, accomplishment, pride—are not necessarily the same as those of its origin, work, the significant fact is that Veblen was speaking of the existence of one instinct, without thereby implying an instinctive explanation for all behavior.

An example of a supposed instinct which does relate to work motivations is found in Parrington's description of the English middle class, which came into being as a result of the Industrial Revolution. Parrington (1927) holds that the philosophy of the English middle class assumed as its determining principle the common instinct of acquisitiveness. Nor does Parrington see this assumption of an instinct of acquisitiveness as merely incidental in that philosophy. He stresses it many times: "The English philosophy of laissez-faire, based on the assumed universality of the acquisitive instinct"; "The Gilded Age recognized only the acquisitive instinct"; or, "It conceived of human nature as acquisitive."

In view of this belief in innate acquisitiveness, it was not surprising that the common view of recipients of welfare, such as it was, was that of people with unlimited acquisitive instincts which they, like everyone else, were naturally and necessarily trying to satisfy by acquiring as much as they could. Welfare laws were thus designed primarily to guard against the acquisitiveness of recipients, and it is to this English middle-class outlook that American social welfare still owes the remnants of Poor Law philosophy which continue to control.

The theory of instinctual acquisitiveness is not derived from observation of economic behavior only. It has also been adduced from studies of child development which cite infant behavior of grasping and holding, as well as from the observed behavior of very young children who guard their possessions and term them "mine." To the extent that this instinct is viewed as phylogenetic, it can be and sometimes is argued that the existence of such an instinct must be one of the causes for human survival. Therefore, goes this argument, the instinct of acquisitiveness should not only be accepted and cherished, but encouraged, as assuring the continuation of the human race; and socialization should, at most, simply attempt to channel as much of the instinct into sharing behavior as is necessary for society. Insofar as acquisitiveness is seen as an instinct, and insofar as the major and only socially approved channel for its satisfaction is through productive employment, then the motivation to work—in the sense of holding a job—can be said to arise, at least in part, from instinctual sources.

In the same manner, the motivation to work can be traced to instinctive bodily needs. Hill (1956) and Kagan and Berkun (1954) have suggested that there is an activity drive which expresses itself, when necessary, in proportion to the time during which the organism has been forced to be inactive. DeMan, in

reaching somewhat similar conclusions, implicitly takes into consideration the societal structure in which the activity expresses
itself, saying (Vroom, 1964): "Inactivity, were it only for physiological reasons, is a torment to a healthy human being. Every
muscle is alive with the impulse to activity. The normal form of
this activity is: in the child, play: in the adult, work [p. 33]."

Freud added another dimension to the impulse to work
with his famous prescription for happiness: "To love and to work."
This placed a value upon work, as upon love, for its own sake, as
a human imperative. It is possible that Freud did not view work
as an instinct, but by classifying work in the same category as love,
Freud indicated that work had value as such, without regard for,
and indeed without need for, any issue or results. For those who
were influenced by Freud's thinking and that of his followers, the
result of this formulation was that the need to work was not seen
simply as a fact of economic life, nor as a relaxation of bodily
tensions, but as a psychological desideratum for self-fulfillment; its
frustration resulted in the same symptoms as do frustrated instinctual drives—tension, unhappiness, psychosomatic symptoms,
and possibly death. Many circles of people who might have rejected
the instinct theory of work as such were persuaded by the im-
primatur of Freud to accept it as a psychic imperative; and many
of these people, not incidentally, were and are the people most
directly concerned with social welfare questions and the assumptions which undergird them.

There is, finally, the view of work as an instinct which
has been implanted in man by God, to serve His purposes. Regardless of the manner in which this view has been exploited, there
are, nevertheless, immense numbers of people who see work as
Divinely inspired, and not just as a duty, but as an urge or an instinct of the same order as man's desire for salvation. In this view,
God requires work of man, and man therefore desires to work.

Regardless of which of these, or other, reasons lead one
to accept an instinctual theory of work, the very essence of such
a theory is that work is seen as a value in human life for its own
sake. It then follows that absence of work, or being prevented from
working, results in—*must* result in—unhappiness, illness, and
deterioration. In the early days of organized social welfare in

America, this view was stated by Lowell (Breul, 1965): "Human nature is so constituted that no man can receive as a gift what he should earn by his own labor without moral deterioration [p. 12]." In more recent times, the same view was stated before a Senate committee, in 1965, by the chairman of the Kentucky Medical Rehabilitation Committee (Massie, 1965): "The best possible thing for a worker is to work. He is more satisfied and he is happier, but he does not understand this [p. 740]."

In a similar vein, the findings that aged retirees have been found to become ill, or to die, at higher rates than nonretirees have been attributed, by implication, to the denial of their instinctive need to work.[1] Friedmann (1964) speaks of a "toxic condition" caused by a long period of unemployment, and Field (1953) says that lack of expected motivation may be resolved by assumption of the "sick role." Anything, then, which prohibits people from working, or which entices or induces them not to work—that is, to overcome their natural desires and instinct to work—renders them unhappy, immoral, or ill.

From this belief in an instinctual basis for working, and in the damaging effect on the individual of denial of expression of this instinct, arises the "moral fiber" viewpoint concerning unearned income. This is the belief that income-maintenance programs generally, and the non-insurance-type programs particularly, in which money is made available to recipients without requiring work of them in return, is damaging to their moral fiber, or personalities, or psyches. This belief is one of the historic bases for work-relief programs rather than outright relief, and manifests itself today in the current emphasis on trying to provide jobs for the poor, rather than payments. One of the fundamental concepts underlying the insistence on work relief was the belief that relief to able-bodied men was demoralizing, and one of the current proposals for ending poverty is that the government become the employer of last resort because, as Levitan puts it (1965), "Most observers would agree that it would be preferable to provide income to impoverished families through the creation of jobs rather than providing cash assistance [p. 51]."

[1] See, for example, Busse, 1961.

The instinct theory of work motivations has proliferated, at one extreme, into postulations of instincts for mastery of materials, craftsmanship, creativity, and "good workmanship"; and at the other extreme, the word *instinct* has fallen into disrepute, being replaced by such terms as *predispositions* and *imprints*. One writer (Lerner, 1957), for example, simply speaks of "The pervasive hunger for commodities and material satisfactions [p. 252]," without defining further the nature or the basis of such hunger.

A second assumption generally held concerning the motivation to work does not see labor as an end in itself, as does the instinct theory, but rather as a necessary means for the satisfaction of material needs. In almost all times and places, most men have needed to work to acquire the wherewithal to remain alive. Holders of this view see man as subject to his physical environment, which requires work in order to yield products. Indeed, in preindustrial society the majority of people worked in order to produce their own necessities, and if these did not suffice, suffered from lacks. It was rarely possible to produce with one's own labor much more than one could consume, and there was little practical value in doing so. Thus, Weber (1952) holds that it was characteristic of the precapitalist era that the peasant who achieved with less labor that which he had previously achieved with more could not be persuaded to work to acquire greater returns, but would instead reduce his work, and thus achieve his traditional and desired amount of recompense. Whyte (1955) holds that this traditionalism continues to exist in economically underdeveloped countries.

On the American continent, the need to work for bodily sustenance was reinforced for the first settlers by the unfamiliar conditions, the hostile climate, and soon-unfriendly population which they found. As the frontier began to move westward, physical labor was the only method of wresting riches, or at least a living, from the existing resources. Caudill (1965) points out that the frontier, while it lasted, required work rather than education and sophistication, and when it disappeared it left the uneducated and unsophisticated workers in a poverty lag from which their descendants have not yet recovered. In the same way he points out that the immense resources of the frontier allowed for inefficient and wasteful work methods, but as the resources dwindled, users of such methods could no longer maintain themselves.

Only in the South did a different situation prevail. There a Greek-type aristocracy, built on slave labor, eschewed personal participation in work. This veneer of an aristocracy, however, was very thin, and both slaves and the majority of whites (who owned no slaves) were expected, and found it necessary, to work. When the Civil War destroyed the pretense of an aristocracy and bankrupted the region, the labor required to rebuild the South reemphasized the place of work in the acquisition of need satisfiers.

The continual flow of immigrants to America, most of whom had been peasants or workers and knew no other life also emphasized the importance of work on the American scene as the key to sustenance. In addition, the masses of immigrants gave up, for the most part, on their own possibilities for vertical mobility in American society, but they invested themselves in the sweat-shops, the railroads, and the mines so that they would assure not only their own survival and that of their children, but would also create better opportunities for their children and grandchildren than they themselves had enjoyed.

Finally, the motivation to work to satisfy physical needs was further affected by the changes in methods of production which came about as a result of the Industrial Revolution. These placed an intermediate step between labor and consumption, bringing masses of people into a wage economy. One result of this was that the direct issue of work was no longer goods, with a limited utility, but money, with unlimited utility. Motivation to work was stimulated by the greater utility of money wages, which could be spent for a variety of goods; saved; invested; or hidden away. Second, the product of a collectivity of workers was much greater than the aggregate sum of their individual production would have been, due to division of labor, rationalization of tasks, and specialization. Consequently, the amount of goods available for consumption both increased in quantity and dropped in price, reinforcing the motivation to work, in order to acquire such pre-viously inaccessible items. Increases in production and availability of goods led to heightened desires, or newly felt needs, which in turn made for greater production.

From this cycle sprang the theory of consumption as the key to a prosperous economy, with the concomitant effect that those who would not or could not consume in sufficient quantities (that is, the poor) were seen as a drag on the economy. One effect of this view was that plans to aid the poor began to be viewed with an eye toward their impact on the economy. On the one hand, the fact that the poor tend to spend a larger share of their income than do the nonpoor (who have a tendency to try to save and invest) was and is offered as a reason for trying to transfer income from the latter to the former, whereas the need to utilize the manpower represented by the unemployed poor is part of the rationale for training courses and other rehabilitative measures.

Another result of the increased availability of a greater variety of goods was the emergence of the theory of the insatiability of human wants, which became a key concept in the development of an industrial economy and an article of faith concerning the basis of work motivations. According to this theory, visible examples of new products and ways of living which are at least conceivably attainable lead to new wants and aspirations which men endeavor to satisfy. Thus a straw mattress is no longer comfortable enough to induce sleep in those who try the new cotton-filled mattresses, and these, in turn, become uncomfortable or unsatisfying to those who prefer foam rubber. Corn liquor burns the throat accustomed to Scotch, and radio is boring when television is available.

The question which arose around the theory of insatiability was whether men are motivated to work as hard for nonsustenance or "created" needs as they are for primary or physiological needs. Although, according to classical economic theory, any notion of necessary versus unnecessary or important as against unimportant good was rigorously excluded, such distinctions became of primary importance in investigations of incentives, and represented one of the basic limitations of classical economic theory as applied to contemporary life (Galbraith, 1958).

In this connection, Arendt (1958) distinguishes between "labor," which is related to the cyclical and biological nature of man and which produces articles which are essential to life but immediately consumed, and "work," whose products are lasting and a source of satisfaction in themselves, not only because they fulfill biological needs. Keynes, too, distinguishes between those needs which are absolute in the sense that we feel them whatever the situation of our fellow human beings may be, and those which are relative in that their satisfaction lifts us above, or makes us feel superior to, our fellows (Galbraith, 1958). More crudely put, the question which arises is, does the hungry man work harder for food than the well-fed man does for social prestige? Or, are the results of socialization as strong and as lasting as are inherited or biological needs?

Keynes felt that while absolute needs could be satisfied, relative needs were insatiable—hence his economic theory. There seems to be a logic to this distinction. Nevertheless, both observation and the findings of social psychology indicate that relative needs might even be more compelling than the absolute ones. Life offers too many examples of people depriving themselves in the biological area in order to satisfy what seem to be the needs of vanity, altruism, or filial responsibility: the girl who stays hungry to maintain a slender figure, the military volunteer, the mother who denies herself needed medicine in order to help her children achieve their desires. Indeed, the interaction of psychic and somatic phenomena has been too well documented to be susceptible of serious doubt; social situations change even autonomous body conditions as well as overt behavior, and biological needs and conditions influence the social situation. Consequently, a division between bodily and social needs is a spurious division for an examination of incentives[2] unless—as may be held to be the case— the poor are seen as being in a social situation which does not give rise to needs that can be satisfied by work.

In this connection, Maslow's theory of hierarchies of need is helpful. Maslow (1954) posits needs as potent and prepotent, with the latter becoming potent as the previously potent are satisfied. Although Maslow assumes that physiological needs are initially potent, other needs become potent when and as these bodily needs are met. In other words, to the person whose bodily needs are

---

[2] For this reason, no distinction between work and labor is maintained in this study, the terms being used interchangeably.

provided for, the desire for a status symbol may be just as strong as was the previous desire for food. In this view, motivation remains constant, as it were, while the need which it attempts to satisfy changes. Since, as pointed out above, biological needs cannot be separated from social needs, the order of appearance is not the important factor, but rather the concept that as certain needs are satisfied, other needs appear.

In this sense, the motivation to work to attain material items would appear to be equally strong in the person living below the subsistence level, whose potent need is for subsistence items, and in the person living above the poverty line, whose need for status symbols, or to satisfy newly acquired tastes, has become relative—in Keynes' wording. Further, crossing the poverty line upwards would mean that new wants become potent, rather than that all wants are then satisfied.

In modern society, few need-satisfying methods other than work are provided. The fact that work may be unobtainable, or not result in income sufficient to meet needs, does not change the basic structure of a work-oriented society as the vehicle by which men are supposed to attain satisfaction of their wants. The society —and certainly the state—are under no legal obligation to do more than to provide a work-satisfaction linked system. As Simmel (1965) points out, the state may create legal bodies which are obligated to the state to assist needy individuals; but they are not so obligated to the latter, who have no legal claim on them. In fact, under Common Law a person has no *legal* claim on the community for subsistence. Even large-scale federal programs, like OASDHI, do not provide a legal and enforceable right to even bare economic existence (Smith, 1955). On the contrary, it has been held that an important element in the American philosophy of social insurance is that benefits should be related to previous earnings (Brown, 1956). The principle of linkage to previous earnings obviously denies the principle of sustenance as a right. Consequently, in our society, the only acceptable legal and dependable method (contingent on capacity and opportunity) to fulfill needs is through work, and such needs seem to be unending and insatiable.

The motivation to work as a means of acquiring material goods is supported not only by observation and logic, but by some empirical evidence as well. Kornhauser (1965), for example, studied 635 manual workers in depth, and found that "When the working men were questioned about what they really want in life, their answers overwhelmingly specify financial and material goals. . . . There are strikingly few expressions of interest in personal achievement, self-development, and self-expressive activities [p. 268]." From his survey of a number of studies of workers, Dubin (1958) also found that "Income remains the all-important means for satisfying human wants and needs. Income from wages and salaries is the major incentive to work [pp. 240–241]."

Since, however, man is a social being, his instinctual and physical needs must be worked out within a social matrix. Society not only provides and condones certain ways in which such needs can be met, but by its own existence also creates additional needs. The motivation to work, as a social need on the American scene, can be understood only as part of the total socioeconomic system, for which a look at the historical roots is necessary. These historical roots of the American economy and society include the inheritance of the Protestant Ethic, the triumph in America of laissez-faire capitalism, and participation in the Industrial Revolution.

The Protestant Ethic had its beginnings with Martin Luther, who attempted to endow work with religious dignity by defining it as a vocation, or a calling. In this view, each person serves God best by doing most perfectly the work of one's profession or vocation, regardless of earthly rewards. For those responding to Luther, work, of no matter what nature, became a religious duty. John Calvin went a step further: not only was work a religious duty, but men were called upon to work without desire for the fruit of their labor, simply because to work is the will of God. Such work would establish God's kingdom on earth, and this was its value and its end.

Such was the attitude toward work which the Puritans brought with them to New England—an attitude toward labor as "not simply a requirement imposed by nature, or a punishment for the sin of Adam. It is in itself a kind of ascetic discipline . . .

a spiritual end, for in it alone can the soul find health, and it
must be continued as an ethical duty long after it has ceased to
be a material necessity [Tawney, 1958, p. 274]."

Whyte (1955) also interprets the Protestant Ethic as
saying that a man "*should* want to work hard and get ahead. He
should want to make money. Furthermore, money should not be
viewed simply as a means to some other end, such as the enjoyment
of life. The acquisition of money is believed in almost as an end
in itself. Making money is simply a good thing and people should
be encouraged to do it [pp. 12–13]."

The religious implications which the Protestant Ethic
added to work, by tying it to salvation, deepened its roots and
intensified its fervor. In addition, the Protestant Ethic served other
purposes. As Tawney (1958) dryly remarks: "A society which
reverences the attainment of riches as the supreme felicity will
naturally be disposed to regard the poor as damned in the next
world, if only to justify itself for making their life a hell in this
[p. 284]." From the latter point of view flows the natural extension that work is not only moral in its own right, but is also a
means for instilling moral discipline. Consequently, requiring work
of delinquents and criminals seems not only very just and very
moral, but also highly efficacious as a means of reforming the individual wrongdoer (Martin, 1966). And, it might be added,
work is the best thing in the world for the physical, psychological,
and moral betterment of the poor.

In America, the Protestant Ethic first took root in New
England, where the later burgeoning of industry gave scope to investment, as well as provided opportunities for wage employment.
Consequently, well-bred young New England ladies were not
averse to working for a few years in a factory, while living in
strictly run boarding houses and saving money for a dowry. Indeed,
in the Puritan tradition such work and such savings were Christian
duties. New England settlers in other parts of the country, and
Protestant and Neo-Protestant groups like the Mormons, carried
the principles of the Protestant Ethic to other areas. However,
the affinity between the Protestant Ethic and industrialization
caused it to take root mainly in the cities, whereas in rural areas
the agrarian, humanitarian spirit epitomized by Thomas Jefferson

remained strong. Eventually, however, not only did the Protestant Ethic triumph in the cities, but it became the work ethic for all America. The reason is not hard to find: In 1890, 77 per cent of the American people were rural; in 1960, only 30 per cent (Folsom, 1965).

When and where the Protestant Ethic was strong, there was a religious belief in the efficacy of labor for attaining salvation, which was a powerful reinforcement to the individual motivation to work, as well as the creator of an expectation that everyone else would or should respond similarly. The continuation of this influence continued far beyond the Colonial period, as de Grazia (1962) has noted: "Work was good, or would become so, was the right of every man and a duty as well. . . . The doctrine was that of the Renaissance, the actual time was that of the nineteenth century [p. 32]." The twentieth century, too, continues to be influenced by the Protestant Ethic. That work is good in and of itself is part of the credo of modern America. Groups like those referred to as Proper Bostonians have maintained the Protestant Ethic until the present day. Thus, "If he made what others might feel was a little too much money, he himself felt he was meant to make that much. 'God,' said one merchant, 'made me a rich man!' [Amory, 1947, p. 91]."

A second historic root which has influenced the view of work as a social necessity in America is the inheritance of the laissez-faire attitude toward business.

Weber (1952) pointed out that a belief in hard work as a religious duty, coupled with a belief in enjoyment of possessions as a sin (which together constituted the Protestant Ethic), must have been the most powerful level for the expansion of "that attitude which we have . . . called the spirit of capitalism." Tilgher (1962) goes somewhat further, holding that the Protestant Ethic not only made possible, but *required,* a new economic structure:

> From this paradox—the command to ceaseless effort, to ceaseless renunciation of the fruit of effort—must needs follow a new economic practice. . . . A new use—the only worthy use —has been found for profit. As soon as earned it is used to finance fresh venture, to breed new profit, again to be rein-

vested . . . when we search history for the first germ of capitalistic civilization, we find it . . . unquestionably in the worldly asceticism of Calvin [p. 19].

Whyte (1955) underscores the individualism inherent in the Protestant Ethic: "Man not only *is* an isolated competitive individual; he also *should* be thus individualistically oriented [pp. 12–13]."

By positing work as a duty, the Protestant Ethic overcame the traditionalism noted above by Weber, in which the worker stopped working when he had achieved his previous, or traditional, output. Instead, there were both need and benefit in continued work, and the factory or other type of industrial collectivity provided the opportunity. Since the result of such work was not only income for the workers, but also profit for the owners, the new economic structure needed an economic theory which would justify production for profit, and some of the practices which followed in its wake. This theory was found in the concept of the free market.

According to this theory, the proper functioning of the market was the result of, and therefore required, each person's attempt to maximize his own gains. Such maximization attempts balanced each other, and in such a balanced market, transactions could take place with some degree of secure anticipation of the results. The invisible hand which regulated the market, and averted chaos, was the unrestricted activity by which each pitted himself against all. By maximizing profit and minimizing cost in competition with others doing the same, the individuals in concert made available the goods and services which the acceptance of the public stamped as most socially useful. The more that self-seeking strove against the whole, the more it served the social good.

Under this theory, sections of the economy, or individuals, who do not attempt to secure maximum gratifications upset the balance and disturb the proper functioning of the market. Consequently, it is not only permissible, but necessary and desirable, that people attempt to secure as much income as possible. People who do not choose to work to their fullest capacity not only thereby indicate lack of ethics and morality—which might conceivably be between themselves and their consciences—but they upset the economic system, and thereby do damage to others.

There naturally flowed from this conception of the market the image of the "economic man," controlled purely by rational behavior in an attempt to achieve the greatest economic benefit possible. The only incentives which work—and which should work —on the economic man are pecuniary incentives, and he can be depended upon to respond to such incentives, no matter how minute, regardless of any other pressures playing upon him. Although no one purports to believe in this mythical creature any longer, his previous incarnation structured societal expectations concerning work, acted to limit many of the social welfare programs which still exist, and continues to haunt many planners of new or changed programs, guiding their hands as they write. In addition, insofar as this image has been internalized by individuals, they may be expected to respond more strongly to economic incentives than to any other kind, and to expect others to do the same.

From laissez-faire as an economic doctrine there also flowed the concept of "rugged individualism"—each person being responsible for himself, with neither the right to call upon others nor the responsibility of responding to such calls. Glazer (1965), in seeking reasons for differences between American and foreign welfare systems, sums up the peculiarly American style of response to social welfare questions with a single word: individualism. A man's work was considered his only channel to success; all others depended upon other people, and such dependency was a sign of weakness. This doctrine, understandably, might have been more popular with the successful than with the needy. Tawney (1958), with his usual pungency, says that the "Individualist complex owes part of its self-assurance to the suggestion of Puritan moralists, that practical success is at once the sign and the reward of ethical superiority. . . . The demonstration that distress is a proof of demerit . . . has always been popular with the prosperous [p. 284]." Yet this attitude is not limited to the wealthy. One of the strong underlying values in our total society is the concern for the importance of individual effort through work in the open market.

"A man must exchange his services for income and contribute to the economy; leisure, recreation, and enjoyment of life should be earned [Hansen and Carter, 1966, p. 99]." Implications of this attitude continue to exist in current programs. Lichtman (1966) points out that tying Medicare to Social Security was a "capitulation to the conservative values of 'individual self-concern.' 'personal initiative,' and 'the responsibility of each for his own well-being.' "

Another important aspect of the theory of the free market was the implied limitation of the powers of government. Interference of any kind in the operations of the market could only disrupt it, and government intervention came to be looked upon as mischievous interference with the laws of nature. It was not the government's proper role to interfere with business, as any problems which existed would work themselves out to their solutions through the operations of the free market. Traces of this theory continue to crop up in American history: a President who holds that "The business of America is business"; a Cabinet member who declares that what is good for General Motors is good for America; or faith in the growth of the Gross National Product to eradicate unemployment, poverty, slums, and mental illness. The expectation concerning workers, and thereby—via socialization—the expectation of workers, was that their own work was their only defense and support in the economic sphere.

The importance of the influence of laissez-faire capitalism on American society is emphasized by Parrington's reminder that this development was not historically inevitable. Rather, it was a triumph of English Puritanism over French agrarianism and humanitarianism, which Parrington (1927) terms the Romantic tradition. In his words, the French tradition was "a passionate social idealism . . . that a juster, more wholesome social order should take the place of the existing obsolete system; that reason and not interests should determine social institutions; that the ultimate ends to be sought were universal liberty, equality, and fraternity [pp. 267ff]." The rival tradition, again in Parrington's words, "was of English middle class origin . . . it embodied the principle of liberalism as that principle was understood by men of affairs. It conceived of a social Utopia that must result if economic forces were done away with and individual enterprise were free to buy and sell in the open market [p. vii]."

It is difficult to judge to what extent American society, and especially the social welfare system, would have differed had the French been the victors in the French and Indian Wars. It is interesting to note, however, that one of the major differences between the French welfare system as it is now constituted and the present American system is the emphasis on the family in France, as compared with the above-noted emphasis on the individual in the United States. It is the latter emphasis which tends to see lack of motivation or capacity to work as an individual matter that the individual can control, rather than being caused by familial or societal conditions.

French social welfare is officially described as having the strengthening of the family structure as its goal. A publication of the French government (*Social Security in France,* 1964) begins by stating that "French social security has a definitely family nature [p. 14]," a fact which has been remarked by Schorr (1965), among others, and a situation further evidenced by the existence of legally recognized family associations for welfare purposes and by the fact that the French utilize family allowances in great measure—to the point that such allowances may be paid out in amounts greater than the basic salary of recipients. This is consonant with Parrington's conception of the Romantic tradition.

On the other hand, despite Stein's (1964) contention that American society is noteworthy for its emphasis on the family, the evidence does not seem to bear out this contention. Schorr has pointed out that American programs have usually begun with the individual, and only later have they taken into account the fact that individuals are parts of families (Glazer, 1965). A direct example of the predominant American view of families as treatment means, rather than ends, is contained in Davis's (1965)' statement: "To deal with the children of the poor, one must also deal with adults . . . that is, with the *parents* of the children [p. 299]."

Salary structures in the United States do not take into account the size of the family, and neither do severance pay and retirement funds. Since Unemployment Compensation and Workmen's Compensation are both based on previous salary, size of family does not affect these benefits. Although OASDHI has begun to be cognizant of families (as reflected in Schorr's comment, above), primary benefits are based on previous employment record. In addition, the implementation of AFDC has even been said to be antifamily, through the pressures to get mothers to work, to get fathers out of the family as a condition of eligibility, and through the enforcement of provisions of the Notification to Law Enforcement Officers rule, which requires that mothers inform law enforcement officers of the probable whereabouts of putative fathers. Even discussion of family structure has caused a heated controversy,[3] and family planning efforts remain in legal limbo. Glazer (1965) says that because we think of the individual worker alone, rather than the family, we find it easy to accept as a public policy that sixteen-year-old dropouts without experience should be paid the same wages as heads of families.

In this same vein, Wickenden (1965) says that the provisions whereby the aged and the disabled may receive assistance for which financial reimbursement to the states is two and a half times greater than that for payments to families with needy children is simply an evidence of prejudiced public attitudes. Indeed, the American attitude toward families, as expressed in social welfare programs, borders on the punitive, since attention is paid to families almost entirely in terms of enforcing relatives' responsibility rulings. Even social work services have long had an individual bias, and are only slowly moving toward family casework, counseling, and other services. This American attitude toward families works itself out, demographically, so that the larger the family in the United States, the poorer it tends to be.

Another difference between the American and French social welfare systems—that is, the difference between the Puritan and the humanitarian traditions—has to do with the participation of the public, including recipients, in the administration of programs. Whereas social security in France is administered by worker/employer bodies on the local level, it is completely the province of

---

[3] For example, see Rainwater and Yancey (1967).

government civil servants in the United States. The attempt to give recipients of services a policy voice in program administration in the United States has evoked more vociferous opposition than any other phase of the war on poverty.

Thus, the differences between the French Romantic tradition and the inheritance of English Liberalism may have been, and may continue to be, substantial, especially insofar as social welfare policies are concerned. Certainly, the triumph of laissez-faire capitalism in America created public expectations concerning individual attitudes and behaviors which have impact on work motivations and on the manner in which they are viewed.

A third tap-root of the American socioeconomic system which has ramifications in work motivations is the influence of America's participation in the Industrial Revolution. In regard to work motivations, three factors are important: the emphasis on production, the change in the nature of work, and the effect on work attitudes of labor in industrial collectivities.

One result of the growth of industrialization has been the emphasis on production which grew with it. This emphasis was not necessarily inevitable; Wilensky and Lebeaux point out that human societies have displayed great variations in their priority lists, some emphasizing commerce, others military expansion, religion, or something else. Economic development is not always at the top of the list (Wilensky and Lebeaux, 1958). In America, however, both the ancient preoccupation with production and the pervasive modern search for security have culminated in our time in a concern for production. Continually expanding production has come to be seen as the touchstone of the nation's well-being, and invocation of the growth rate of the GNP in defense of various measures takes on the nature of a talismanic incantation. In this way, certain social welfare programs are proposed and defended because of their influence on productivity, for example, "The factor that will permit a child to stay in school, or a mother to work or become literate . . . will have a payoff in increased productivity of labor [Kershaw, 1965, p. 56]."

A sufficient growth rate of the GNP will, it is held, solve all of the country's problems. Maximum production thereby becomes an overriding goal, and maximum production is held to

require full use of the country's human resources. Lerner (1957)
terms this attitude "the swaggering American sense that in a
dynamic society a mounting productivity will absorb all social
ills; that those who fall by the way are lazy or weak [p. 339]."
This emphasis on production has led to the creation of a social
role called "productive person." The productive person receives
approbation and self-satisfaction, both of which become positive
incentives to work. By contrast, the nonproductive person is stigmatized as harming the growth and prosperity (and thereby both
the happiness and security)' of the country.

Another result of the Industrial Revolution was the divorce
of workers from the fruits of their labor, thus divesting work of
any creative satisfaction which it might have held. Also, in many
cases work was transmuted into dull, repetitive chores which
further robbed work of any redeeming interest. The supposed
deadening effect of this kind of work on the human being has
been graphically depicted in fiction, and attested to by respondents
in some studies. Gurin's study (Gurin et al., 1960), for example,
found that in a nationwide survey, only 13 per cent of unskilled
workers were "very satisfied" with their jobs; 27 per cent of the
semiskilled; and 22 per cent of the skilled.

Paradoxically, a third feature of the Industrial Revolution
led to satisfactions at work, although these satisfactions derived
from the work group rather than from the work itself. They were
the result of work performed in and by collectivities. Work in a
factory, for example, had different overtones when performed as
part of an interacting whole than when performed by individuals
unrelated to a group. The enterprise could not allow each worker
to decide how much, or how fast, or how long he would work, or
to quit when he felt that he had done enough. Even the growth
and intervention of labor unions did not and could not operate
to allow each individual in the collectivity to determine his own
work pattern. Work therefore took on an interactional aspect—
the work of the individual was no longer seen as necessary for
his needs alone, but necessary for the well-being of others as well.
Therefore, the way in which an individual worked became the
proper concern of others. Specialization, as has been pointed out,
leads to interdependence, because of the need for coordination.

Hence, the worker who cannot do his share or who is felt to be deliberately shirking can expect to be stigmatized and penalized by his fellow workers, unless working below capacity is part of the norm established by the work group. Conversely, the work group can become a social group, even a primary group, in which the worker not only receives personal satisfactions, but in which he interacts on various levels with others, and in which he is accorded normative societal rewards—acceptance, recognition, friendship, and so on.

These social group aspects of working have been investigated in a number of settings since Roethlisberger and Dickson's seminal study (1939) of the men in the Bank Wiring Room. Although in some cases work was seen as drudgery from which the workers wanted only to escape as soon as possible, in many cases there were social satisfactions, or at the very least the opportunity for social satisfactions, within the work group. Whyte's study (1955) recounted how in a large machine shop of one plant in a giant corporation only nine individuals in a department of some three hundred production workers did not abide by the group limits on production norms. Herzberg and associates (1959) point out that the tremendous growth in studies and use of human relations techniques in industry are in themselves recognition of the non-economic factors in job satisfactions and productivity.

Such work "togetherness" may be encouraged or stressed by management through company ball teams, bowling leagues, picnics, and—on the executive level—an almost mandatory round of social affairs. Or, social groups may grow up within work settings which affect the way the work gets done, and/or spills over into after-hours friendships. Aside from the social activities, however, there are also the hours spent on the job, the interaction experienced during those hours, and, in most cases, enough concern for and about each others' feelings to create status, role, and relationship concerns. Homans (1951) has pointed out that, other things being equal, interaction almost invariably leads to interpersonal relationships. Also, the desire to be part of an affective network, or, being a part, to maintain self-satisfying relationships with others, seems to be an important part of individuals' social lives.

In addition to the small-group implications of work brought about by the results of the Industrial Revolution, there are also larger societal considerations. New industries and new jobs, as well as the division of labor, created new conditions of work. Consequently, the fact that men work, the kind of work which they do, and sometimes the manner in which they do their work, all began to have implications for the way in which they were regarded and the way in which they regarded themselves. Pfouts (n. d.) puts it succinctly:

> In our work-oriented society all adult males are expected to be productive wage earners. In most cases, gainful employment is a necessary though not a sufficient condition for a man to consider himself and be considered a responsible and respected member of the community. In addition, the kind of job he holds helps to determine both his self-image and his status in society. In short, work is a major life task and unless a man performs it adequately, he is a failure by his own standards and those of society.

Work thus takes on functions for the individual which are additional to discharge of instinctual needs or the mere provision of goods. Five such functions of work, held to be present in any situation defined by society as a job, have been given as (1) the provision of income; (2) regulation of life activity; (3) identification; (4) association; and (5) meaningful life experience [Friedmann and Havighurst, 1954, p. 5]. Vroom (1964) holds that work roles provide financial remuneration; require the expenditure of energy; involve the production of goods and services; permit or require social interaction; and affect the social status of the worker. Barlow and associates (1966) similarly speak of jobs as giving their occupants a sense of belonging, or a sense of power, or social status, or the satisfaction of meeting self-imposed standards of performance. Dubin (1958) adds to financial rewards the concept of psychic rewards, which include work assignments and privilege pay, and position rewards, which include power, authority, and status. In Herzberg's study, too, the respondents who were defined as having high (positive) attitudes towards their work reported as important factors in their jobs such items as achievement, recognition, responsibility, advancement, possibility of growth, and the like, as well as the work itself and the salary. In fact, recognition was rated as more important than salary by both high and low attitude holders (Herzberg et al., 1959). Friedmann and Havighurst (1954) also found that the majority of workers (72 per cent) found meanings in their work other than earning money: "Many of the workers . . . have told us what their work means to them. They have found other and more pleasurable meanings in their work [pp. 173, 189]." Kwant (1960) puts it: "It is quite evident . . . that individual profit is not the only, and not even the main motive for working. The emphasis on the individual profit of labor has been one of the worst aspects of the economy of the nineteenth century, and we have not yet completely eliminated this attitude from our thinking [p. 153]." In short, the industrialization of the economy brought about an emphasis on the social aspects of, and the necessity for, work.

Added to such direct social needs met by work, there are also the symbolic meanings which attach to work and which become part of the motivation to work. Symbols, being man-made, may arise from instinct or from biological or social needs, but they become symbols—in the manner used here—when they become reified and invested with a significance of their own. Thus, Burke (1965) speaks of purely necessitous labor as drudgery, whereas he holds that symbolic labor is fitted into the deepest-lying patterns of the individual.

An example of the reification of one type of labor into a symbol is found in agriculture. Once considered the most necessary form of labor (possibly as a remnant of the French Romantic tradition, which saw the state of nature as noble; and of the Physiocratic school, which saw agriculture as the basic source of all wealth), it continues to be looked upon as a higher form than many others, even in an economy with an overabundance of agricultural products. Consequently, three million more people than are necessary—in terms of their products—are paid out of the general revenues of the United States to remain farmers. The rationale which approves—or, at least, does not disapprove—of payments to unnecessary farmers, but opposes payments to city dwellers seems to be, in part, the assumption that the very exigencies of farm life require the farmer to work (the needs of farm ani-

mals, the daily and seasonal routines of crops)' and therefore he
is accepted as deserving of unearned income. In addition, however,
there is a *mystique* about farm life as such, which results in approval of measures to support farmers, whether needy or not.

Types of work also take on symbolic significance, as when
jobs are classified as professional, skilled, semiskilled, and unskilled;
or when occupation is used as one basis for determining social
status. For example, an empirical study conducted by Smith (1962)
rated the prestige of various occupations, with the result that a
United States Supreme Court justice was rated as the most
prestigeful and a professional prostitute as the least prestigeful,
although one might contend that the prostitute works harder than
the judge. Even in scales which are used for research, there
appear to be symbolic implications. Thus, Caplow (1954) points
out that the Minnesota Scale appears to contain a general bias
against work which is dirty or strenuous, even when such work is
highly paid and requires a high degree of skill.

Other symbolic aspects of work show up in the facts—
remarked by Caplow—that street cleaners may be as well paid as
policemen, or better paid, but they will not enjoy equal status;
and that young women entering the labor market prefer clerical
employment to factory work, even when it is offered on much
inferior terms. Caplow calls attention to the fact that there is an
assumption

> . . . that personal service is inherently degrading. To this
> there is sometimes attached the related notion that it is less
> honorable to be employed by an individual than to be employed
> in the same capacity by an organization. The census classifica-
> tion of Edwards places all servants at the very bottom of the
> occupational heap, below farm laborers and unskilled industrial
> workers [p. 48].

Similarly, although the lifetime earnings of plumbers and electricians
are higher than those of school teachers, the status of the latter
is usually higher (H. P. Miller, 1964).

Symbolism is attached not only to specific jobs and occupations, but various aspects of work as a whole also have symbolic
meanings. For example, it seems a widespread American belief that
men should make more than women—or, more specifically, that a

husband should make more than his wife. The symbolic nature of the family, and the male as the husband and father figure, thus becomes attached to the meaning of work. In the same way, work is perceived as important in and of itself, without reference to the necessity, meaningfulness, or desirability of that which it accomplishes. It becomes the symbol of ambition, thrift, trustworthiness, and other normative values of American life. Schottland (1965) speaks of the prevailing attitude which equates work with well-being. Thus, "good worker" becomes an accolade; "poor worker," an epithet.

Another symbolic aspect of work has to do with the sense of community felt by men—the desire to aid the community to achieve its goals, which in a work-centered society requires work. Sense of community thus becomes a work incentive. The symbolic nature of work is further emphasized by the rites of passage connected with it. Graduation ceremonies symbolizing entrance into the world of work are commonplace, as is the acquisition of a union card in some occupations. Coser (1965) goes further, and calls the granting of relief the assignment of the person to the category of the poor—a type of degradation ceremony. So deeply has the symbolic nature and value of work penetrated into the very warp and woof of American attitudes and behaviors, that Lewis and Brissett (1967) find that even sex relationships have come to be regarded and discussed as a form of work.

Because of the nature of symbols, the symbolic view of work seems to be more charged with passion than is either the instinct or the usefulness view of work. Work thus takes on moral, religious, and almost mystical overtones, leading to discussion of work and incentive questions in terms that are very heavily emotion-laden. Indeed, such discussions are not seen as merely involving jobs, money, or other material entities, but become struggles over deep psychic and cultural commitments to other values which are taken as ultimate goals, shaped in large measure by rigid moral and religious attitudes and beliefs (Martin, 1966). This deep, passionate belief that men should work, without regard for the objective usefulness of their production, will be recognized as the influence of the Protestant Ethic, operating within the socioeconomic structure brought about by the Industrial Revolution. It is one of the factors which not only permits, but which also makes for widespread featherbedding and make-work on the American scene, and the prescription and use of work for crime prevention, punishment, rehabilitation, and character building. Insofar as individuals share in this mystique of work, it can be assumed to be part of their work motivation.

In summary, the instinctual, material, and social needs of Americans—the latter including the inheritance of the Protestant Ethic, the Industrial Revolution, and laissez-faire economics—can be said to have resulted in widely held attitudes and beliefs concerning work motivation: (1) Men work to satisfy their instincts, to acquire psychic self-fulfillment, and to attain religious salvation. (2) Men work to satisfy their material needs, which are continually expanding. The necessity for work in order to attain such satisfactions is constantly reinforced by prevailing American conditions and attitudes. (3) Men work in order to feel accepted as members of society, by fulfilling their expected roles in the economy, proving their independence, achieving the satisfactions which accrue from working with others, and by being productive in a work-oriented society.

In addition, the American work ethic requires that everyone who possibly can should work—for his own mental health, his physical well-being, the good of the economy, and the smooth functioning of society. These beliefs guide the actions of Americans in regard to their work patterns. Persons whose wealth seems to make it unnecessary for them to continue to work nevertheless do so. Inheritors of wealth and self-made millionaires rarely choose to lead the life of the idle rich. Although a Tommy Manville garners much publicity, it is due to the exception that he represents; the working Rockefellers, Kennedys, and others of the same type, who continue working beyond the point where the income is important as such, are the normal pattern. In other words, Americans not only say they would continue working if sudden riches struck them, they really do it.

In the same way, most people who are eligible to retire early in life, with wealth or incomes considerably above subsistence level, elect to keep on working or retire from one career only to begin another. Thus, professional athletes, whose careers are short, but who can amass enough money during their careers for the rest of their lives and who are also the recipients of generous pension plans, almost invariably undertake second careers after the end of the first ones (Bookbinder, 1955). Similarly, over 7.5 per cent of United States Civil Service employees are presently eligible for retirement, but prefer to continue working, and 57.7 per cent of those who have retired have begun second careers or have gone back to work in some fashion (Messer, 1964). The same general picture prevails for military retirees (Biderman, 1967).

The existence of such attitudes toward work has resulted, as most widely held attitudes do, in the creation and modification of social structures. For example, the need to work and the value of work to the individual have been affirmed by laws supporting the activities of labor unions, and by court opinions which have held, in effect, that workers have vested rights in their jobs, an investment which cannot be summarily withdrawn by the employer. In addition, the structure of the economy is such that a 4 per cent or 5 per cent rate of unemployment is held to be necessary in order to avoid inflation. That is, employment of the presently unemployed would, according to economic theory, utilize marginally productive people at pay rates higher than is economic. Therefore, one measure for avoiding inflation is by maintaining a pool of unemployed workers. Similarly, the structure of the economy is such that the difficult, dirty, low-prestige jobs pay least—rather than, as logic would dictate, being compensated and kept filled by higher pay rates. Nor is there much promise of change in this situation in the immediate future. As the then-Secretary of Health, Education, and Welfare reported to a Congressional committee (Ribicoff, 1963): "There isn't a prayer of a chance for the common laborer. The common laborer is the first one fired and the last hired, and more and more this is becoming a great problem [p. 19]."

There is also the social structure to consider. J. M. Becker (1965), discussing unemployment insurance, says that the benefits are regulated by two principles—the competitive (premiums and vestings) and the social (welfare)—and that "Of these two aspects of social insurance, the social, or welfare aspect, has the primacy. The two are related to each other as means to the welfare end.

Important though technique is, it is subordinate to the welfare end and may never be so employed as to jeopardize the substantial attainment of that end [p. 80]." It is clear from even a cursory examination of the structure of social insurance, however, that this is a wish, not a fact. It is difficult to name one social welfare program in which the fear of the loss of work incentive is not a controlling factor in determination of benefit levels. Even the services—rehabilitation, retraining, counseling, and so on—are designed to prepare people to enter or to re-enter the labor market. There are few, if any, programs designed to prepare people for leisure, or to accept their roles as nonworkers with equanimity or satisfaction; and movements designed to remove "vocational" from rehabilitation in order to prepare people for independent living unrelated to the labor market are just beginning to be discussed, informally.

In short, the American work ethic is strong and pervasive, with deep roots in the history of Western civilization and the development of the United States. It is not only a means by which a desirable society might be attained, but is an ideology in itself, a vision of the kind of world which would be desirable.

Despite the ubiquitousness of these views throughout American society, variant and sometimes antithetical views concerning work motivations nevertheless exist. Some of these are held to belong to specific groups; others are in the nature of a minority view; some are seen as old-fashioned, or avant-garde; while still others are held alongside and in juxtaposition to the major views. These differing views concerning work motivations and their sources can also be classified, for purposes of convenience and comparability, as instinctual, material, and social.

As often happens with other theories concerning human behavior, the postulation of an instinct to work is paralleled by an assumption of the precisely opposite instinct—in this case, an innate aversion to work, a type of "avoidance instinct," a basic drive to avoid work, an inherent laziness in man. Thus, men are held to want little beyond their immediate needs and must be prodded and stimulated by advertising, social pressure, and motivational techniques to desire more. This, it will be recognized, is the direct antithesis of the acquisitive instinct. Indeed, although Freud held that work was indispensable for human happiness, he also said that "As a path to happiness work is not valued very highly by men," and that, indeed, there seems to be a "natural human aversion to work [1958, pp. 20–21]."

This aversion is attested to by the fact that there have always been ways of attaining satisfactions other than through that which is generally defined as work, and there have always been people participating in these other ways. Biblical strictures against usury bear witness to the antiquity of one such method, and the labor of slaves in ancient Greece, in the American South, and in modern Africa provides another example. In addition, many people partake in activities that are defined, at least by nonpartici-pants, as nonwork: intellectual activity, creative endeavors, fiscal operations, housekeeping, and even management and administration.

Use of such methods and participation in such activities would indicate that work does not necessarily arise from an in-stinctive need. Indeed, there seems to be a law of parsimony in work efforts—the desire to do as little work as possible to attain desired ends. Men do not seem to work overtime for the sheer joy of working, or to choose to work longer hours for the same remuneration as they receive for shorter hours. Seeking easier methods, using labor-saving devices, and utilizing resources in new ways are seen as not only legitimate, but desirable, traits in work-men. The use of time-and-motion studies and efficiency experts to reduce the amount of work required is evidence of the social legitimacy of work-reduction efforts. In addition, the motivation to do as little work as possible is held to be the father of invention, and many companies pay bonuses to workers who suggest methods of reducing work.

Indeed, the American ethic calls for efficiency, self-reliance, and ingenuity. The worker who works the longest or the hardest to achieve goals is held in lower esteem than the worker who attains the same goals with less work. Finally, mobility in the work world consists of moving away from physical work to supervisory, man-agerial, and more intellectual activities, which are not considered work in the same way. Thus, it can be argued that the basic need is to avoid work, rather than to work in order to fulfill instinctual needs.

The work-avoidance instinct may be held to be rooted in the pleasure-pain principle, where exertion, lack of autonomy, and stress—the concomitants of most work—are painful, and therefore tend to be avoided. In this connection, it is worth noting that Freud's attribution of virtues to work was limited to those people who are free to choose their careers in relation to the whole of their tastes and capabilities. Friedmann (1964) has noted that many of Freud's patients seem to have led idle lives—a fact not generally remarked—and derives from this the notion that deprivation of work activity may play a larger part in the origin of some neuroses than seems generally recognized. However, the contrary possibility also exists—that Freud's emphasis on the importance of work arose because so many of his neurotic patients did not work, and that a more representative sample of patients, including many with the same type of complaint despite the fact that they worked, would have resulted in less emphasis on the importance of work in Freud's thinking. The fact that Freud felt that working-class people, with little opportunity to lead richer lives, might be better left with their defenses and illusions (Friedenberg, 1962) adds weight to this possibility, and at least qualifies the universality of the work portion of Freud's formula for human happiness.

The theory of an innate muscular need for activity is also opposed by the theory of energy-preservation—that the body in its natural state exerts as little energy as is possible and that there exists a tendency to maintain or to revert to that "least effort" state (Vroom, 1964). There has even been a report of evidence that work can cause allergic reactions (*New York Times,* September 3, 1967). The theologically based view of the work instinct as God-implanted has its opposite in the religious version of work as a curse placed upon man, which classifies work as a burden, rather than a joy, and postulates a human, if sinful, desire to avoid it.

Additional evidence bearing on the instinct question is the continual and continuing reduction of working hours. Whereas in some preindustrial societies custom or religion guaranteed a hundred or more holidays a year (Buckingham, 1961), the emphasis on productivity associated with the Industrial Revolution resulted in very long hours for most workers. These hours have been constantly reduced, however, since the early days of industrialization. An industrial report notes that in recent years reductions in the length of the work year through increased vacations and added holidays have been more prevalent than increases in overtime rates (*Methods of Adjusting to Automation and Technological Change,* n. d.). The average American has four more hours of leisure a day than his grandfather had (Kaplan, 1960), and if the ratio of reduction in work hours continues as it has since 1880, before today's children retire the work week will be halved again (Buckingham, 1961). Not only has the long-term trend of working hours in all industrial countries been generally downward (Mangum, 1965), but as the work week has contracted and life expectancy has been extended, the average American has added about twenty-two more years of leisure to his life (Cunningham, 1964). At present, the AFL-CIO Executive Council is calling for a thirty-five hour work week (Perlis, 1963). This quantitative dissociation from work does not bespeak a strong instinct to work.

Finally, the instinct theory of work motivation begs some consequent questions: How work is distinguished, instinctively, from hard play; whether intellectual activity is instinct-satisfying, or only physical activity; whether meaningless work can satisfy the instinct; and how meaningfulness is measured or judged for instinctive purposes.

In short, there are questions about and denial of any instinctive desire to work. Lowell summarized this feeling in her time thus: "No human being will work to provide the manner of living for himself if he can get a living in any other manner agreeable to himself" (V. S. Lewis, 1966). The continuation of this attitude into the present has been verbalized as "No man . . . would take up hard work unless he had to [Bates, 1966/67, p. 66]"; and is manifested, as noted previously, by social welfare programs which peg welfare or other income-maintenance rates at a percentage of human need, saying, in effect, that men do not work because they want to, or because they enjoy it, or because they have an instinctual need to do so, but rather because society is so constructed as to require it of them. This view may be summarized by saying that motivation to work may arise from the necessity to acquire material satisfiers or from the desire for social gratifications, but it is not an inherited, instinctual drive.

Are men driven to work, then, by their needs for sustenance? Since the structure of the American economy is such that most men can only achieve satisfaction of their material needs by working, there does not seem to be any substantial dispute that this need is at least part of work motivation under present circumstances. There is, however, a school of thought which holds that this motivation is artificially maintained, as the amount of human labor demanded is in excess of the amount necessary to produce the same amount, or more, of material satisfiers than are now being turned out. This school of thought is followed by those who see automation/cybernation as one of the great changes of present times, a change that will grow at a geometric rate, if not faster, until the great majority of society's work will be done by mechanical slaves. Lerner (1957) expresses this view rather mildly: "The dogma that idleness is somehow a sin was part of an age that was passing. An age of automatic machines would put a premium on leisure in which the mind would not be idle [p. 249]." The late Representative Fogarty, an expert of many years' standing concerning social welfare matters, told a Congressional committee that automation is gradually eliminating the common laborer, and that we are not going to head off or stop the continuing increase in automation. At the present time automation is eliminating about 38,000 jobs a week (Ellis, n. d.), and some experts believe that it could displace most workers (Carey, 1955).

Although the inevitability of widespread automation and its effects are by no means unanimously agreed upon, the existence of make-work and feather-bedding practices is widespread, and it is no secret that automation and its impact are both feared and resisted by organized labor. Many workers know that their jobs could be done by machines—perhaps faster, better, and for twenty-four hours a day—if society were serious about reducing the work required for necessary production. Some workers seem to view with fear the threat of being replaced by machines, whereas others may feel degraded that they are forced to work in order to acquire material necessities when such work is basically unnecessary. The dependence of men on work, like any enforced dependency, may have ramifications in their feelings about themselves.

Consequently, the mental health of industrial workers is a matter for legitimate and serious concern. Kornhauser (1965)' found that from one-fourth to one-half of the factory workers interviewed revealed extensive enough feelings of inadequacy, low self-esteem, anxiety, hostility, dissatisfaction with life, and low personal morale to raise serious questions concerning the general conditions of psychological and social health of industrial workers.

Being tied to useless work as the only means of sustenance may have mental health effects upon the people forced to engage in it for a living; for example, the fireman on the diesel locomotive, the printer setting never-to-be-used type, the workman producing items which he doubts are either desirable or useful, the researcher engaged in operations which violate his ethical commitment,[4] or the individualist in a bureaucratic structure. This may be part of the reason why the best that can be said about the majority of American workmen is that they do not actively hate their jobs (Cunningham, 1964). Kornhauser's conclusions (1965), drawn from his own work and his examination of hundreds of other studies, are in the same direction—that most working people are moderately contented, often in a passive, unenthusiastic, and accepting fashion. Riesman and Whyte even question whether the social conditions now extant make it possible to change this situation—that is, to develop people who would put a positive value on hard, even if productive, labor (Vroom, 1964).

These feelings which many people seem to have about their own work—questions about its usefulness and necessity, and fear about its continuance—lead to doubts about the necessity of work as such and fantasies about a workless existence. However, since American society is work-centered, such doubts and fantasies must be denied by redoubling one's manifest devotion to the value of work. In this sense, public demonstration of one's devotion to the work ethic might be evidence of lack of belief in the necessity for the ethic.

---

[4] For a revealing account of researchers wrestling with such ethical questions, see Horowitz (1967).

Thus, the strength of motivation to work to acquire material needs is affected by the very structure of the economy, which keeps four to eight out of every hundred employable persons from satisfying this motivation; that is, the official unemployment rate has been around 4 per cent for some years. However, this rate is based upon the number of people actively seeking employment as evidenced by their registering for jobs at employment security offices.[5] It is estimated that there is an equal number of people who would work if jobs were available to them, but who have given up on registering, or who do not know how or where to register. The effect of unemployment, and particularly long-term unemployment, on work motivation is discussed in more detail below. Another serious question concerns the mental health effects of inability to work—due to incapacity or lack of opportunity—in an economy which demands work in exchange for decent maintenance.

Finally, the motivation to work for material satisfactions may become so strong that it overshadows or displaces other motivations, in which case men work to acquire wealth, without regard for their own bodily and health needs, and without regard for the way in which they are viewed by the rest of society. This drive may extend to the point where the ability to acquire satisfiers, rather than the satisfiers themselves, becomes the end, and money, instead of the things that money can buy, becomes the motivating force. In summary, this view of the motivation to acquire material satisfactions holds that there are, at best, deep ambivalences and undesirable side-effects, at least for some people, in the basis of the motivation—a motivation which would not exist in the same strength, or would exist with different effects, in a different system of production and distribution. In short, work to acquire material satisfiers is an artifact of the economic system, and not an innate need of individuals.

There remain the divergent views on work motivation to fulfill social needs, which can be examined within the same framework as were the normative views, that is, the Protestant Ethic,

---

[5] Some states even require evidence of more than one method of searching for work before considering a person unemployed, and thus eligible for unemployment insurance.

laissez-faire economics, and the results of the Industrial Revolution. The effect of the Protestant Ethic is held to be eroding, or to be already supplanted by the consumer ethic. Whereas the goal of the Puritan tradition was work for its own sake, with a prohibition on the enjoyment of its fruits, the very nature of the present American economy demands consumption, and promises enjoyment as its result. The "conspicuous consumption" which Veblen saw as the status symbol of the wealthy class remains, but is present as the status symbol of every American who can afford it, for mass production has brought many such symbols into the reach of all. In addition, income taxes have limited the amount of conspicuous consumption which even wealthy Americans can enjoy, while the democratic ethic has made too-conspicuous consumption almost un-American. Advertising, packaging, built-in obsolescence, credit laws, and the effect of movies and television are all designed to spread the consumer ethic, with notable success. The conspicuous consumption that remains as part of the jet-set or movie star pattern serves to provoke imitation, and further erodes the Protestant Ethic.

A statement by the AFL-CIO refers to this process as the de-Puritanizing, or orientalizing, of the United States (*A Statement on Adaptation to Free Time,* 1963). Lerner (1957) describes the change thus:

> Many of the generalizations about work . . . are no longer true in the New Society. The greatest change has come about in the "gospel of work." Except for the antebellum South there were no Greek notions in America of work as a badge of dishonor, something belonging to a lower caste. . . . The American bourgeois spirit . . . regarded idleness as sinful and the way of work as the good way. . . . The gospel of hard work took long to die . . . with the growth of the big corporation, work became depersonalized; and with the change in the immigrant experience and composition, hard work became associated with the foreign-born, the Negroes, the illiterates, and the underlying social strata. . . . What has replaced it on the employers' side is the ethic of efficiency and profit and on the workers' side the ethic of security and success.

Similar viewpoints hold that work as a religious duty is no longer a major factor in American work motivations, and that self-denial of the enjoyment of the fruits of labor is not only practically non-existent, but would be viewed as un-American.

The laissez-faire philosophy—including the concepts of free market, economic man, and rugged individualism—is also held to be more mythical than real. Myrdal (1965) says, "It is clear that the mythical and irrational conceptions we have built up over generations and preserved in order to defend laissez-faire . . . are crumbling before our eyes [p. 432]." For example, old age pensions have not been left to the exclusive concern of business or of labor unions for more than thirty years; workmen's compensation regulations are laid down by government; minimum wage laws, child labor provisions, and antitrust regulations, among others, have all breached the idea of a free and untrammeled market to the point where lack of government regulations is not only no longer posed as desirable, but the request of many sections of the economy is for more, not less, governmental intervention. Such intervention would include tax concessions, changes in interest rates, participation in housing construction, cost-plus contracts, research grants, and so on. In addition, the idea that the government should become the employer of last resort seems to be gaining support. This proposal says, in effect, that if industry cannot give everyone jobs, then the government should take over that commitment. Similarly, the proposal for a guaranteed minimum income says that if industry cannot pay people enough to lift them out of poverty, the government should. In reply to those people who are still blind to, or in opposition to, such government intervention, Tawney (1958) says:

> Few tricks of the unsophisticated intellect are more curious than the naive psychology of the businessman, who ascribes his achievements to his own unaided efforts, in bland unconsciousness of a social order without whose continuous support and vigilant protection he would be as a lamb bleating in the desert [p. 284].

With this destruction of the free market concept has come the reversal of the idea that workers owe it to society to work as hard as they can and to produce as much as they can. Instead, the worker takes pride in being "a member of the team," and in fitting in with his fellow workers, regardless of the effect on production. Kornhauser's study (1965) points up this change:

A further look at the men's attitudes toward themselves and their life goal discloses a picture that bears little resemblance to the idealized image of sturdy, self-confident, enterprising American working men. Fewer than one-fourth of the factory workers could be classified as exhibiting strong, healthy purposeful orientations [pp. 267–268].

The influence of the Industrial Revolution is also held to have been weakened by the very methods which made the change itself significant. Because work has been robbed of meaningfulness, workers find no satisfaction in the work but instead focus on extrinsic rewards like wages and security. Nor is the existence of, or substitution by, social satisfactions from the work group an unchallenged concept. Kornhauser (1965)' found that only 26 per cent of *all* ideas and only 22 per cent of salient ideas of factory workers centered around the job. Dubin (1962) also found that:

> The industrial workers' world is one in which work and the workplace are not central life interests for a vast majority. In particular, work is not a central life interest for industrial workers when we study the informal group experiences and the general social experiences that have some affective value for them. Industrial man seems to perceive his life history as having its center outside of work for his intimate human relationships and for his feelings of enjoyment, happiness, and worth. . . . When measured in terms of valued social experience, the workplace is preferred by only 25 per cent of the workers studied. When measured in terms of primary human relations, only 9 per cent of the workers report that the workplace provides their preferred associations [pp. 262–263; 257].

Along these lines, it has been held that what a man does, or how he works, no more determines his social status than reflects his self-image, which may be determined largely by how he spends his leisure. Musician or golfer, baseball fan or skier, hi-fi bug or sports car buff—these leisure-time pursuits define for him his friends, his area of interests, and the way in which he is judged by those whom he considers significant others (Kaplan, 1960). A further evidence of the fading impact of the Industrial Revolution on men's work motivation is the fact that American working people do not define themselves as the proletariat, or the workers in contradistinction to the bosses, or in any way which might be expected to give or evidence a sense of group identification, or pride, or direction.

Even the symbolic aspects of work may be questioned when examined closely. The symbolism exemplified by agriculture, for example, is sustained only insofar as farm owners or—in many cases—agricultural businesses are concerned. Farm workers, who might be thought of as the essence of that which is being symbolized, are systematically left out of social security, minimum wage, and even collective bargaining laws. Even farm subsidies are paid, in the main, to the largest and most successful agricultural corporations. For example, 70 per cent of all cotton farmers are small farmers whose allotment is ten acres or less; the average subsidy they received in 1961 amounted to about $60 for the year. In the same year, 322 farmers had allotments of 1,000 acres or more; their average subsidy was $133,657 each. Two great corporations received more than $2,000,000 each, and the 13 farms with allotments above 5,000 acres averaged $649,753 in subsidy (Bennett, 1965). The symbolic value of farm work as such is not evidenced by such a payment schedule. Similarly, the symbolic value of hard physical work in general is denied by a wage system which pays such work at lower rates than it pays skilled, intellectual, or managerial tasks.

In addition, the incentive to work which might arise from a shared sense of community may be absent when large segments of the community are alienated, or subject to anomie, as certain segments of American society seem to be today. In short, this view holds that work is highly overrated as a determinant of status, as a creator of social satisfactions, and as a symbol.

In summary, the divergent or dissenting view of work motivation holds that: Men have an instinct to exert themselves as little as possible, and work as such satisfies no instinctive need or drive. The necessity to work to achieve material ends is resisted and resented; results in ambivalent attitudes toward work; may adversely affect mental health; and is increasingly an anachronism which is perpetuated by societal inertia and by vested interests. Men's feelings about themselves and their social status and goals are derived from nonwork activities, rather than from work or work settings; or, insofar as they are related to work, they have to do with the work group rather than the work itself.

The existence of such varying views concerning work motivations results in a series of contradictory assumptions widely held in America today. The simultaneous existence of contradictory views is not surprising. No society is monolithic in its ideology, and policy arises from the interaction between ideas, rather than from universal consensus. Katz (n. d.) explains this phenomenon thus:

> Wars are made in the minds of men, but this statement can be deceptive if it equates the declaration or prosecution of a war with the aggressive impulses of the members of the warring nation. The nation is not an aggregate of similarly minded aggressive individuals acting in parallel, but a complex organization of many criss-crossing cycles of social behavior [p. 4].

Insofar as assumptions concerning work motivation are concerned, the following are some of the existing contradictions: (1) Men work in order to satisfy instinctual and biological needs and drives, and are unhappy to the point of sickness if they are denied such opportunity:—Men are inherently lazy; no one wants to work or does so unless he has to; and efforts to avoid work are the basis for all social and mechanical progress. (2) Men work basically to achieve material ends, and any other supposed motivations are rationalizations which would not support work motivations if material needs were provided by other means:—Men work even when their material needs are satisfied because of personal needs and social pressures. (3) Only people whose sustenance needs are unmet are motivated by needs to work; other people must be stimulated by advertising, social pressure, and other devices, or else they would be satisfied:—Men's needs are insatiable, and therefore men will always work to achieve more satisfactions. (4) Men work because of the satisfactions inherent in working; the sense of creativity, fulfillment, productivity, and performing an expected and useful social role:—Most men find their work boring, unsatisfying, and uncreative, and constantly seek to reduce the hours they must spend at it. (5) Men work because in their work groups they find primary group relationships, companionship, enjoyment, status, and recognition:—The major focus of men's lives is outside their work places; major interests center on nonwork activities; and most satisfying personal relationships are not found with fellow workers. (6) Men work because of the social identity which it offers them, the regulation of daily life activity which it entails, and the way it defines them to the rest of society:—Men define themselves and are defined according to their leisure-time activities, their interests and expertise, and their familial and ethnic backgrounds.

Explanations for the paradoxical existence of these and other contradictory assumptions which are widespread throughout American society, and upon which social structures and institutions are built, can be sought through the use of theoretical frameworks. Six such possible explanatory frameworks are examined below.

First, just as individuals can simultaneously hold opposite or divergent desires, emotions, attitudes, and beliefs, so the concept of *ambivalence* can be applied to the society as a whole, insofar as work motivations and beliefs about work motivations are concerned. It is possible for an individual to believe in a supernatural, omniscient God, and at the same time to reject the concept of supernaturalism as contrary to reason, nature, or science; or to believe simultaneously in the desirability of cooperative men and a competitive society. So it is possible to believe both that work is ennobling, necessary, and useful; and demeaning, unnecessary, and meaningless. One method of living with such ambivalences is simply not to attempt to reconcile them, but to maintain both beliefs implicitly, or one belief implicitly and the other explicitly, with whatever discomfort this may cause. Such societal discomfort may be the reason for the heat with which work motivation is discussed in public media, the insistence on only one aspect, and the denial of nonpopular views. Another method of handling ambivalent feelings is to dissociate the beliefs upon which they are based, or to maintain that they are rooted in different realities. This method also involves not bringing the two beliefs into juxtaposition with each other. Thus, it is possible to believe and to maintain that work is a necessary and desirable socializing experience for all youth, when the frame of reference is lower-class teen-age youth; and an undesirable consumer of limited time when the frame of reference is middle-class college-aspiring youth. Still another method is to bring forward, dwell upon, or believe the version which is most comfortable under the circumstances, for example, to assert that work is a highly desirable phenomenon in a setting where this is an a priori assumption, and to question the value or necessity for work in the context of a research project on unemployed youth. Finally, it is possible to hold one belief intellectually (for example, work is ennobling and everyone should engage in it)', and another belief emotionally (for example, work is difficult and anyone who does more than he has to is crazy)'. The result of such ambivalences concerning work motivation in American society is social welfare programs which purport to do one thing but actually do another—for example, AFDC, which is intended to allow mothers to make homes for their children, but which often operates to induce mothers to leave home for work; or OASDHI, which is intended, in great part, to make it possible for elderly people who want to do so to retire from work, but concerning which the then-Secretary of Health, Education, and Welfare told a Congressional committee, "It is important that the retirement test not interfere with incentives to work [*Social Security*, 1965, p. 116]." Ambivalence regarding work is not only a phenomenon of society as a whole—individuals may be equally ambivalent, wanting to work and not wanting to work; getting satisfactions from work and being bored by or indifferent to it. Such ambivalence on an individual basis expresses itself in absenteeism, periods of poor work, moving from job to job, and even occasional vandalism directed at the equipment or buildings, as well as strikes and walk-outs occasioned by relatively insignificant incidents. Unfortunately, research has given little consideration to the concept of ambivalence in dealing with work motivation; most questionnaires call for a choice between answers and measure, at best, the strength of choice, but not the ambivalence.

Second, another possible explanation of the contradictions in American attitudes toward work may be found in the phenomenon of *goal displacement*. Most organizations, structures, or institutions which are devised to achieve a defined end—that is, to transform certain inputs into certain outputs—also develop processes which are designed to keep the structure in being, to maintain it intact, and to ensure the continuation of whatever side-payments have developed, such as personal relationships, power structures, financial and psychic payoffs, and other latent functions. Such maintenance needs may exist parallel with the production goals, or they may come to displace them in large part or entirely. Sills (1965) speaks of the near-universality of the phenomenon of goal displacement within organizations. A similar process may take place within societal structures too large or inchoate to be termed organizations; Perry (1954) says of societies: "The collective action originally organized to serve a need other than itself becomes the supreme value of the group [p. 69]." Thus, it is possible to view the motivation to work as having arisen from an original need to subdue nature, wrest a living from the soil, and create goods with one's own hands. Consequently, a socioeconomic system grew up which used work as the means to attain desired ends. However, insofar as these ends have since become, at least in part, attainable by other means such as machinery, power, or symbols, goal displacement has taken place, and work is valued for ends other than necessary production. The motivation to work to acquire goods and satisfactions—an artifact made necessary by the structure of the system—becomes accepted as necessary for maintaining the system, and is thereby reified into seeming to be an independent need, a need not only of the system, but of individuals. In other words, in addition to the amount of work which is actually or technically necessary for production, the view of work as needed by men has led to and reinforced an economic structure which attempts to provide work for and demands work of everyone who is capable of it; and this structure is rationalized on the basis that the work is necessary for the provision of goods. Thus, in effect, a self-fulfilling prophecy takes place in which work by everyone is assumed to be necessary to the functioning of the economic structure; the structure is therefore constructed to provide work opportunities for everyone; and the existence of such opportunities proves the necessity of everyone working. Even the absence of opportunity for some does not obviate the necessity for everyone for whom the opportunity exists to work. As a consequence, changes in the economic system which would reduce the need to work are resisted on the basis that they will harm the economy and thereby the workers, or harm workers and thereby do damage to the economy. So deeply ingrained is the assumption that men must work that, "It is indeed difficult, in this environment, to examine freely some of the alternative methods of providing transfer payments. . . . Negative tax plans, family allowances, simplification or elimination of the means test for eligibility—such alternatives inevitably raise value questions about incentives to work [Hansen and Carter, 1966, p. 99]." The viewpoint that motivation to work is in part a reified artifact would be of limited and pedantic interest were it not for the fact that this attitude toward work motivation may cause resistance to changes in the economy, and militate against efficiency, automation, and methods of allocating the resources and products of society different from those now in use. This fear of the tyranny of the status quo seems to have some justification. As long as work as such continues to be seen as beneficial, the structure of the economy, which is geared to providing work, will be maintained, defended, and strengthened; and not only will automation not be pursued by every effort, but it will be resisted by more or less subtle Luddite methods. Burke's comment (1965) is thus relevant: "If we are to revise the productive and the distributive patterns of our economy to suit our soundest desires, rather than attempting to revise our desires until they suit the productive and distributive patterns [p. 66]," the "occupational psychoses" and "trained incapacities" will need to be broken through. A society which is convinced of the desirability of work as a mode of human behavior can be expected to resist changes which lessen the need to work. This resistance is exemplified by the fact that the present material needs of all Americans could be satisfied to a point well above the subsistence level by production of all the agricultural products which the American soil can put forth; distribution of all the consumer goods which power, machinery, and raw materials could produce; and consumer determination to use and reuse goods until they were no longer functional, coupled with production of goods built to last. However, there is no likelihood that such changes in production and distribution will come about, for despite the material benefits which they would bestow, these changes would completely disrupt the present socioeconomic system, the method of government, and the philosophic basis of most of the country's institutions. Thus, the means have become more important than the end, representing what has been called the triumph of "imbecile institutions" over social capabilities. One reason for the contradictory assumptions about work in American society, then, may be that the original goals and the displacing goals have become confused in the public mind.

Third, another reason may be understood through the theory of cognitive *dissonance* (Festinger, 1957). According to this theory, two opinions or beliefs or items of knowledge are dissonant with each other if they do not fit together; that is, if they are inconsistent, or if, considering only the particular two items, one does not follow from the other. Dissonance is postulated as a source of discomfort, and three ways of reducing dissonance are generally used: The person may try (1) to change one or more of the beliefs, opinions, or behaviors involved in the dissonance; (2) to acquire new information that will increase the existing consonance; or (3) to forget or reduce the importance of the cognitions that are in a dissonant relationship. Applying this theory to work motivations, it seems that people, having chosen to work rather than face the consequences of not working, but nevertheless having come to question the value or necessity of working, either resist and deny the basis for their questioning or prove to themselves how important work is. In this way, people who do not want to work, who get no pleasure from it, or who question the usefulness of what they do eventually perceive their work as something which they want to do, get pleasure from, and hold important. And, according to the theory of cognitive dissonance, they do not simply say that they want to or like to work, or pretend to see it as useful, but they actually do perceive it in that way. Since most other people are in the same condition, they receive social support and confirmation of the correctness of their views or behavior. The more dissonant the belief is with cognitive reality, the more outside support is solicited; and as it is received, such mutual support reduces the dissonance and the belief is reinforced. From this viewpoint, the American attitude toward work as expressed through its major institutions is an example of mass dissonance reduction in the face of new realities.

Fourth, it is also possible to explain the contradictions in attitudes toward work motivations by viewing them as a case of *cultural lag*. Burke (1965) says:

> Veblen is perhaps most responsible for bringing out the aspect of moral confusion called the "cultural lag." In its simplest form, his doctrine is concerned with institutions which, developed as a way of adequately meeting a past situation, became a menace insofar as the situation has changed. Naturally, also, as long as the institutions survived, the ethical values that reinforced them would be upheld [p. 47].

Merton (1949) speaks of the same phenomenon when he says, "Governing concepts can, and often do, lag behind the behavioral requirements of the case. During these sometimes prolonged periods of lag, misapplied concepts do their damage [p. 92]." As an example of such cultural lag, it has been remarked that all the available evidence points to the fact that people continue to believe in the "equalitarianism" of American society despite their daily familiarity with economic inequality and status distinctions (Lipset and Bendix, 1959). Another example of cultural lag is the philosophy of the frontier, which enables the dwellers of the city to equate themselves with the dying yet romantic figure of the cabin farmer. They are able to live in a very comfortable way and still regard themselves as frontiersmen, and to develop massive corporate enterprises while speaking of the individual entrepreneur (Lerner, 1957). Consequently, it is possible to see certain attitudes toward work as being those which were applicable at a time when men could only with difficulty provide for their own basic physiological needs by their own labor; when rugged individualism, ruthless competition, and laissez-faire economics were dominant; and when full employment was seen as a goal, rather than as a danger. The continuation of these beliefs and concepts and the structures which are based upon them in the face of radically changed conditions are an example of what has been termed the "regressive" or "atavistic" tendency—to see that which came first as necessarily more important or desirable. Cultural lag may thus account for some of the contradictions mentioned above: some existing beliefs stem from the past, whereas others have risen from confrontations with new situations.

Fifth, still another way of accounting for the paradoxes is contained in the theory of *norms and behaviors*. Norms are the accepted, often articulated, standards by which members of a society are normally expected to live. The strength of norms has been experimentally demonstrated in small groups in which members literally changed their perceptions of reality to conform to the norms of the group. The norms of work groups have also been the subject of considerable investigation. That the larger society has norms hardly needs emphasis; for example, Americans are expected to be religious, attending the church or synagogue of their choice: girls are expected to remain virgins until married; conception is to be followed by birth; and mothers are supposed to be married. The norms of society, however, and the behavior of its members do not necessarily coincide, nor are they really expected to. The person who believes that America should be a religious country does not necessarily himself belong to or attend a church or a synagogue; female premarital virginity is, according to the Kinsey report, in large part mythology; abortions have been estimated to be in the millions annually; and unwed motherhood has become a phenomenon of considerable proportions. Katz (n. d.) discusses this aspect in terms of individual and system values and ideologies:

> Individual values are internalized in the personality. System ideology is the set of values accepted as appropriate general guides for the behavior of members of the system. These values may or may not be internalized by a majority of system members and certainly are not internalized in their entirety. When a social system collapses, its ideology often collapses, which would not be true if there were a one-to-one correspondence between personal and system values [p. 6].

In like manner, societal norms call for people to work, to want to work, to enjoy working, to attain their satisfactions only by working, and to be judged by their work; but individuals, while upholding these as desirable norms for the society, avoid work, use other means to obtain satisfactions, and are judged by nonwork standards. The norms, in short, are for other people, while the behavior is the individual's own private affair.

Finally, an explanation of the contradictions in attitudes

toward work which are apparent on the American scene is contained in the postulation of *two cultures*. In this formulation, the majority of Americans share and are guided by the traditional views concerning the meaning of work. They are hard-working, self-reliant, thrifty, productive people who take pleasure in their work and receive their major satisfactions from the work which they do and from the relationships which they have with others at work. Their activities keep the economy sound and the society healthy. There is, however, another element in American society, often vaguely referred to as "they." "They" do not really want to work; find all kinds of excuses not to work and methods of living without work; stop working as soon as they have enough for minimal needs (often defined as beer and cigarettes); and are immune to desires for upward mobility, more material satisfiers, and respectable social status. "They," in fact, have their own culture which puts premiums on different activities and values than does the majority culture, and within their own culture they find social and psychological satisfiers that do not arise from work. The vague "they" are a mixture of colored people, new immigrants, urban slum dwellers, rural (usually Southern) farmers, dwellers in areas like Appalachia, welfare recipients, Medicaid participants, teen-aged dropouts, dope addicts, alcoholics, derelicts, and hippies. The one thing that they all have in common is poverty, which not only leads to individual dependency, but is often family-wide, and is passed on from generation to generation. Hence, this group has come to be referred to as "the culture of poverty," which is either in contradistinction to, or a deviant subculture within, the larger American culture. The postulation of a culture of poverty serves many purposes and answers many questions on the American welfare scene, as well as demanding certain understandings and approaches. It is particularly germane to income-maintenance programs and policies, for with the exception of the retirement provisions of OASDHI, such programs mainly serve poor people. The feelings and beliefs of poor people are thus of the essence in planning and administering programs intended for their benefit, and their attitudes toward work are critical in such programs. In short, to the extent that the culture of poverty is a reality—that is, that there is a real cultural group made up of poor people—feelings about the poor and treatment of them as different have some basis in reality, and perhaps justification. To the extent, however, that there is no clear culture of poverty, the assumption and subsequent exploitation of its existence lend credibility to the view that poverty in America is basically a scapegoating phenomenon. The next chapter is devoted to the evidence on the existence of such a separate culture, and subsequent chapters examine its existence specifically and exclusively in terms of work motivation.

5

Culture of Poverty

*T*he manner and extent to which the poor differ from the nonpoor in America are currently being discussed and investigated in a number of ways. Some of these ways are anecdotal and impressionistic, others draw on documentation and interviews, still others are surveys, investigations of specific areas, and logical extrapolations and categorizations. Underlying these various explorations, however, there are discernible at least five different assumptions concerning the poor. These form a continuum from the view that the poor are almost completely different from the remainder of American society, to the assertion that they are indistinguishable as a group or class.

One viewpoint holds that there exists a distinct culture of

poverty which transcends ethnic and other reference group features and is peculiar to the poor. The roots of this view seem to be in the theory of the stratification of American society, ranging—in at least one formulation—from lower-lower to upper-upper (Lynd and Lynd, 1929).[1] Methods of ascertaining the existence and size of various classes have differed, but have resulted in a generally accepted measure of socioeconomic status. Much empirical investigation, both quantitative and qualitative, has been directed toward identifying the attitudes, behaviors, and social structures associated with each class, but that classes exist in American society seems to be generally accepted.

Less clear is the extent to which each social class shares with others a common value system, and/or is differentiated from them on the basis of different values. Parsons (1959) and Merton (1949) assume a common value system in their definitions of society, whereas Hyman (1953) and Davis (1946) represent the class-differentiated view. Nevertheless, no one seems seriously to postulate a stratified American society with each stratum representing a completely different set of values, behaviors, and structures, without commonalities or overlaps between strata. The operative question seems to be whether the differences which exist constitute a separate class, or, conversely, whether the commonalities deny it. The assertion of a culture of poverty, beyond merely a class of the poor, is obviously of the first persuasion.

Oscar Lewis (1966), who has been the most prominent advocate of the culture of poverty thesis, is clear in his assertion that it is a culture in the traditional anthropological sense. He goes further, and explicates the conditions which he considers necessary for the existence of such a culture: a capitalist economy with unemployment and underemployment; a nuclear family pattern; and upward social striving which attributes failure to shortcomings in the individual. Given such conditions, Lewis defines the components which he sees as important in the culture as those having to do with family systems, interpersonal relations, spending habits, value systems, and time orientation. However, although Lewis is explicit that he sees the culture of poverty as transnational, at least in

---

[1] Rainwater numbers the lower-lower class as 15 per cent of the population, which is one-fourth of the working class (Rainwater, 1960, p. 4).

the Western world, and therefore complete as a culture, it is clear from the components which he specifies as unique to poverty that he is not actually speaking of a culture in the sense that it is completely different from the culture of other American classes or of America as a society. Elements which are classically and strictly considered part of a culture—religion, language, ethics, artistic expressions, and recreational forms, among others—are left out of his formulation, presumably because they are not peculiar to the poor. Indeed, despite his strict definition, Lewis refers to his concept interchangeably as a culture and as a subculture (O. Lewis, 1961).

Nevertheless, the phrase "the culture of poverty" is, as Lewis acknowledges, a catchy one, and has been used by others in even less precise fashion to describe and explain such phenomena as intergenerational poverty, multiproblem families, underprivileged children, unwed mothers, and other societal problems. As Irelan and associates (1967) point out, it has been "used as a summarily descriptive term, as an explanation of behavior, and as a basis for programs both of exhortation and of action. . . . Most frequently, it appears as a shorthand term referring to the variety of ways in which economic deprivation can influence ideas and actions within a single society."

In addition to its use as verbal shorthand, the concept of a culture of poverty also seems sometimes to be used with evaluative overtones. This use may be basically negative, ranging from the generalized "They don't want to work," to the specification of lack of familiarity with work routines or functional illiteracy as caused by the culture of poverty (Himes, 1965). On the other hand, a culture of poverty may be assumed and discussed in positive terms, as when Glazer holds that the standards of the white Protestant majority are inhumane or inadequate or ineffective for large parts of our population (Glazer, 1965); or when Riessman discusses the strengths of the poor (Shostak and Gomberg, 1965).

Among the findings which tend to support the concept of a culture of poverty, or which take it for granted in identifying differences between the poor and others, is Martin's contention (1966):

> There has developed in America a Negro-Mexican-Puerto Rican lower class which, more or less isolated from the tradi-

tional routes of vertical mobility, does the dirty work at the lowest rung of the occupational ladder, while at the same time pushing up to the next rung or to the lower-class whites, especially those who are native born . . . a submerged, exploited, and very possibly permanent proletariat [p. 8].

Burgess and Price (1963), in discussing the intended targets of criticisms or legislation designed to "alleviate or correct" so-called weaknesses in the AFDC program, note that these appear to be parents and/or more specific racial groups who deviate from certain white middle-class norms regarding family structure, marriage patterns, and living standards—in short, a separate culture.

The conception of a culture of poverty has both theoretical and practical implications. On the theoretical plane, it indicates a shift in traditional thinking concerning poverty. Poverty is no longer seen, in this view, as something which people may drop into and work their way back out of, but a condition into which one is born and in which one remains locked. From a pragmatic point of view, the acceptance of the existence of a culture of poverty may have programmatic implications—the implicit assumption that poverty-stricken families present a generalized syndrome which is then susceptible to modification by a generalized service, without regard to the differences in causes or meanings of poverty among the population. Or, it might result in or strengthen the stereotype that every person who needs financial aid also needs services in order to manage his own life (Smith, 1966).

Again, the assumption of a culture of poverty might include beliefs concerning the ability of the poor to live on small sums or to acquire other, surreptitious sums elsewhere. The result of such stereotypes may be, "To go on thinking that a family of four in California can exist on $185 a month for food, clothing, housing, utilities, personal expenses, and so on, which is as realistic as believing that storks bring babies [Smith, 1966, p. 97]."

It is with these theoretical and practical implications in mind that examinations concerning the validity and reliability of the evidence for a culture of poverty have been made. This evidence seems to indicate that the more rigorously we examine individual items—which are presumed to be different for the poor— the less tenable is the case for a distinct culture of poverty.

Kimmel (1966), for example, using a combination of experimental design, sociological survey, and participant observation studied need for achievement; time perspective; interpersonal relations; deferral of gratification; occupational, educational, and marital aspirations; control of reinforcements; family relationships; self-image; anxiety; verbal I.Q.; value hierarchies; and social participation among 131 white members of 61 poor families, including 43 members of 11 AFDC families, to find that there was more variance than homogeneity in the responses, and, where there was homogeneity, the bulk of the responses and behaviors were in the direction of the middle class. Differences between AFDC recipients and middle-class respondents were only in time perspective, differentiation of self-image, social participation, and "perhaps" in verbal I.Q.

Dunmore studied the factors which influenced acceptance or nonacceptance of an educational opportunity extended to residents of a poverty area, with particular reference to the manner in which the possible culture of poverty affected acceptance and rejection. She found that social psychological factors were not significant correlates of nonacceptance of the opportunity offered by either the poor or the nonpoor, and that insofar as the culture of poverty was concerned, the data failed to support its existence among the families of school-age children (Dunmore, 1967).

Kronick (1963) found little support for the concept of a lower-class subculture in her study of AFDC families; and Hylan Lewis (1961) found that neither the quality of life in most low-income neighborhoods nor the child-rearing behavior of low-income families can be interpreted as generated by or guided by "a cultural system in its own right . . . with an integrity of its own [pp. 10–11]." Gordon interviewed the mothers, and some children, in multiproblem families in Harlem with special reference as to how they relate to their neighbors and relatives, and to the more structured areas of life. She found that despite the fact that they share certain characteristics—all are Negro, women, mothers, poor, slum dwellers, and the concern of welfare and community agencies—they show marked differences in the way they relate to the formal structures of the larger society and to the informal structures of neighborhood and kin (J. Gordon, 1965).

Irelan and associates approached the question from another angle, and explored whether members of ethnic groups who were also poor showed greater similarity to other members of their own ethnic groups, or to other poor people, in regard to: alienation; rejection of certain occupational values; fatalism; dependent behavior; high evaluation of close contact between a man and his parents; autonomy of children; and low responsibility for children's behavior. Their conclusions were that for five of the above areas the "poverty-stricken were found to vary more among themselves than did the Negro-, Anglo-, or Spanish-speaking Americans with different income sources. For at least this sample and these attitudes, poverty does not override ethnicity as a cultural determinant [Irelan et al., 1967, p. 15]." Miller even holds that a clearly defined lower class does not exist (S. M. Miller, 1965).

Although neither the findings which support a culture of poverty, nor those which reject it, have been on a scale large enough or in sufficient depth to justify firm conclusions, Thomas's comment (1966) seems apropos:

> The alleged "culture of poverty" should be excluded . . . for without denying its intrigue and plausibility, the hypothesis of such a culture has been seriously questioned by informed observers, and the social and psychological elements of the assumed culture have not been specified and researched adequately to allow us to draw many strong inferences [p. 108].

In any case, the idea of a group which is virtually immune, at least in certain aspects, to the socialization processes of American society, and which has its own set of values and beliefs, is difficult for some observers to credit, especially when applied to numbers as large as one-fifth of the American population, and in the face of data which do not support the existence of such a distinct culture. Consequently, a definition of a subculture of poverty has been put forth, in which poor people subscribe to the great majority of the values of the total society, and differ in very limited areas insofar as their values are concerned. Another definition holds that the poor share all of the values of the middle class, or of the total society, but because they lack the opportunities that others have to achieve these value-goals, they use deviant means to do so. The theoretical base for the latter viewpoint has been best explicated by Cloward and Ohlin (1960), and is generally referred to as "opportunity theory." Deviant behavior such as juvenile delinquency is not seen in this view as a rejection of societal values, but on the contrary, as a determination to reach the same goals as the rest of society, using, if necessary, means which are punishable, punitive, or pathological. Thus, though behavior differs, values remain the same.

For example, in discussing the economic behavior of the affluent, Barlow and associates say (1966):

> Those who own property have many opportunities to realize investment income that is either tax free or taxable at only a fraction of "ordinary" rates. In addition to these opportunities . . . there is tax-free interest on state and local bonds, tax-exempt accumulations of interest on life insurance policies that are paid at the death of the insured, deductibility of "losses" incurred by "hobby" farms and other enterprises . . . rental real estate on which book losses are accompanied by large cash payouts . . . generous depletion allowances unrelated to capital costs . . . and many others. Tax liabilities may be substantially reduced by distributing income-producing property among the several members of one's family . . . by forming specious partnerships, and by establishing corporations whose primary function is to receive property income so that it will be taxed at rates far lower than it would be if it were taxed to high-income individuals. People of wealth may indulge their tastes for certain forms of consumption and at the same time avoid income taxes [pp. 151–152].

The value, thus epitomized, is the maximization of one's economic position.

In contrast to this behavior by the wealthy is Levitan's (1967) expressed fear that in the event of a guaranteed minimum income paid through the income tax machinery, recipients might divide their families or take other steps to increase their incomes. The implication is that the means the lower class uses to achieve the same values which are held by the wealthy class are seen as immoral, if not illegal. In the same way, the subculture of poverty may be seen as simply substituting playing the numbers for gambling on Wall Street; aimless cruising in an automobile in search of excitement for taking a cruise; the candy store for the country club; beer and wine for highballs and cocktails; television for theatre, concerts, and opera; and less formal arrangements for the otherwise acceptable marriage/divorce/remarriage cycle. In every case, it is obvious that the values are those of the larger society, but the means distinguish the subculture of poverty.

Another conception concerning the values and behaviors of the poor has been put forward by Rodman (1963). In this view, the poor hold the same values as do the nonpoor, but hold other values in addition. Thus, in Rodman's illustration—drawn from field work in the Caribbean—both marriage and cohabitation without marriage ("Livin' ") are seen as desirable by the poor. Marriage is often unattainable, in which case livin' is acceptable. Rodman (1966) refers to this as the lower-class value stretch, in which the dominant value is stretched to accommodate another version.

Irelan and Besner, although ascribing to the poor power-lessness, meaninglessness, anomie, and isolation, nevertheless hold that they seek and value the same things as other Americans. Insofar as their moral code is concerned, however, they agree with Rodman's conception, and posit "An adapted version of society's rules and behaviors. . . . A sliding scale" of values (Irelan and Besner, n.d., pp. 5, 7).

Still another view of reactions to poverty holds that it is useless to speak of "the poor," or the lower class, in global terms, or, indeed, as a group in any sense. This view holds that poor people differ in their reactions to poverty in accordance with demographic and/or group differences, and that discussions of values must specify the group and the circumstances. Martin, for example, in discussing the determinants of crime and deliquency, points out that the question is really not only the degree of poverty or unemployment, but also certain psychological traits or inculcated cultural definitions (Martin, 1966).

In the same vein, Miller combines class and style-of-life criteria in order to subdivide and categorize the poor, while emphasizing that there is much flux between the categories. His typology consists of the stable poor, the strained, the copers, and the unstable (S. M. Miller, 1965). Engel (1966), using the dimensions of world-view, style of expression, social-psychological constriction, and social-emotional instrumental response, categorizes the poor as strivers, consistent copers, inconsistent copers, reliefers, and holdovers. Incidentally, Engel equates reliefers with the culture of poverty, but paints a much more deviant and difficult life than does Lewis. Kronick (1965) distinguishes between the alienative, the calculative, and the moral poor in somewhat the same manner.

Into this category of views of the poor would fit the study of Irelan and associates (1967), mentioned above, in which ethnic group background was seen as more important than poverty as such in differentiating behaviors.

The final view on this continuum rejects the thesis that the poor can be classified together on any basis, or that they differ from other classes or American society as a whole along any significant dimension. For example, Ulman (1965) writes of "The general refusal to regard the poor as intrinsically or potentially inferior to or different from the successful majority (p. xx)" although it is not clear whether he is referring to "liberals," policy-makers, or the general public.

Rainwater (1960) quoting from a 1959 study of 2,713 women, refutes the idea of different family aspirations among poor families: "The American ideal is a three- or four-child family, and the family actually desired by women ranges from two to four . . . the ideal does not seem to vary greatly with social status; young women of all social classes seem to want about the same number of children [p. 25]." And in a more startling challenge to conventional views regarding the sex habits of the poor (insofar as the poor tend to be the least educated), Kinsey found that American women in lower-educated groups do not have sex relations more frequently than higher-educated women, and the lower the educational level, the *less* likely it is that premarital relations will occur (Rainwater, 1960): Along these same lines, May (1964) points out that the unreported illegitimacy rate among whites and middle-class women may eradicate the differences which exist in this respect between them and the reported illegitimacies of the poor.

Thomas (1966) approached the problem of the "difference" of the poor from point of view of psychological dependency, and found that at least five behavioral phenomena referred to as dependency are unrelated. "It is *our* reactions as members of the behavior-defining community and not the behavior itself of those so classified that appears to be the behavioral coherence and unity in psychological dependency [pp. 105–106]," he says. Kimmel (1966) comes to the same conclusion: "Like any other social evaluation, poverty is as much 'in the eye of the beholder' as it is 'in' the individual or group being judged [p. 57]."

In his study of morale factors, Herzberg (1966) says, "It did not matter whether a man was . . . old or young, educated or uneducated, or in a high-level or a low-level job. The same kinds of objective situations led to low morale among all our respondents; they led to the same effects [p. 98]." Whyte's study (1955) also found that the differences between workers spurred by incentive plans and those not so motivated were rooted in backgrounds, psychological make-up, and other such individual differences.

Lipset and Bendix (1959) posit a factor in regard to behavior generally which would militate against the emergence of any culture or subculture of the poor or the otherwise disadvantaged: "Apparently, there are imperatives which prompt men to resist and reject an inferior status and these imperatives persist regardless of the way in which any society has legitimated inequality . . . the stronger the norms against social mobility, the greater the desire for it [p. 63]."

In summary, the extent to which a culture of poverty seems to exist depends in large measure on the way in which culture itself has been defined, and one book has reviewed 160 definitions of culture in English (Kroeber & Kluckholm, 1952). Others have investigated specific aspects attributed to the poor, including family size, the single-parent family, color, age of head of household, and educational level of the father (Berliner, 1965); family structures (Rainwater and Yancey, 1967); and behaviors, such as consumer practices (Richards, n. d.).

For purposes of incentive research, however, the most important factor concerning a culture of poverty seems to be whether, or to what extent, poor people react to the same incentives to work, to make money, and to acquire satisfiers as do the nonpoor. The assumption that poor people are untouched and untouchable by the factors which mold and influence the rest of the population's desires—mass media advertising, the life-styles portrayed in movies and on television, consumer fads, and emulation of public figures, among others—is the postulation of a distinct culture of poverty, at least insofar as incentive is concerned. This view necessarily denies the insatiability of human wants among the poor, and the emergence of prepotent needs as formerly potent needs become satisfied. Consequently, it is based in part on the so-called "wantlessness" of the poor.

The wantlessness of the poor is an important part of the belief-system concerning the culture of poverty. One of the methods by which it has been assailed is through studies which find that the aspiration levels and desires of the poor are no different from those of the nonpoor. Thus, Kimmel (1966) found that the need for achievement, the ability to defer gratifications, and occupational aspirations were no different among the poor whom he studied than among the nonpoor. Irelan and associates (1967) found ethnic factors to be stronger than poverty factors in regard to certain occupational values, dependent behavior, and fatalism.

Another method of attacking the imputation of wantlessness to the poor is to explain the apparent wantlessness in terms of present circumstances which additional income, opportunities, or ability would overcome. Kornhauser (1965) takes this tack when he speaks of the tendency of men to accommodate their aspirations to their appraisal of the opportunities open to them—hence the frequently commented-on "wantlessness" of the poor. It will be recognized that this attitude is analogous to dissonance theory: Being denied the opportunity of achieving more income, more satisfiers, or more status, the pain of the denial is itself denied by not wanting that which is considered unattainable.

In this connection, it can be said that attainment is generally composed of three elements: motivation, ability, and opportunity. Each of these is necessary for successful attainment, but no one of them, nor even two in concert, are sufficient. For example, one who has both motivation and capacity, but who finds no opportunity commensurate with his ability and desire, may change his motivational attitude—perhaps as a necessary psychological defense mechanism—toward work. In other words, lack of proper opportunity leads him to not to want to work. Provision of the proper opportunity may then change the motivation to work. This is the reverse of the traditional thinking that change efforts must concentrate on motivation (through salaries, conditions, and so on) to get the person to take advantage of opportunities. In this dynamic, perceived opportunity changes motivation, and income guarantee or no guarantee may be irrelevant to motivation.

Similarly, one who has both motivation and opportunity, but who lacks the required ability—psychological, vocational, physical, or social—may prefer to substitute lack of motivation for lack of ability, and thus appears to lack incentive, when the real lack is capacity. In this case, too, an income guarantee might be irrelevant in affecting the ostensible lack of incentive, since the real problem is lack of ability.

Attainment contains three dichotomous elements, and makes it possible to categorize the population into eight types:

1. That portion of the population which has capacity, opportunity, and motivation is presumably working, and thus might be properly termed the *employed*. There is little to say about this group except to point out again that approximately five million of the poor are endowed with these three attributes and are in poverty nevertheless; and that it is only upon them that the major disincentive effect of an income guarantee might be expected to have impact.

2. Those with both the capacity to work and the opportunity to do so, but lacking in motivation, are by definition the *unmotivated*. These people are probably the cause for most concern about work incentives in the event of a guaranteed income—that their lack of motivation will be confirmed and become chronic. Paradoxically, since it is probably their present condition—whatever that may be—which has robbed them of motivation, the assurance of income could hardly have an adverse effect upon them. Indeed, it is the contention of one school of thought that provision of income might even revive motivation within them, particularly since the opportunities open to most of them consist of very distasteful work, or completely insufficient salaries.

3. Those with both the capacity to work and with sufficient motivation, but lacking the opportunity, make up the *unemployed*. This group is officially four to every hundred of the employed, a

fact that raises doubts about the reality base of the whole concern about incentive, since not even all of those with both incentive and ability can find work.

4. Although there are those who suffer from lack of both opportunity and motivation, it is difficult to see how lack of motivation can *cause* lack of opportunity. However, as pointed out previously, lack of opportunity might easily lead to lack of motivation. The group thus affected can be termed the *discouraged.*

5. Those who have the opportunity to work and the desire to do so, but lack the ability, are the *incapacitated.*

6. It is difficult to envision any persons with neither capacities nor motivation who have work opportunities. Such opportunities are more likely to be illusory than real, so this group might be called the *dreamers.*

7. Those who are motivated, but whose incapacity is matched by lack of opportunity, are the *frustrated.*

8. Finally, those with neither capacity, opportunity, nor motivation might be termed the *resigned.*

If wantlessness is truly part of the lack of motivation to work, then an income guarantee might improve the *situation* of the *incapacitated,* the *dreamers,* the *frustrated,* and the *resigned,* without affecting their motivations, since they are barred by lack of capacity from working in any case. Technically, then, as mentioned in Chapter Three, the motivation of only those who are employed should be affected by an income guarantee, since others are either *unmotivated* already; *unemployed* despite their motivation; or *discouraged* and withdrawn from the labor market.

However, the issue of wantlessness seems wider than that of lack of work incentive. Here the question is whether the unmotivated and those who have become discouraged would develop wants once given the capacity to achieve them. Rather than feeding wantlessness, an income guarantee would probably change it, thus moving people from the discouraged and unmotivated groups into the unemployed group (for whatever psychic satisfactions might accrue to the nonpoor in this event), and eventually —at least so runs the argument—into the employed group.

It seems clear from the foregoing that the question of whether poor people are affected differently by the values and pressures of American society than are the nonpoor is not at all clear or agreed-upon among those who have studied the problem, and yet the postulation of a group which does not respond to normative American values concerning work, desires, and ambition is an important, even major, factor in the thinking of both laymen and professionals concerning the effect of an income guarantee. The tenacity with which this vision of a different group is held, its imperviousness to logic, its pervasiveness and influence, all bespeak a need for such a group to exist, a need which is that of the nonpoor, and which is not influenced by the actual attitudes or actions of the poor. Consequently, it is worth examining further whether at least in terms of work incentives, there is empirical evidence that the poor differ from the rest of society. Whether such evidence does or does not imply a complete culture of poverty is not important here, but the attitude of the poor toward work is a basic question for the determination of a guaranteed minimum income.

6

Incentive Research

$\mathcal{D}$espite the importance assigned to incentives in social welfare planning, and despite the safeguards against adverse affects on work incentives which many programs contain, little research has been done on the existence or nature of incentives to go to work or to continue working (in contradistinction to incentive plans designed to increase the amount or the efficiency of work being done), and still less concerning the effect of unearned income on such incentives. Almost no such research has been done among those designated as poor.

A search of the literature fails to reveal any instance in which members of one group are experimentally given varying amounts of unearned income which is not given members of another group, and their subsequent work records compared.

Only one study has been found in which the work records of individuals receiving unearned income from nonexperimental sources were compared with the records of similar but uncompensated individuals (Salzberger and Shapira, 1966). The few studies bearing on the incentive factor which are available include econometric models that examine correlations between labor force participation rates or transfer payments, among other factors, and a set of variables chosen from demographic, economic, and sociological statistics; logical extrapolations from existing situations; anecdotal and impressionistic studies; and hints and fragments in studies basically concerned with other subjects.

This lack of data has not escaped the notice of those concerned with social policy. Dahl and Lindblom (1953) put it thus:

> The amount of useful, systematic, verified knowledge on the relation of income to incentives is small. . . . Deficiencies in knowledge are specific. Only short-run effects can be observed, and even these only with difficulty. . . . In addition, empirical information usually describes how some people respond to changes in distribution; how representative their responses are is not yet known. Moreover, no one has yet attempted a systematic examination of available empirical data for evidence of the degree to which advantageous changes in incentives offset adverse effects [pp. 149–150].

Howard (1963) puts the question differently: "Who really knows whether public assistance undermines or strengthens individual initiative? Or whether Blue Cross, Blue Shield, or automobile insurance may not be undermining the insured person's sense of individual responsibility [p. 56]?" Burns (1967) says that we "really know very little about the incentive to work [p. 18]." Many other experts, concerned with the field of research on poverty, speak of the need to know more about poverty and its effects. Even raw data about poverty and the poor are notable for the deficiencies: In 1964, Schultz decried the lack of available information concerning poverty; and in 1967 Drew noted the lack of basic information necessary to plan income maintenance programs that was available in and to the Department of Health, Education, and Welfare. Rainwater and Yancey (1967) comment on the same situation: "The question of the adequacy of our knowledge at the level of basic data-gathering implicates both the social sciences and the government. . . . Why has it been that the agencies involved have not been prodded and given the necessary resources to collect decent data [pp. 309–310]?"

This paucity of research may spring, in part, from the comparatively short time during which the attention of the public and the research community has been focused on poverty. The most seminal book—Harrington's *The Other America* (1963)—and the most famous article—Macdonald's *New Yorker* essay (January 19, 1963)—both appeared in 1963. There may be a considerable amount of other work in progress which has not yet been published. In addition to the time factor, however, research findings in the area of poverty may be sparse because of the difficulties which valid and reliable research into this area presents. These difficulties include those which are generic to all research, and those which arise from the nature of the subject matter itself. The former will be discussed below, as a preliminary to examination of research findings, and the latter in Chapter Twelve.

Although all research may be said to involve the use of value judgments, research which purports to investigate the factual basis of a widely held ideology tends to be affected by the emotions aroused in respondents, researchers, the consumers of research, and its sponsors. As Smith (1955) puts it, "He who would take issue with a popular legend is likely . . . to find all society conspiring to defeat him [p. vii]." Since incentive to work is inextricably bound up with part of the basic ideology of America, it is small wonder that investigation into the existence or extent of factors which encourage or discourage incentive seems to stimulate emotional responses and bring about unacknowledged value judgments on the part of researchers.

Respondents among the poor are said to be another source of bias insofar as they tend to reinterpret the role of respondent to research in familiar terms, for example, as client to public assistance investigator, and therefore not to report certain information, such as outside sources of income, if they see a threat to cut their assistance (Scott, 1966). Among the nonpoor, too, questions concerning income have been found to evoke consistent underreporting (Barlow et al., 1966). Along these same lines, youngsters undergoing training to prepare themselves for the labor market in the future prefer to speak of themselves, and perhaps see themselves, as being presently employed (Krosney, 1966). Evidence of attitudes, drawn from social work practice, is subject to the same type of distortion. In Kahn's words (1965), the social welfare check is often exploited, by workers, as bait for the use of social services, and it is therefore not surprising that clients have been found willing to accept services (including answering questions which they might feel to be somehow linked to their checks, even if labeled "research") in a manner designed to be acceptable to the worker/questioner. Friedmann and Havighurst (1954), for example, felt that some respondents were giving "socially respectable" answers for why they wanted to continue working past retirement age, when they really needed the income, whereas others who had deeper motives for wanting to remain on the job rationalized them in terms of wanting money. It seems to be a rare client who will refer to his own real interest, rather than that indicated by the worker, by saying something like, "Let's not talk about my kid anymore. Let's talk dollars and cents [Elman, 1966, p. 292]."

Researchers' biases when dealing with the area of poverty have been pointed out by S. M. Miller (1965): "A good deal of the tone of the discussion of the 'lower classes,' even by sociologists, has a negative quality. On the other hand, a few seem to have a romantic feeling about the 'lower class [pp. 37–38].' " More specifically, some studies ignore, or at best acknowledge in passing, the existence of incentives to work other than or in addition to economic incentives, and thus interpret their results, or come to conclusions, exclusively on the basis of pecuniary factors. Levitan (1967), for one, has done so, and Klein (1966) ignores all other possible influences, stating flatly that preservation of incentive is incompatible with the achievement of an adequate level of welfare, and that "If they want to keep poor people in the work force, they have no alternative but to preserve an adequate financial incentive to work [p. 23]." In both of these cases, it will be noted, the conclusions are based upon an assumption that poor people will not work for the same or a lesser amount, or perhaps even a somewhat greater amount, than they would receive as welfare, although no evidence is presented to indicate to what extent this is true universally, true in great part, or true at all.

In a similar fashion, Vadakian (1958) discusses family allowances in France, and with no citation of data before or after the statement, says, "In France, the evidence points to the conclusion that family allowance payments would seem partially responsible for this adverse effect on incentives situation," and, "A worker who is guaranteed an income from family allowances whether he works or not might well tend to regard his job responsibilities somewhat more lightly," and, finally, "It may be reasonable to conclude that family allowances have adversely affected incentives in France [pp. 134–135]." Although Vadakian acknowledges that inflation, the housing shortage, and general adverse economic and political conditions may, in fact, be causes of disincentives to work in France, there is as little evidence in his study to support this theory as for his suppositions about family allowances. Friedlander (1962), on the other hand, denies the very existence of work disincentives in France, insofar as the evidence allows:

> Any available data about the rise of productivity in various industries in France after the Liberation of 1944, the major reconstruction of industrial equipment and machinery, and the recent economic prosperity in France provide, however, no definite proof of the discouraging effect of Social Security and family allowances. Production in the coal mining industries shows a substantial increase in productivity, for example. . . . The increased output may be in part the result of the use of skilled labor and better mechanical equipment, but it is certainly the result of reliable work as well [pp. 156–158].

Burns (1966) is more outspoken as to her own bias when she refers to those who foresee a society in which all production is carried on by 5 per cent of the employable population while the other 95 per cent live in idleness, though supported by some universal income guarantee, as "extreme prophets of gloom [p. 11]" whereas others, of a different bias, might refer to them as optimists and utopians.

Econometric studies in particular, and any study dealing primarily with statistical correlations, are by their very nature subject to researcher bias, as the independent variables presumed to be important get chosen. Collins (1967), for example, correlates assistance expenditures with state income levels, urbanization, unemployment rate, racial composition, age composition, social insurance coverage, and rate of population growth, but not with educational levels, cost of living, climate, in-state migration, historical tradition concerning welfare, political coloration, labor union practices, type of economy, discriminatory attitudes, or other variables which investigators making different assumptions about the causes of poverty might have chosen. As Vroom (1964) says,

> It is seldom possible to determine conclusively from correlational studies whether a statistical association between two variables, A and B, is attributable to the fact that A causes B, B causes A, or whether A and B are caused by some third variable, C. The associations obtained in correlational studies may be a useful source of casual hypotheses, but a rigorous testing of such hypotheses requires the use of other methods [p. 274].

When the researcher assumes, a priori, that receipt of income adversely affects incentives to work, then many results may be attributed to this assumed lack of incentive—results which may, in fact, be caused by enforced retirement, ill health, societal expectations, or lack of suitable job skills. In the same way, assumptions that poverty is a symptom, and not a cause, of lack of education, ill health, lack of job skills and experience, or discrimination may lead to neglect of studies of the effect of increased income (or plans to bring about increased income) as insufficient ("palliative" is Hirsch's phrase [1965, p. 89]), irrelevant, or even counterindicated (since if income is assumed to create work disincentives, it would militate against the acquisition of job skills and experience). This assumption is diametrically opposed to the view that unearned income, or a guaranteed minimum income, would have a positive effect on acquisition of education, skills, and jobs—and research based on the latter assumption would involve using a different type of design.

Similarly, the assumption that anyone who really wants a job can find one leads to conclusions which are based upon examining unemployment as a function of incentive alone, without taking into account considerations of opportunity and ability; whereas, the researcher who assumes that there is a separate culture or subculture of poverty—or, in less sophisticated terms, that the poor are different from the nonpoor in their needs, wants, reactions, attitudes, and behaviors—may arrive at logical conclusions which are empirically incorrect, and to study designs based on false premises.

In addition to the assumptions, biases, and value judgments of the respondents and the researchers, the viewpoint of the consumers of research is also to be considered. Walinsky (1965), for example, holds that the middle-class majority *does not want* to improve significantly the lot of the poor. Consequently, research which throws doubt on the disincentive effect of unearned income might need to be stronger, clearer, and supported by more evidence than research indicating the reverse, and thus require a different design, more resources, or different sponsorship. Gans (1967) has pointed out that one of the reasons for not improving the lot of the poor is society's need to ensure people who do the "dirty work." Perhaps it is for this reason that the lower class is thought to be immoral, uncivilized, promiscuous, lazy, obscene, dirty, and loud (Rodman, 1959). Research that points out ways in which people can extricate themselves from the position of doing such dirty work is discouraged, and may involve the researcher in extended explanations, defenses, and controversy that some may find distasteful, causing them to avoid this area of research.

Finally, the attitudes of the sponsors and funders of research must be considered. Most income maintenance programs are carried out by governmental agencies, and, like all bureaucratic organizations, they develop their own maintenance goals and latent functions. It is not surprising, therefore, that research which might indicate that their work is ineffective or harmful does not have first priority on their lists of research programs. Even with outside funding, such research might not be approved in terms of examining records, interviewing workers and clients, or otherwise using the agency's resources.[1] This is not to suggest that all research is

---

[1] Executives of two agencies with whom this investigator discussed the possibility of empirical research among their beneficiaries concerning

based upon the "law of anticipated reactions," and that researchers avoid studies which might result in unpopular conclusions; there is too much evidence to the contrary. On the other hand, it seems improbable that researchers are completely immune to the possible implications of their anticipated findings, and, more to the point, to the reaction of sources of research funds and facilities. Research proposals, after all, get written so that they will be accepted, and designs are developed to interest a probable sponsor.

In addition to the value judgments, assumptions, and biases of researchers, respondents, consumers, and sponsors of incentive research, the very way in which incentive is defined structures, in great part, the manner in which it is investigated. Insofar as incentive is defined as an attitude, its investigation involves problems germane to attitudinal research. One such problem has to do with the extent to which attitudes can be inferred from behavior, or, conversely, the extent to which behavior can be understood or predicted without assuming underlying attitudes. When, on the other hand, incentive is defined as a behavior, research problems involve those of observation, including field observation or participant observation; the possible distortions between reported behavior and actual behavior; and the limitations of studies of correlation.

When the focus of the study is on incentive as an attitude, the possible distortions between attitude and report are even more severe than those between behavior and report. Deutscher (1966) has indicated how much sociological theory is based upon reports, despite the prevalence of known distortion, rather than upon observation or experimentation. These distortions include the difficulty of distinguishing between basic, or continuing, or pervading conditions, including the research situation; between the various strengths of attitudes, ranging from passionate conviction to near-indifference; and the problem of respondents who are unable to verbalize their attitudes, or who hold conflicting or mutually exclusive attitudes simultaneously. In addition, like all motivation, incentive affects various people differently and also changes with

_____

incentive effects expressed reservations on the grounds that it is a "sensitive" area for their agencies.

time. Conventional research rarely takes these variables into account.

These differences between incentive as an attitude and as a behavior are not purely pedantic. Historically, the difference between the "deserving" and the "undeserving" poor was the existence of a willingness to work on the part of the former. In early days, a work test was used to test whether an applicant for aid was willing to work, even if the work itself was never very valuable and often positively harmful. More recently, work-relief plans were used to give applicants minute quantities of work, or make-work, to do, rather than outright relief. Thus, in the absence of suitable work opportunities, the *desire* to work was made the operative factor in giving relief, and the assumed absence of such an incentive was often punished under the title of vagrancy.

Continuation of this emphasis on proof of willingness to work is visible in the regulations which, even in times of unemployment widespread enough to be officially labeled a recession, or in areas of unemployment so drastic as to be designated a disaster area, require the unemployed to report personally to the employment office once a week. By this action they would express their pro forma willingness to, and availibility for, work, in order to receive unemployment compensation—which, incidentally, was deliberately structured to insure against just such contingencies. It seems reasonable to believe that it is at least mechanically possible to have the unemployed register only once, and thereafter to receive checks by mail until informed of an employment opportunity or called for a job interview, but the public seems to expect a periodic ritual avowal of willingness to work as a prerequisite for benefits.

A further definitional problem involved in incentive research concerns the meaning of *work*. For example, if managing one's wife's estate, which consists of reading stock prospectuses, market analyses, and stock market reports, and contacting brokers with orders to buy and sell various holdings constitutes working— or, at least, is not defined as not working—then the question arises as to how this differs, if at all, from betting on horse races with a portion of one's wife's wages, which is rarely defined as working.

Similarly, the corporation executive and the street-corner hustler might each characterize the other's activities as not really working.

On a more complex level, the components of work and leisure, as Kaplan (1960) points out, become constantly more intertwined: The psychiatrist uses his knowledge as a member of the PTA; the insurance salesman does business on the golf course; the lawyer who dabbles in ESP uses it in the courtroom. Some executive positions entail an almost formal round of cocktail parties, whereas other workers participate on bowling teams, engage in tavern-hopping, or play poker to function effectively in an office or on an assembly line.

Consequently, it is quite possible to see welfare recipients as working for their grants: They wait in interminable lines, fill out endless forms, participate in repeated interviews and home visits, and need to keep constantly informed of changes in laws and administrative regulations, exceptions made for others which might have practical implications, and opportunities inherent in new situations, such as housing projects, agency mergers, and the like.

Defining work requires taking into account those situations which have come to be considered work through tradition or agreement, although they involve neither effort nor output. The third, and sometimes fourth, person in the airplane pilot's compartment built for two; the fireman on the diesel locomotive; the printer setting type just to break it up again (Jacobs, 1962); and government employees who do not report to their offices (Bailey, 1966; Cleveland et al., 1960), are all spared the stigma of laziness and the classification of unemployed through appropriate societal conventions. Contrariwise, the con man, the hustler, the criminal, the small-time gambler, and others of similar occupations are viewed as not working, and lacking incentive to work, although they may, in fact, work very hard at what they do, and be conspicuously successful at it.

In addition to the purely semantic problems in defining incentives and work, there are also operational problems involved in incentive research. Rimlinger (1965), for example, points out that incentive and disincentive are not necessarily antonyms, for it is possible to discourage disincentives without thereby encouraging incentives:

Increasing the incentive to work has never been singled out as a basic goal of American social security. The main concern . . . has been the avoidance of measures which might hurt individual incentive and self-help incentive. . . . This differs very significantly from . . . designing eligibility conditions and benefits for the express purpose of achieving particular incentives and controls [p. 102].

This viewpoint is very much in line with Herzberg's major findings (1966), which were that there are some work conditions which are "motivators," and some which are "satisfiers" or "hygiene factors." The presence of the latter does not motivate men to work, although their absence makes them more dissatisfied at work. For example, lack of a drinking fountain may make employees dissatisfied, but its presence will not induce them to work or to work harder, nor will twelve drinking fountains make them any happier than one. Similarly, although the motivators may be necessary conditions for inducing men to work, additional quantities of the same do not serve to make men more satisfied. Thus, a sufficient salary may be necessary to motivate men to go to work, but additional salary may not take the place of desired recognition, opportunities for advancement, or acceptance by the work group. Conversely, the opportunity to do creative work might motivate some people to take a job, whereas no amount of money would induce them to take another kind of job; but a salary obviously below what others doing the same work command might act as a dissatisfier, even in the desired job. The implications of these findings for incentive research is that a distinction may have to be made between incentive to take a job ("motivators") and incentive to hold a job, work well, or aspire for advancement ("satisfiers" or "hygiene factors").

Finally, the distinction made in Chapter One between incentive below the subsistence level and above it needs to be emphasized in incentive research; that is, whether the incentive being discussed or measured is the inclination to work for the same amount, or less, than can be received as an income guarantee, or the inclination to work for salaries which are greater than the income would be if guaranteed. In seeking clues to these two questions, a further distinction must be applied to incentive or disincentive to work for the same amount, or more, or less, than is being or can be received as unearned income which is less than the subsistence level—unemployment compensation, relief payments, and so on. The difference between wanting to make more money in order to reach or to get closer to a bare level of subsistence, and the desire to make more money once subsistence is guaranteed, is one of the important definitional differences in incentive research. Failure to make this distinction can lead to what Geiger (1964) calls the "Fallacy of the initial predication [p. 109]."

Another area of research difficulty insofar as incentives are concerned is the cause and effect problem. The search for causes and effects in human behavior has been confounded by increasing knowledge of the complexity of human beings, both as individuals and as members of society. In addition, the advent of computers has made possible new methods of handling such complex data. As a consequence, the assumption of and search for causes of behavior have been increasingly superseded by emphasis on correlations between a large number of variables. Economists have been in the forefront of efforts to examine the relationships between transfer payments of various kinds and different aspects of the economy, including the effect on labor force participation, perhaps because computers complement what Whyte (1955) calls "one of the basic assumptions of orthodox economic theory: that man is a rational animal concerned with maximizing his economic gains. Of course, no economist believes this assumption to be true to the facts, but the tendency has been to reason from the assumption as if it were close to actuality [p. 2]."

In any case, after correlations have been found, there is a tendency, perhaps a need, to interpret them in cause and effect fashion—an interpretation that often gives rise to questionable conclusions. Thus, Galloway (1966) argues, in effect, that the provision of Social Security benefits has made it possible for numbers of the aged to retire (although on only 20 per cent of their current earnings, according to his figures), and that since the increased amount of such retirement does not arise from relatively greater unemployment nor from relatively smaller earnings among the aged, it is a "voluntary" change in work patterns. Ignoring the implication that even 20 per cent unearned income is a more powerful incentive than 100 per cent earned income, the argument is analogous to saying that if an increase in widows' benefits under Social Security coincided with an increase in the number of widows, the correlation means that a large number of women chose to become widows to qualify for the grant. Social Security, as the man in the street knows, made it possible for a large number of the aged to *be* retired by their employers.

Other examples of such spurious causality regarding work incentives can easily be imagined: The recent effort by New York City social workers to bring pressure to bear on the welfare system by inducing clients to file applications for every benefit available, qualified or not, resulted in an increase in applications filed. Had this coincided with or followed a period of weak market conditions, civil rights demonstrations, increased draft calls, or inclement weather, correlation of these factors with the increase in relief applications could have led to false interpretations. In this way, the finding of Morgan and associates (1962) that higher wages are associated with shorter hours could be (falsely) interpreted to mean that working shorter hours will result in higher pay.

Kaspar (1967), on the other hand, is careful to point out that the mutual relationship between variables in his study might be taken to indicate that the level of relief payments affects the number of recipients, but, given a fixed sum for relief, it is just as possible that the number of recipients affects the level of payments. It is also possible, although Kaspar does not take it into consideration, that large numbers of recipients might constitute a visibility, or a power force, strong enough to induce higher payments. In short, the complexity of incentive to work does not seem to lend itself to simplistic studies or to cause and effect formulations.

The general problems of research applied to the area of work incentives and the specific problems of this type of research, discussed below, may be a factor in determining what aspects of the total question are investigated, as well as what methods are chosen.

Gilbert (1966) implies that services may move in the direction of the measurable when research or accounting is a strong orientation in an agency or an organization, even though, as

Lichtman (1966) warns, a quantitative measure cannot be directly employed to measure value, and can only corrupt such judgments when the mistaken attempt is made to apply it. In the same way, research may move in the direction of the more easily "computerizable," or at least in the direction of the quantifiable, rather than in the direction of what Hansen and Carter (1966) term the less measurable but more humane values.

Cyert and March (1963) use the terms "problemistic search" and "uncertainty avoidance" to describe certain aspects of organizational decision making. Although the dynamics are somewhat different, the same phrases can be used to describe what seem to be certain aspects of research concerning incentives. In some cases, the problems to be investigated seem to be those which deal with the most easily available data, handled in the simplest manner possible. The result is a set of findings that are fragmentary, inconclusive, and possibly misleading in the total context of the effect of unearned income on the work incentives of the poor. The need for large-scale research and some of the factors which need to be built into such research are examined in Chapter Twelve.

7

Findings

*L*ittle specific research has been done on the incentive factor as it relates to the poor, and that which has been done is beset with many problems. Herzberg (1966) found the same thing to be true of research concerning job attitudes generally:

> In 1957, my colleagues and I . . . published a book that was an attempt to summarize the research and opinion that had been garnered in the area of job attitudes in the past half-century. The book was a saddening experience, because the major conclusion . . . was that we could document almost any position one wished to take with respect to what affected people at work [p. 148].

Consequently, any generalizations concerning the incentive of poor people to work, arising from such research as exists, must be regarded as highly tentative.

In examining the general evidence, the three-fold division concerning incentive outlined previously must still be made: (1) The inclination to work or not to work for an income the same as or less than a subsistence income guarantee. (2) The inclination to work or not to work for an amount greater than the amount guaranteed. (3) The inclination to work or not to work for an income greater than the present amount of unearned income, which is below the poverty or subsistence level; or to do so only in order to reach the subsistence level, but no more.

The first two classifications above refer to the nonexistent situation of a guaranteed minimum income, and therefore research based on existing situations and experience can only be within the third classification, from which extrapolations can be attempted concerning the previous two. The existing situations include, among others, AFDC and general assistance, disability compensation, and unemployment insurance, each of which will be examined separately in subsequent chapters. This chapter will focus on the more general evidence which points to whether people receiving a guaranteed income would or would not work for the same amount or less, or for more.

Since many of the examinations of work incentives use, as it were, a "one-tailed test"—that is, look for and measure results only in the expected direction—there remains not only the possibility that unearned income may have no effect on work incentives, but that it might have a positive effect. Therefore, each of these possibilities will be examined.

Finally, it is possible to divide such evidence as exists into the logical, the qualitative or impressionistic, and the quantitative. Logical evidence arises from extrapolations of present feelings or attitudes concerning human behavior, including behavior in fields other than work and in regard to items other than incentive. The second type of evidence may arise from experience or from studies, and includes evidence drawn from impressions, as well as from carefully derived research conclusions. The final category of evidence includes the types of studies from which measurements and mathematical correlations can be drawn, as well as experiments.

The logical conclusion that people will not work for income the same as or less than they can get as an income guarantee is so compelling as to need little explanation. It stems from the theory of the free market—that men *should* try to maximize their economic positions; from the vision of the economic man—that men *will* try to maximize their economic positions; and from assumptions concerning the real world—that men *do* try to maximize their economic positions. To the extent that the American economy is a money-based economy, with income the major symbol of respectability, social status, and recognition, people are believed to respond primarily to that which is most advantageous financially. Reiss (1961), among others, studied the items involved in assigning a rank order to a list of jobs and found that financial rewards and social prestige are primary. Since the jobs available to the poor (or jobs paying less than the poverty line) rarely offer either of these, there is no logical reason why they should prefer them to an income guarantee. Senator Byrd (Gilbert, 1966) was clearly acting with this logic in mind when in 1935 he resisted a federally established minimum grant standard, in order to protect low Southern wage levels, by giving workers no real alternative.

Morgan and associates (1962) point out that it is logical to believe that those who work the hardest are more likely to feel that hard work, rather than luck or help from friends, is the surest, and perhaps the only way, to success; whereas those who have been deprived of such work opportunities through discrimination, poor education, illness, or other societal factors do not share this value of work for its own sake or for its purported rewards. In summary, conventional wisdom, the thinking of the rational man, or logic, indicates that anyone who can get more money by not working than working will opt for the unearned income, especially if the work available to him offers little other satisfactions.

Qualitative studies or impressions arising from professional activity, which lead to conclusions that poor people do or would prefer unearned income to work which pays the same or less, have little evidence to back them. Perhaps this situation exists because the conclusion seems so obvious that it seems fatuous to document it; or perhaps the bias of those doing studies of the poor causes them to overlook or deny it. Yet, the bulk of popular sentiment that people will not work if they can get the same income from not working seems to stem from logical extrapolations and anecdotes. There is no end to stories, newspaper letters, and published incidents in which people refuse "honest" if underpaid work, because they can make more money illegally, or from nonwork activities, or from various welfare programs. Dubin (1958) is one of the few whose views arise from an extensive review of the literature regarding work incentives and from documented work experiences. He feels that income remains the all-important means for satisfying human wants and needs; "Income from wages and salaries is the major incentive to work [p. 241]."

In quantitative studies which support the disincentive effect, the most fruitful—or, at any rate, the most thoroughly covered— areas seem to be those of the unemployed, the disabled, and relief. Each of these will be discussed in subsequent chapters; however, one study, of a rather general nature and with a tenuous conclusion, should be mentioned here. This study found that forty of fifty employees chose to take the severance pay which was offered rather than continue employment in the same company when it moved, although the new quarters were on the same block as the old building. The implication is that the employees preferred cash and unemployment to salaries with employment. Unfortunately, details concerning employment conditions in the company, prospects elsewhere, and like information are not given (*Seminars on Private Adjustments to Automation and Technological Change*, 1964).

The middle position concerning the effect of unearned income is that it has neither incentive nor disincentive effects; that it has various effects, depending upon a number of variables; or that the effect is masked by, or substituted for, other factors.

As indicated above, in 1964, 12 per cent of the employed poor were farmers or farm managers. The question arises as to how many of these people would, in the face of an income guarantee, live on their farms and do no work at all; how many would leave the farms; and how many would work their farms in an effort to acquire an income larger than that of the guarantee. From 1960 to 1966, the farm population of the United States declined by four million persons, or 26 per cent, a decline that shows no evidence, as yet, of slackening (*Current Population Reports*, 1967).

This exodus from the farm is not confined to the poor farmers, nor do these figures indicate how many of the poor are included. Nevertheless, it seems reasonable to assume that those who have the hardest time will give up farming in greater proportion than those who are more successful. This assumption is, of course, tenuous, if logical, and requires investigation into the causes of farm abandonment, and the participation of the poor in such abandonment. There are undoubtedly reasons other than economic as to why people leave farms; and whether a guaranteed income would induce people to stay on farms or would facilitate their leaving is an open question. Insofar as the nonfarm poverty line is set considerably higher than that of farmers, it is possible that an income guarantee based on those lines would induce farmers to leave farms, particularly the uneconomic ones. On the other hand, since the poverty line is set lower for farms because of the food presumably produced there, others might make the calculation that the lower figure would enable them to live better by remaining on the farm. In any case, the logic of guaranteed income resulting in cessation of work is not applicable to poor farmers without more investigation.

Another population to which disincentives cannot be logically assumed to apply in great numbers is the 9 per cent of the poor listed as professional and technical workers. Logic would indicate that young persons entering into a career with at least middle-class aspirations and possibilities, although poor at the beginning of such careers, would not give up their work for a minimal guarantee. Young doctors, lawyers, and other professionals cannot be logically regarded as those who would give up their work in exchange for a somewhat higher income than their present ones; nor would aspiring actors, musicians, or other artists, who have less assurance of, but nevertheless great hopes for, much greater future incomes.

Still within the professional and technical category, as well as among some of the other categories, there are people listed as poor whose poverty is part of their jobs—certain priests, for example—and who would not give up these jobs for higher salaries. Finally, there are those who are devoted to their jobs, their employers, or the service which they are rendering others, and who would not give up being teachers, social workers, nurses, and like professionals for somewhat larger salaries doing other work or no work.

The same considerations which apply to professionals might be applied to some of the 8 per cent of the poor who are proprietors of businesses. Included in this category are probably some businesses which are just getting under way, for which the owners have high hopes; and some businesses which have had a bad year, from which recovery is expected. Again, the number is not known, but proprietors of such businesses would probably not go out of business in large numbers in order to qualify for the income guarantee. The same factor must be applied to those members of the clerical and sales group (7 per cent of the poor) who are beginning careers, such as new insurance and real estate salesmen.

However, there is very little reason to believe that many laborers, operatives, and household workers (45 per cent of the total employed poor), or the restaurant, hotel, and hospital employees contained in the 11 per cent in other service categories, see their jobs in terms of careers with better futures. On the contrary, logic would dictate that the large part of these groups would opt for the income guarantee, a result in line with Martin's findings (1966) concerning youthful offenders, which seem to be equally applicable to the poor. They seem less interested in work as such, particularly the kind of work which borders on exploitation, the dirty jobs, the positions with no possibility of advancement or future, which is the only kind of work they can find, than they are interested in obtaining satisfying, decent-paying, steady jobs which they may even define as jobs with a future. Since these aspirations are unrealistic—and, what is more important, they know them to be unrealistic, despite what Halleck (1963) calls the dishonesty of professionals who posit honest, steady work as the road to middle-class status—present material benefits would seem to outweigh both future considerations and present nonmaterial ones.

It is also logical to believe that the same behavioral dynamics operate in regard to the area of work and nonwork behaviors as in other life areas. Thus, because behavior results from multiple causes, it is reasonable to assume that the effect of unearned income is dynamically related to other situational factors, some of which might be masked by the factors of poverty or unearned income. For example, lack of education might disincline one to seek or accept work which is beyond one's abilities, and concomitant poverty or unearned income might nevertheless be seen as the cause. There is also some evidence of the converse: Education can be a disincentive factor when the job is not commensurate with the educational attainments. Thus, the requirement by one large department store that stock clerks be high school graduates led to high turnover in the job, while relaxation of the requirement resulted in longer job tenure. The salary was less important as an incentive than was the perceived use of capacity.

Similarly, support by families might logically be seen as a disincentive factor, with an income guarantee simply shifting the source of income from the family to the government, thereby not affecting the individual's incentive or employment situation. The extent to which relatives do, in fact, support the disadvantaged has been but little examined. M. Gordon (1963) states, as a fact, that many beneficiaries of welfare payments would otherwise be partly or wholly supported by relatives, although she presents no evidence to support this contention. However, she builds upon it to the extent of stating that the requirements of OASDI beneficiaries for staple food items would, for the most part, be met in the absence of such programs. She even faults empirical studies for not taking this "fact" into account. Schorr's findings (1966), however, that many of the aged, instead of receiving help from their children, are actually giving them such aid, paints a different picture. Langer (1965), too, found that only in the case of parents helping single children were relatives' responses a factor in relieving the financial situation of the unemployed.

Perhaps the most cogent evidence concerning the extent and impact of relatives' help, however, is that quoted by Steiner (1966):

> One bit of evidence does exist that seems explicitly to deny the hypothesis that a diminution in public welfare would mean a resurgence of family responsibility for the very poor. . . . Relief was terminated [in Clermont County, Ohio] . . . in April, 1961, when the voters rejected a proposed tax levy.

Clients did not magically become self-sufficient, nor did responsible relatives come out of the woodwork when the pressure was intense. Instead, the burden of support was shifted from the public fisc to landlords, grocers, physicians, churches, schools and other civic groups. A study showed a 54 per cent increase in money owed to landlords, grocers, physicians, and hospitals . . . the sheriff's office reported an increase in the number of evictions, and voluntary agencies . . . reported a rise in requests for aid [p. 9].

It is not clear to what extent relatives' support is a real factor in the poverty/incentive picture. Insofar as there is an effect, it should be among those who spurn help from relatives but would accept it from the government; and among those who previously supported relatives but now have smaller income needs and therefore possibly less work incentive.

There is also reason to believe that the depth of poverty and family status might influence the incentive of workers. For example, a single person making a hundred dollars a year less than the income guarantee, who is receiving some satisfactions from the work itself, from the work situation, or from being defined as a worker, might be more inclined to refuse the guarantee than the head of a family whose income is two thousand dollars below the poverty line and on whose family members much of the burden falls.

Then there are the satisfactions which come from work, other than or in addition to money. Lincoln (Herzberg, 1966) feels, as do many others, that money is valued less for what it will bring than as an evidence of successful skill in achievement. Consequently, undoubtedly at least some of the poor would prefer to work for the same amount as a guaranteed income, or for less, in order to be like everyone else. Indeed, this has been used as an argument against guaranteed income generally—that poor people do not want to be different, in being guaranteed an income, but prefer jobs like everyone else; or that poor people should not be made to seem different, to constitute a caste, as it were, by being given income in a different manner than anyone else. The counterargument is contained in Bernard's study (1964) of AFDC mothers, who found that they were so deprived and so anxious about money that the source of the money—the purported stigma—was the least of their worries.

Finally, there is the logical argument that no generalizations are possible because: (1) people differ too greatly as individuals, and (2) not enough research has been done. Morgan and associates (1959), speaking of return to work, say that a wide range of variables seem to influence the decision, with no one variable playing a predominant role; whereas Smith (1955) says:

> Some alleged realists say that if individuals had the assurance of what they need to keep them going, they, the majority of them, at least, would lie down and do little or nothing. Another group says that, by and large, they would build on that base—they would use their released capacities for constructive purposes, either to make higher economic ground or to achieve higher and more permanent values from their productive capacities. Others, and they may be in the majority, say no generalization is possible. It depends on the individual and no doubt on environment [pp. 20–21].

Insofar as empirical evidence for this differential reaction is concerned, in Herzberg's summary (1966) of ten studies of seventeen populations concerning motivation factors, salary was found to be significant only for certain hospital workers; salary was found to be more potent as a job dissatisfier than as a job satisfier, except for Negro housekeeping women in a Veterans Administration hospital.

Another piece of empirical evidence which would tend to indicate that unearned income would not affect work incentives is the report, by Morse and Weiss (Nosow and Form, 1962), that 80 per cent of their respondents said that they would continue working even if they came into much money. This kind of conjectural answer is subject to many kinds of distortions; and in addition, respondents were not asked if they would keep working *in preference* to receiving much money, but only in addition to, so that even these answers are not completely to the point concerning the effect of income under an income guarantee which would require no income-producing work as a condition. Dubin (1958) underlines the difficulty inherent in incentive research by pointing out that different incentives operate at successive stages in working life histories: "At the lowest reaches of most work organizations the nonfinancial reward of job satisfaction probably does not operate generally as a significant incentive [pp. 242–243]."

The third position regarding unearned income is that it results in positive work incentives. As with the other positions, arguments may be logical, qualitative, or quantitative.

Despite the emphasis on the efficacy of work since the early days of American social welfare, there has also always been the concomitant idea that "People in need, far from responding well to punishment and deprivation, do best when they receive encouragement and have adequate means to secure basic necessities [Sarah Joseph Hale, Boston, 1830, quoted by Pumphrey, 1965, p. 24]." This is the logical position that takes as its premise trust in people, which is basic to a democracy, and postulates that people will do that which is best for themselves and for the collectivity, even when faced with opportunities which might make it possible to do the "wrong" thing. In this vein, Buckingham (1961) points out that "Any philosophy that has a trust in humanity must also hold that humanity is to be trusted with idleness. A philosophy that recognizes individual human dignity cannot at the same time preach that idle hands are the devil's tools and idle minds his workshop [p. 155]."

In discussing the differences between theories which require persons to "contribute" in order to be eligible for benefits, Dahl and Lindblom (1953) point out that there is no evidence that contributory programs maintain desirable incentives and that, logically, " 'Contribution' theories might easily produce such inequality as to demoralize a population rather than develop desirable incentives [p. 136]."

There are other logical arguments that can be adduced. For example, it might be argued that leisure costs the individual more than working. Being at loose ends requires expenditures for entertainment, snacks, transportation, and the like, simply because time needs to be filled, whereas working gives structure to the time, makes certain expenditures impossible during working hours, and offers social satisfactions which obviate some of the need for commercial entertainment. Thus, insofar as purely economic considerations are assumed to be paramount for the individual, logic would dictate work rather than nonwork as a more economical activity.

There have been, as noted previously, almost no controlled or rigorous studies of the effect of unearned income. There is one, however, which has been reported. Salzberger and Shapira (1966) studied Israeli army veterans receiving and not receiving compensation. After matching two groups, their post-discharge employment records were compared. The conclusion was that compensation had a positive effect on retention of jobs and quality of work, especially among those who were otherwise disadvantaged. However, compensation was paid whether the veteran worked or not—that is, in addition to rather than in place of earned income— and thus, the results are not strictly applicable to the problem being examined here.

The question of whether an income guarantee would result in large-scale resignations among those making *less* than the guarantee is unanswerable on the basis of the data presently available or of studies already being done. At best, one can only say that the result would not be unanimous—an unknown number of people would continue their careers or businesses; remain on their farms; elect to help or serve others; prefer the time structuring, status, social setting, and economy of remaining on the job; and use the income guarantee as a base to change jobs, or to overcome the anxieties and difficulties which kept them from taking jobs. What the effect of the *same* amount of unearned as earned income would be is not clear, but the number who would receive exactly the same amount is probably quite small, and therefore not significant.

We turn now to the effect of an income guarantee on the incentive to work for sums greater than the guarantee. The assumption that people will refuse to work at all, even for sums larger than those guaranteed them, rests—as pointed out previously —in large part on the belief that the poor do not react in the same manner as the nonpoor, and on anecdotal material. Whether the "culture of poverty" is invoked in all of its ramifications or whether the assumption is unspoken and perhaps incoherent, the belief that poor people will not seek to maximize their economic positions at the cost of going to work underlies much of the resistance to a guaranteed minimum income. This belief is reinforced by anecdotes in which individuals preferred income from what the observer defined as nonwork to that from work; or, they involved people who were content with incomes drawn from income-maintenance programs, and who thereby refused equal or higher income from work. Finally, knowing some of the kinds of jobs which are open to the poor—and would presumably be open to the uneducated, untrained, and discriminated-against regardless of salary—there is probably some feeling that no one would undertake such work if their bare subsistence were otherwise assured.

Perhaps the best documented and well-remembered incident of this kind allowed literally millions of Americans to put off the necessity of working. This was the so-called "52-20 Club" under the G.I. Bill of Rights, whereby at the end of World War II veterans were given unemployment compensation of $20 per week for a maximum of 52 weeks, and took advantage of it in varying degrees and for differing lengths of time. It is probable that many who took advantage of this program in order not to go to work immediately now assume that others would naturally do the same under similar programs.

Although there seem to be no careful studies which indicate that poor people would refuse to work for more income if they were guaranteed less, there is a body of folklore, logic, anecdotes, and experiences which add up to a widespread assumption so deeply believed that the burden of proof would seem to be on any theory or study which purports to put forth the opposite view.

Yet, there is a view that, regardless of the effect of an income guarantee on work paying the same or less than the guarantee, there would be no effect upon work paying more, or that there would be some, but not a total effect. In this view, people receiving the guarantee would not refuse *en masse* to take higher-paid work, nor would all of the people making more money resign their jobs in order to get the lesser guarantee.

On the other hand, it is possible that there are people so satisfied with their present conditions that they see no need to try to improve them, at least by working. This attitude, to the extent that it exists, is truly deviant from the mainstream of American culture, but there is little reason to believe that it is confined to the poor, or even widespread among them. The number of the wealthy, whose life conditions are much better than those of the poor, who are satisfied with what they have, appears to be minimal. Barlow and associates (1966) found that the higher the income, the more frequently were second jobs reported. H. P. Miller (1964) found that in 1960 only one family out of a hundred in the top 5 per cent lived entirely on unearned income; the other ninety-nine did paid work or were self-employed. The same situation obtained in 1966 when nine out of ten in the high-income group were working as members of the labor force, most of the rest being retired (Barlow et al., 1966). Bookbinder (1955) interviewed 121 former major-league baseball players and does not record a single one living on savings and/or retirement pay.

Being satisfied with one's lot is not, therefore, the conspicuous earmark of the wealthy, nor, as observation attests, of the middle-class, so projection of this attitude almost exclusively onto the poor or onto large numbers of the poor has little basis in fact.

If people receiving an income guarantee would give it up for the opportunity to achieve more income, one of the unanswered questions concerns the amount greater than the guarantee which would be necessary to act as an inducement. Would people work for $50 a year more than they could achieve by not working? $100? $1,000? Conversely, would people making only slightly more than the guarantee give up work and prefer slightly less income and no work? How much less? How many people? On these questions the data stand silent.

Finally, perhaps the single most convincing argument against the anticipated lack of work incentives which would arise with an income guarantee is the employment experience in the United States during World War II. Not only did the unemployment rate drop to the lowest point in history, but numerous people who considered themselves and who were considered out of the labor market rejoined the work force. The meaning of that experience has been held to be that if proper kinds of work are available, paying good salaries, offering conditions which include a feeling of doing useful work, the motivation to work is not a problem.

The final position is that a guaranteed minimum income

will create positive inducements among recipients to seek and undertake jobs which pay more than the guarantee. In this case, the guarantee is seen as a change factor operating to create greater motivation. This view sees the difference between the poor and the nonpoor as primarily one of income, and postulates that increased income to the poor will make them more like, if not completely like, the nonpoor. This position rests upon the general psychological theory that people who are relieved of ever-present tension and anxiety about elemental needs are more apt to respond in normative fashion, to aspire to be like others, to have the psychic energy, the time, and the desire to prepare themselves for meaningful work, and to look for the kind of work they can do and from which they receive satisfactions.

This view also holds that sufficient income, even at a subsistence level, would enable recipients to overcome material difficulties which militate against their work chances at present. Such difficulties include those of education, job skills, and work habits, by enabling recipients to engage in educational and training programs in the knowledge that their families are provided for.

It is also held that receipt of sufficient income would change the self-images of some of the recipients so that they would be encouraged to undertake new kinds of jobs, or even to apply for jobs. It is also felt that the opening of the hitherto blocked opportunities to acquire luxury goods or to engage in certain activities would whet the appetites of recipients for more, thus motivating them to seek large incomes.

The logical argument for this position might be stated as follows: The feeling that if people were offered income guarantees larger than their salaries, they would quit work, assumes a motivation which is consonant with that of most other Americans—the desire to improve one's economic position. Consequently, it should follow that once they had improved their positions in this way, people would continue to want to improve their economic condition, as most Americans do, by taking jobs that paid more than the income guarantee. To argue that the poor act like all other Americans while in poverty, but become nonrepresentative when no longer poor, is a logical inconsistency.

The general feeling that people do want to work has many

and vociferous proponents. This feeling has been explained by Rimlinger (1965), quoting others,

> . . . that the provision of a basic level of security encourages work incentives. This argument now seems to have fairly wide support. Professor Galbraith goes so far as to suggest that "the notion that economic insecurity is essential for efficiency and economic advance was a major miscalculation—perhaps the greatest in the history of economic ideas." In his view, "A high level of economic security is essential for maximum production." Some students of long experience in the social security field, including Professor Eveline Burns, question the incentive effect of differential benefits, especially in view of the fact that in America the wages on which benefits are based often have little to do with individual incentive and initiative [p. 119].

Moore (1951) approaches the same problem somewhat differently:

> If it is extreme poverty that pushes the worker into modern enterprise, it may also be poverty that keeps his efficiency at low level. A number of investigators, commenting on the low efficiency rating of Indian workers, given comparable capital equipment, attribute this result to pre-existing poverty, confirmed by low wages and continuing poverty, thus completing the cycle. On the basis of less intensive studies, like conclusions have also been reached with regard to factory workers in China, Iran, French North Africa, and Egypt. In a sense, this constitutes a physiologically mediated relation between low wages and the level of incentive to work, or to work effectively [p. 108].

Dahl and Lindblom (1953) also point out that apathy is a probable product of great inequality in incomes: "Even where rewards are obtainable, it does not follow that the more rewards, the better for effective incentive. For when too many of the rewards of life are contingent upon performance and too few granted outright, insecurity and despair may be more common reactions than the responses which the rewards are designed to bring forth [p. 151]."

Other attitudes about lack of a disincentive effect, or creation of incentive, as a result of payments center on a number of different aspects. Thus, Morgan and associates (1962) discuss time-orientation, or the ability to make future plans: "The largest number of reasons given by people who felt that they were unable to plan . . . concerned their financial positions [p. 429]." Rehn

(M. S. Gordon, 1965) expresses the same idea in the context of training programs: "Training is most effective when the trainee is already employed and free from economic insecurity [p. xviii]." Shyne (unpublished) speaks of the effect on the recipient of casework services: "I believe that effective service is contingent upon an economic base of adequate assistance." Aftercare is the subject of another comment (*Social Security in France*, 1964): "The continued payment of daily indemnities and pensions to former patients who have resumed the exercise of a professional activity tends to help them take all the precautionary measures necessary to prevent relapse [p. 64]." M. S. Gordon (1965) gives examples of liberal unemployment compensation policies in other countries that nevertheless have low unemployment rates as a proof of the general desire to work. Richardson (1960) holds that any loss of self-reliance due to welfare benefits among a minority of the recipients is greatly offset by the removal of the fear of extreme privation from large numbers of people. Dubin (1958) qualifies the effect of income in terms of its reference group component: "If wages and salaries are comparable to the going community or industry rates, then they are likely to be taken for granted. . . . If employees feel that their basic financial payoff is at an acceptable level, then and only then will they rate other incentives as more important to them [p. 240]."

There are other experienced—even expert—commentators who are prepared to make flat statements about willingness to work, as a result of their experiences. Thus, Pusic (1965) says, "The basis of security . . . is material security [p. 80]"; Smith (1955), "The principle of minimum guarantee is, I believe, sound gospel [p. ix]"; Ginzberg (1964), "People want to work [p. 121]"; Goldberg (1962), "Men want work [p. 6]"; and Nathan (Goodman, 1966) says:

> Most individuals prefer the dignity and respect associated with economic independence and self-reliance and with the opportunity to contribute to, as well as to participate in, economic activities. Perhaps we have focused too much attention on abuses and too little on the benefits of social measures. Maybe we have concentrated too much on the "economic man" and too little on the human being [pp. 226–227].

The mere parade of such a list of expert opinion is not, of course, proof of the correctness of their contentions; but in the absence of more empirical proof of the results of unearned income on incentive to work, these indications of "consensual validation" deserve consideration.

8

Relief Payments

$\mathcal{S}$ince the focus of this study is on the effect that an income guarantee would have on the work incentives of the poor, an obvious place to look for clues is among those who are categorized as poor to the extent that they are receiving unearned income. For this purpose, it is worthwhile examining the areas of AFDC and General Assistance.

AFDC[1] is part of the Public Assistance portion of the Social Security Program, which was originally established to aid the needy aged, the blind, and dependent children. It has since been ex-

[1] Originally called Aid to Dependent Children, this program has undergone several changes in title, including Aid to Families with Dependent Children; Aid and Services to Needy Families with Children, and others. For purposes of simplicity, it will be referred to herein as AFDC.

154

panded to include the permanently and totally disabled, and medical care for the indigent. General Assistance is a local and/or state program to aid those not covered by the federally supported programs, or to supplement them. Since, however, the work incentives of those who have reached retirement age are of only peripheral interest in this study, and since the disabled will be discussed separately and medical care is not considered unearned income for purposes being pursued here, this chapter will be confined to the AFDC program and to General Assistance.

The justification for examining the effect of unearned income on incentive to work among recipients of AFDC is manyfold: For one thing, there have been a number of studies of various phases of this program at various times, and a number of documented experiments, so that more information is available concerning AFDC recipients than concerning most other program clients. Second, the changes which have taken place in the recipients of this program since its inception, no less than the change which has occurred in the public image of such recipients—from impoverished white widows with orphans to unmarried colored mothers of several children—have caused public attention to focus on the effect of this program on incentive to work. Finally, eligibility requirements for this program are such that, with rare exceptions, every recipient can be considered to be *ipso facto* in poverty as a condition for receiving such aid, making further definitions and qualifications unnecessary.[2] Since, however, the great bulk of recipients of AFDC funds are women,[3] findings concerning the General Assistance Program (GAP), which includes both men and women, will also be included here.

In April 1967, there were in these programs, for a total of 1,578,400 families containing 6,031,000 individuals, 1,193,000 families, consisting of 4,946,000 individuals, receiving AFDC; 68,400 families, consisting of 398,000 individuals, receiving

[2] "A vast majority of ADC families can be considered as living in extreme poverty with incomes of less than $2,000 a year," and, "It is clear . . . that the public welfare agencies' estimates of the needs of ADC families fell far short of what is considered a minimal budget [Burgess and Price, 1963, pp. 182, 66]."

[3] In 1960, only 2.2 per cent of AFDC homemakers were men (Burgess and Price, 1963).

AFDC-UP (Aid to Families with Dependent Children with Unemployed Parents); and 317,000 families, consisting of 687,000
individuals, receiving General Assistance ("Program and Operating
Statistics," 1967).

The AFDC program, as originally conceived, was established
primarily to make it possible for mothers of dependent children
not to have to work; that is, the purpose of this program was to
enable mothers not to work, or, at least, to give them viable choices
between working and staying home to take care of their children.
However, the attitudes of the social workers dealing with AFDC
parents seem to affect the way the program actually operates. One
writer assumes that caseworker attitudes may have to be changed
so that they cooperate in, where they presently resist, allowing
AFDC mothers to work (Hausman, 1967), whereas other reports
seem to indicate that social workers judge and publicize their success on the basis of how many AFDC mothers they have persuaded to go to work.[4] In either case, financial incentives are obviously not the only factor operating.

Hausman (1967) distinguishes between "employability,"
which is not simply lack of employment, but which involves absence
of handicaps, presence of attributes such as experience and skills,
a state of the economy that provides opportunities, and willingness to work; and "self-supportability," which is the ability to earn
enough not to need unearned income, and not, therefore, simply
the ability to earn as much as the AFDC or GAP grant, which
does not usually represent sufficient support. Thus, to characterize
someone as employable means that he is capable of earning some
money, given the proper circumstances. It does not necessarily mean
that he will thereby become self-supporting and need no unearned
income, as the previously quoted figures concerning the employed
poor will indicate.

---

[4] There is some evidence that professionally trained social workers
try to dissuade AFDC mothers from going to work, in order that they should
stay home and care for their children in accordance with the original intent
of the law, and perhaps in accordance with their own training concerning
childhood needs, whereas nonprofessional social workers attempt to prove the
efficacy of the program by persuading mothers to go to work, and thus lower
the relief rolls and costs. See *Employment Incentives and Social Services*,
1966.

Therefore the state of the employment market is important as a factor in the examination of relief, and has been so noted by a number of writers, who take into account the rate of unemployment in assessing the effect of relief payments. What is not generally remarked, however, is that the *definition* of employability is changed by extremely high aggregate demand. Acceptable handicaps, usable skills, level of education—all have different effects on the employers as well as the employees when manpower is urgently needed. The number of people who are not only unemployed, but unemployable, is a partial function of the labor supply/demand situation. Consequently, persons given relief as unemployable (and several states do not give relief to persons rated as employable, regardless of the cause of their unemployment) may not only be linked to the size of the grant and the ease of eligibility, but to such definitional factors. This is probably why Collins (Eckstein, 1967) notes that unemployment appears to be a significant determinant of the cost of AFDC, whereas Hausman (1967) says that "The proportion of 'unemployable' . . . male family heads on welfare is probably inversely related to the level of aggregate demand [p. 132]."

In this connection, then, the skills represented by these clients are also important factors. Experience indicates that they are usually those least needed in the labor market. Among the fathers whose usual occupations were known, fewer than 17 per cent were in skilled, clerical, or white-collar types of occupations, while 38 per cent were unskilled laborers. Among mothers, only 8 per cent were skilled, clerical, or white-collar, while the remainder were concentrated largely in unskilled labor and service jobs (Burgess and Price, 1963). Of the total, 71.2 per cent were unemployed when they entered the AFDC program, while only 6.1 per cent were employed full-time permanently (Burgess and Price, 1963). In 1961, only 15.7 per cent of all AFDC mothers were employed, and in 1965 (AFDC-UP having been inaugurated much later than AFDC) only 5 per cent of all AFDC-UP fathers were employed, and in both of these categories, most of those who were employed were working only on a part-time basis (Hausman, 1967). In general, the families within the AFDC program can be described as faced with lack of work experience or marketable skills, poor health, emotional instability, discrimination, isolation, or rejection. They do not present an optimistic picture in terms of potential for independence (Burgess and Price, 1963).

In addition to the attributes of the AFDC and GAP clientele, situational factors should also be taken into account. Causes other than incentive to work, or its lack, affect the number of clients in the AFDC program; for example, cyclic variations in employment, seasonal variations in employment, family and personal disorganization, changes in rules and conditions of eligibility, and changes in definitions of minimal living requirements, among others (Hausman, 1967). Then there are the varying amounts of pressure caused by outside circumstances; Burgess and Price (1963), for example, attribute the higher proportion of Negro mothers who are in the labor force to greater (unspecified) pressure upon them.

Insofar as the evidence drawn from the areas of AFDC and GAP is concerned, the paucity of knowledge about incentive effects seems to be no smaller than it is in other areas. Burgess and Price point out that there is very little substantive knowledge available on the problem of dependency-independency among recipients of welfare funds, although there is a sort of intuitive feeling about many of the sociocultural, economic, and psychological factors which may be operating to move needy AFDC families away from or toward continued support, as suggested by innumerable reports and statistical analyses (Burgess and Price, 1963).

Hausman (1967) says, "In none of the surveys are attempts made to get at the behavioral responses to alternative levels of income provided independent of work or to alternative tax rates in transfer programs [p. 36]." About his own study, he says, "Whether . . . AFDC heads are deliberately reducing their work in response to the high welfare tax rate is a problem that we do not . . . answer satisfactorily. . . . The data merely indicate that they are likely to be and even seem to be doing so [p. 14]."

Turning to the evidence concerning work incentives in the AFDC and GAP programs, the same factors are operative as in the previous general examination of data, that is, that there might be disincentive effect, no effect or mixed effects, or a positive incentive, and that the evidence might be logical, qualitative, or quantitative. Since, however, the same logical factors apply to AFDC and GAP as to work incentives generally, this chapter will concentrate on the studies, both qualitative/impressionistic and quantitative, which have been done in these areas, rather than on the logic. In addition, since we have at issue the extent to which AFDC and GAP clients are working, and the effect which this has upon their grants—and conversely, the effect of the grants upon their work—the previous exclusive concentration on the employed poor will not be operative in this chapter.

The studies used here include those by Burgess and Price (1963) of 5,517 closed AFDC cases in 1961; by Hausman (1967), using AFDC figures, census data, and a survey of 131 AFDC mothers in one slum area in New York City in 1966; Joan Gordon's study (1965) of poor families in Harlem; Kronick's study (1963) of AFDC families in Philadelphia County in 1959; Brehm and Saving's mathematical model (1964; 1967; Stein and Albin, 1967) concerning GAP payments, and the correspondence which resulted from publication; Kaspar's mathematical model (1967), which was an attempted correction of the Brehm and Saving study; the so-called incentive budgeting plans in Denver (*The Incentive Budgeting Demonstration Project,* 1961) and Cleveland (*Employment Incentives and Social Services,* 1966); the Geary County, Kansas, exemption for working expenses (*Operation Fairplay,* 1967); Green's study (1967) of the effect of negative taxes generally; and Collins' analysis (1967) of public assistance and general assistance programs of 1960, relating per capita expenditures, recipient rates, average payments, and average administrative costs with income level, urbanization, unemployment rate, racial and age composition, social insurance, and population growth.

It is easy to conclude, on a logical basis, that persons getting welfare grants would not work for less than that amount, especially if such income were to be deducted in its entirety from their grants. Thus, J. Gordon (1965) found that one-half of her respondents thought of laundry and domestic services—the kind of work they could most often get—as poor jobs, and as they moved from job to job, they remained in domestic service, factories, and service industries. The category was not as significant as the fact that all of the jobs were low-paying, unskilled work with no security.

Burgess and Price (1963) came to the same conclusion: "Since in most cases whatever was earned was taken into account in the budgetary needs and deducted from the assistance check, many families may have found that there was little incentive to work since they made little progress financially [pp. 164–165]."

Empirical data to support the same position are offered by Hausman (1967), who reports that two-thirds of the 131 AFDC mothers interviewed would not accept a job at which the net monthly wage was beneath their monthly assistance income, and, not incidentally, 65 per cent could not realistically expect to earn as much as their assistance income. Brehm and Saving (1964), correlating salaries, ease of getting on GAP roles, size of assistance payments, and unemployment rates, come to the conclusion that the level of payments is an important variable in explaining the percentage of a state's population which is on the GAP rolls. In their words, "In addition to the 'hard core' of unemployables and low-income earners the set of GAP recipients should contain consumers who deliberately have chosen to bring their earned income below the minimum set by the society [p. 1017]."

This finding has been challenged by Stein and Albin (1967), who suggest a recipient rather than a case analysis as more accurate, and who, on this basis, find no relationship between number of recipients and levels of payment per recipient, a correction which has, in turn, been challenged by Brehm and Saving (1967). Kaspar (1967), too, has challenged the Brehm and Saving finding by pointing out, on the one hand, that size of the GAP roll may determine the size of the grant, and not necessarily only the other way around; and on the other hand, that certain of their assumptions are faulty, for instance, that manufacturing wages would be appropriate predicted earnings for GAP recipients rather than, say, domestic service earnings; or their use of the insured unemployed rate, rather than the total unemployment rate—since GAP recipients are not likely to be among the insured unemployed. With such corrections, Kaspar concluded that differences in labor market conditions, rather than the differences in the level of average GAP payments, seem to be the major explanation of interstate variations in the proportion of a state who are receiving General Assistance. He also found that there may be some fifteen to twenty thousand instances in a population of nearly fifty million families, or four-hundredths of one per cent of the population, who may be in some sense taking advantage of the GAP program, or some 5.6 per cent of the GAP cases. It should be noted that Kaspar's findings, in turn, have been attacked on the basis that he did not take into account the family heads transferred to AFDC-UP or to work-training programs, from GAP (Hausman, 1967).

Hausman (1967) concluded that 73 per cent of all AFDC mothers and about 41 per cent of all AFDC fathers could expect no financial benefit—over their grant income—from working, and, surveying a number of studies, came to the conclusion that labor force participation among AFDC mothers is very much a function of the effective wage rate they face. Bernard (1964) found that women in non-AFDC families were more willing to take on irregular work, for small amounts of money, than were the AFDC women, from whose grants such amounts were deducted. Burgess and Price (1963) add empirical data when they point out that approximately 50 per cent of the regularly employed AFDC homemakers reduced the extent of their employment on receipt of benefits, and about half of these to complete unemployment. (In the interests of perspective, it might be pointed out again that the original purpose of the AFDC program was seen as reducing the necessity for mothers of dependent children to work.)

The middle view—that effects of welfare payments the same or greater than salaries are mixed or nonexistent—derives from observations and studies which indicate the differences between people who are on relief. Yet, even these differences, as well as some commonalities, are of interest. J. Gordon (1965) found, for example, that when her respondents were offered jobs by the State Employment Service, they queried and stressed the wages and conditions involved, but when they found jobs through friends, they were interested in the interpersonal relations that they could expect. Wages were *not* the only or the most important factor in all or nearly all cases.

This is somewhat like Overs's distinction (1967) between contractual and familial relations in domestic household jobs. Some of the dissatisfaction with such jobs was found to arise from the fact that one side saw the job as a contractual arrangement, with fulfillment the expected behavior, whereas the other saw the job in familial terms, expecting mutual accommodation. In such cases, although the amount of payment might have been used as the presenting problem, it was not the real one, and reverting to AFDC support was not necessarily a purely financial calculation. J. Gordon (1965) also reports that "None of the women in our sample are glad that they are on welfare, most feel uncomfortable about it, and one-fourth find the experience extremely humiliating. These women appear to feel that their frustrations or humiliations in dealing with the system are inevitable consequences of not being able to "make it" on their own [p. 77]." This attitude hardly seems calculative. Further, three-quarters of Gordon's respondents felt that when one has a job, one should go to work even if one does not feel like it. Krosney (1966) found that in January 1966, there had been a 43 per cent decline of families on relief since 1961, and concludes that "The clear relationship of general relief to the booming economy indicated that many of the men on relief were 'employable' and willing to find work if work existed [p. 134]."

Despite these findings, it is nevertheless difficult to draw firm conclusions concerning incentive to work among AFDC families, as noted in the following three instances: (1) Although, as quoted above, 50 per cent of AFDC homemakers reduced their employment on receipt of benefits, it appears that 50 per cent did not. Further, approximately 18 per cent of those who were unemployed *increased* the extent of their employment on receipt of AFDC payments (Burgess and Price, 1963). (2) Since two-thirds of the 131 AFDC mothers queried by Hausman would not accept a job at which the net monthly wage was beneath their monthly assistance income, it appears that one-third would *not* so refuse (Hausman, 1967). (3) Although, as Burgess and Price discovered, many families may have found that there was little incentive to work, 60 per cent of the participants worked or attempted to find work *during* their AFDC period, even though they did not earn enough to be ineligible (Burgess and Price, 1963).

Orshansky (1965b) cites a California study of AFDC-UP clients and a low-income nonwelfare group, to the effect that "There was no difference observed in willingness to work or in work history [p. 24]." Mangum (1965) also found that there is no evidence that any substantial number of welfare recipients prefer public aid to employment, and Joan Gordon (1965) found that a majority of the women interviewed said that they would like to be working, and there are data to support the willingness to work. Burgess and Price (1963) summarized this aspect of their study by pointing out that 74 per cent of the homemakers continued in the same employment status during the AFDC period as during the crisis period which immediately preceded their entry into the program, and that although 13 per cent changed to working less, practically the same percentage began working more.

Another way of looking at the evidence that the welfare payment has no disincentive effect, or not a complete disincentive effect, is provided by Hausman (1967), who notes that in California, about 360 per 1,000 active AFDC-UP cases were closed between January 1, 1965, and June 30, 1965, because of the increased earnings of the AFDC-UP father; that is, they chose work, which paid more than relief. Despite the smaller employment opportunities for mothers and their comparative lack of ability to be free for work, and the goal of AFDC, which was to free them from work, 27 per 1,000 of the AFDC mothers left the rolls during the same period because of increased earnings.

Kaspar (1967) provides another viewpoint in holding that even if GAP payments rose to $250 per month (the equivalent of $3,000 per year), the average number of GAP cases per thousand population would only rise from 1.63 to 1.90; whereas if the GAP rate fell to zero, only 5 per cent of the cases would increase their supply of labor, and the remainder would have to become wards of the private sector, "tighten their belts," engage in crime, or do something more drastic.

Finally, Green (1967) surveys the experience in New Zealand, and concludes that it is not clear whether the 100 per cent take-away rate has adversely affected the incentives of benefit recipients. However, it does not seem to have reduced the average amount of work done per worker.

Although the case for the third view—that welfare payments create positive incentives for work—is not strong, there are some indications that this may indeed be the case for some clients.

Unfortunately, the data do not indicate, in the cases quoted above of clients who sought employment on being accepted into the AFDC program, whether these work incentives resulted from the stigma of being on relief, the pressure of social workers, the security of dependable income, or other factors.

Kimmel (1966) offers a possible explanation in his expressed belief that AFDC families may be more like middle-class families than poor non-AFDC families because of the former's interaction with social workers and the social welfare structure. To the extent that this is true, we might expect AFDC cases to prefer income from working, even if it were equivalent to their grants, in order to be more like the middle class.

Hausman (1967) mentions, in passing, the difference between the effect of a given level of income and the given degree of security attached to its receipt. This may be interpreted as meaning that for many clients the low level of the welfare grant is compensated for by the security of knowing that it will be received. On the other hand, it is possible to view welfare grants as very undependable, since many clients lose their grants for reasons which they do not understand, because of actions which they did not know were forbidden, changes in regulations which seem arbitrary, new social workers with different attitudes, and other, almost arbitrary reasons. Consequently, a salary which pays less than the welfare grant, but which is seen as more dependable, would be a positive incentive to work for some people.

However, the most compelling evidence for a positive incentive effect is more circuitous. Burgess and Price (1963) found that some form of family breakdown accounted for 36 per cent of the white cases and 40 per cent of the Negro cases of AFDC, and Kronick (1963) interprets her data as suggesting that family life is directly affected in specific ways by restricted economic resources, a condition of life implicit in continuous existence as a recipient of public assistance. In turn, the disturbance of family life results in an increased incidence of pathological behavior, and an increase in the difficulty of maintaining economic independence. Thus, the receipt of unearned income should result in less difficulty, less family disorganization or breakdown, greater ability to work, and therefore greater income, or, at least, income enough to get off relief. Consequently, the effect of economic security on family life may be analogous to the effect of jobs or income on the "wantlessness" of the poor discussed above: the very intervention of an income guarantee may change the situation that seems to counter-indicate such a guarantee.

Examination of the incentive to work for sums greater than the relief payment indicates that, despite the folklore, there seems to be little evidence that receipt of relief payments disinclines recipients from *wanting* to earn more than the amount of those payments. This is easily understandable in light of the fact that such payments are usually deliberately pegged below salary averages, and that most recipients, as noted above, could not earn more than their grants in any case, given their skills and opportunities. Again, this does not mean that they necessarily would want to earn more than a subsistence guarantee—payments are not at the level of subsistence, and the evidence concerning wanting to earn more than relief payments is not directly applicable to the desire to earn more than subsistence income. Thus, the factor of opportunity may be the operative one, even if masked by seeming lack of motivation. Many AFDC family heads may be capable of greater work effort than they are making, but in any case would be incapable of self-support (Hausman, 1967), so the receipt of relief has no effect on their incentive to make more than this amount. In addition, relief clients do move off the rolls. A 1961 study showed that one-third of the AFDC clients remained for one year or less, and that 16 per cent were on the rolls for under two years. The median was 2.1 years (Wickenden, 1965).

In addition, the evidence that relief clients are willing to work to increase their incomes over the grant level is compelling. Both Denver and Cleveland have experimented with letting relief clients retain some of their earnings, under a plan called "incentive budgeting." Although the Denver plan did not result in any significant increases in number of clients working, this has been attributed, in part, to the general increase in unemployment at that period (*The Incentive Budgeting Demonstration Project,* 1961). However, it was found that although physical, social, and mental problems kept recipients from becoming self-sustaining, desire, motivation, and concern on the part of recipients were present.

In Cleveland, moreover, 137 persons in the group gained employment, an increase in the employment rate of 134 per cent. This occurred while the employment rate in the comparison areas was declining 11 per cent (*Employment Incentives and Social Services,* 1966).

In a somewhat similar fashion, some areas have allowed clients to keep, from their employment income, the expenses involved in going to work. In Geary County, Kansas, for example, where a $50 exemption was established for working expenses before the deduction from grants, the feeling is that while it is difficult to evaluate in dollars and cents the effects of the project, the agency staff is convinced the project has provided incentive to either take employment or to continue in employment. Some of the working mothers probably would have had to stop working if this kind of a provision for deducting the costs of employment before considering the earnings available to meet need had not been made. Literally, they could not afford to work unless the reasonable costs of that employment were considered.

Although some states deduct all of the earned income of a relief client from their grants, some of those which peg rates below need allow clients to earn and keep enough to reach the need level. There are some indications that the latter system has resulted in increases in work incentive, but a full-scale survey of this situation has yet to be made.

Although 50 per cent of Morse and Weiss's unskilled laborer respondents, quoted previously, said that they would quit work if they inherited enough to live comfortably, 50 per cent said that they would continue working even under such circumstances. Hausman (1967) is more emphatic in his feeling that it seems possible to more than double or even triple labor force participation among AFDC women by allowing them to keep their earnings. Quoting Greenfield, he points out that it appeared easy to secure the cooperation of mothers in cases in which the earnings would exceed budgetary need.

There is some reason to believe that money may be a more significant motivator among those who have little than among those who have more, reasoning which sets the law of diminishing utility against Maslow's hierarchy of needs. In this theoretical vein, it might be well to point out the reasoning applied by Musgrave (1959) to transfer payments. He posits that taxes above the poverty line have a substitution effect, making a substitution of leisure for work easier, but that they also have an income effect, creating incentive to work to make up for the taxes paid. Below the poverty line, he holds that the substitution effect exists, but since making more money does not increase one's income, due to the deduction from the relief grant, there is no counterforce to the desire to take leisure rather than to work. This logic is applicable, however, only to income which still leaves the recipient below the grant level. If the income that can be obtained by working pays more than the relief grant, then there is a gain in absolute income, and the income effect operates. Thus, incentive to work when no real income results might be inhibited by welfare rules, but incentive to work which takes one out of poverty is not negated by Musgrave's law.

In summary, although the proportion of relief clients who are theoretically employable may be larger than generally believed (Hausman, 1967), the number who can be self-supporting is very small, and even those who are theoretically employable may have great difficulty in finding jobs. The jobs which they find will not pay as much as their grants, and although an unknown number who would prefer work to the point of suffering financially (and at their income level, the suffering is very real), the majority will not. However, given the opportunity of making money which, together with the grant, would give them the income defined as that which they "need," a large number would undertake such work. If they were not allowed to keep all of their earnings up to the need line, but only a proportion of them, then the hours of work and the type of work necessary to attain a comparatively small income increase would be a factor in their decision to work or not. It seems that when the opportunity to earn enough to be self-supporting, even by a limited definition, is offered, those who are capable of work would, by and large, seize the opportunity.

9

Disability Payments

*T*he evidence concerning the effect of disability compensation on incentives to work is difficult to assess, and more difficult to generalize. In the first place, the fact of disability has its own effects—in some cases a determination to overcome the disability; in others, acceptance of realistic limitations; in still others, rationalization of nondisability effects; and in still others, ambivalence.

In addition to its subjective effects, disability causes real limitations in employment opportunities, to the point that the Court of Appeals has ruled that disability determinations must take into account not only what the applicant can do, but also what employment activities exist for one who can do only what the applicant can (*Summary of Court Decision—Disability,* 1960–1961).

Further, the determination of disability is itself a highly subjective matter. As Nagi (1967) points out,[1] evaluation of disability requires information, criteria, and judgment, and almost total reliance is placed upon the rehabilitation counselors' judgments and criteria, "derived from their training and experience, in determining whether or not a disability interferes *substantially* with employment, what constitutes *suitable* employment, and whether or not an applicant offers *reasonable* expectations [Ch. III, p. 23]." Such judgments, as well as rehabilitation itself, are often and perhaps inevitably influenced by socioeconomic factors as well as by physical ones (Massie, 1965). Age, for example, is an important factor—the older the applicant, the greater his chances of being allowed benefits (Nagi, 1967). Again, psychological disabilities are not as well compensated, or judged as important, as physical limitations. There is an inverse relationship between psychological limitations and rates of allowances granted, since applicants who "do nothing" with their time are more often judged to be lazy or cheating, rather than psychologically incapacitated (Nagi, 1967).

Another difficulty is the confusion concerning the goal of disability compensation and rehabilitation efforts generally—whether it is to replace lost wages, to pay workers damages for injuries sustained, to facilitate employment at the previous income rate, to bring about employment regardless of income as a desirable thing in its own right, or to aid the disabled to accept their condition.

Then there is competition between, and differences in handling by, Workmen's Compensation, Social Security, and private insurance carriers. This has been known to result in attempted isolation of the client from one service by the other, as when insurance carriers feel that contact by the insured with the Vocational Rehabilitation service will adversely affect their interests. Finally, the lack of information concerning this whole field is another limitation in drawing conclusions from it concerning work incentives. Day (Jaffe, 1961) has summarized these lacks by saying, "Little

[1] Quoting F. P. Frutchey, "Evaluation—What It Is," in D. Byron (Ed.), *Evaluation in Extension* (Washington: U.S. Department of Agriculture), p. 2.

is known . . . about the employment . . . of the disabled in general [p. 57]," due to the fact that most studies in this area have used small samples, failed to separate men from women, used nonrandom selection of cases, and failed to separate cases by nature or severity of the disability.

Yet, the extent of the disability compensation and vocational rehabilitation programs makes them the most suitable areas for examining the incentive factor under conditions of reduced capacity. In 1963–1965, 22.6 million noninstitutionalized civilian personnel experienced limitations in activities they once were able to perform, and of these, 4.1 million were unable to carry on their major activities—employment, housework, or school work (Nagi, 1967).[2] There are about 80,000 annual cases of permanent impairments from work accidents (Jaffe, 1961), and by the middle of 1966 slightly over one million workers were receiving disability benefits under the Social Security program, with an additional 829,000 benefits being paid to beneficiaries of disabled workers (*Health and Welfare Indicators,* 1966). In the face of these numbers, it has been estimated that 76 per cent of all disability applicants for rehabilitation are screened out as having low potential, and eventually only 1 per cent of those aged 50–64 and 6 per cent of those under 50 are accepted for service. Of this group, only 40 per cent of those under 50 and 20 per cent of those over 50 receive vocational training (*The Disabled Worker under OASDI,* 1964). To what extent these disabled then follow the trade or vocation for which they have trained is not clear, but a national study of 10,000 deaf persons—nearly all of whom were white, and between the ages of 20 and 59—found that most of those who had studied for a trade never followed it (Day, in Jaffe, 1961).

The evidence concerning the incentives of disabled persons includes as much folklore as does incentive evidence generally, as well as the familiar conflict between stated public policy and general attitudes. Thus, although programs such as Aid to the Permanently and Totally Disabled presumably deal with people

---

[2] Quoting *Age Patterns in Medical Care, Illness, and Disability, United States, July 1913, June 1965.* National Center for Health Statistics, Series 10, No. 32, U.S. Department of Health, Education, and Welfare, Washington, 1966.

who are completely and forever incapable of working (or, at least, did so until the definition was recently relaxed), the reports on and justification offered for this program invariably include the boast of how many beneficiaries have been reemployed; and benefits of this program are deliberately kept low in order not to interfere with the incentive to work of people who have been officially adjudged permanently and totally disabled. Other such programs also base their payment rates on a fear of disincentive; to receive Workmen's Compensation of $57 a week in Michigan, the worker must have been earning $85 per week and have no less than six dependents (Morgan et al., 1959).

Two small pieces of evidence concerning a disincentive factor from disability payments are the findings of Morgan and associates that basic personality dispositions had no relationship to whether or not the person returned to work, from which they assume that the need for more money was more important than any feeling that it was an achievement to get well; and that special sample studies carried out by the Social Security Administration indicate that persons denied disability benefits are about twice as likely to be rehabilitated as are those allowed benefits, although this, in turn, is based upon the fact that such persons are twice as likely to be accepted for rehabilitative services (*Summary Data on Operation of OASI Vocational Rehabilitation Referral Program,* 1964).

The three major areas in which incentive effects might be sought are those dealing with payments vis-à-vis rehabilitation, the effect of double payments, and lump-sum vis-à-vis regular payments.

The feeling that fear of loss of compensation is a disincentive for rehabilitation on the part of the disabled has been expressed by Cheit, Jaffe, and Gulledge (Jaffe, 1961). Payments during the rehabilitation period are generally less than compensation, and Gulledge has found that many industrially injured workers cannot afford to accept vocational rehabilitation service: "Their family needs are such as to make the maximum maintenance allowance of $100 a month from the Vocational Rehabilitation Service inadequate to meet their needs [Jaffe, 1961, p. 117]." He goes on to call for a minimization of this conflict in motivation arising from the relationship between vocational rehabilitation and rights to benefits. That this conflict may be real is illustrated by the experience of the Ontario Rehabilitation Clinic, which is described by Horovitz (1959): "As nearly as anybody has reached a successful solution to rehabilitation, the Ontario Workmen's Compensation plan is the most commendable. Injured workers voluntarily come there in large numbers. The percentage of rehabilitable employees using their center is high. The results on the whole are excellent [p. 496]." Among other factors, the success of this program is held to rest upon the principle that compensation is paid for the loss of capacity, rather than the loss of earning power. Consequently, a person who is rehabilitated but still physically maimed receives a pension for life. Insofar as the effect of this system upon work incentives is concerned, Horovitz concludes that the guarantee of income whether the injured person returns to work or not results in more people working.

The relationship of work incentives to the desire for rehabilitation is complicated, however, by the nature of disability compensation. Thus, from the point of view of the insurance company, a disabled workman who is unwilling to undertake rehabilitation is either malingering, or is neurotically attached to his disability. In either case, these are situations to overcome. From the point of view of the injured workman, however, the employer has a contractual obligation to compensate him because of the injury, a cost which will not even be borne by the company, but by an insurance company. The employee's attitude toward rehabilitation may therefore be based upon feelings about the company, insurance companies, justice, physical pain, and other such matters, rather than exclusively on desire to return to work or not. Employees' attitudes have been expressed by Horovitz (1959):

> Most workers feel that the employer (and hence his insurer) is somehow responsible for the accident and has a duty to make complete financial reparation. Where the workmen's compensation act provides payments for life for a worker's injury and he then learns that rehabilitation will or may cut down his employer's financial responsibility, the worker often resents the rehabilitation suggestion. In short, if a worker knows his injury will eventually cost the insurer $50,000 in medical and weekly compensation, he cannot understand why he should reduce the insurer's liability to $10,000 or less by going through

a painful and disconcerting rehabilitation program. He feels that to do so would be relieving the insurer and employer of their rightful responsibilities [p. 493].

The area of payments vis-à-vis rehabilitation and/or work can be summed up by saying that there are no hard data available for the number or proportions of disabled persons considered acceptable for service who are deterred from undertaking rehabilitation, or work, purely because of receipt of compensation payments.

The second major area of incentive evidence in the disability programs concerns the results of overinsurance and double payments. The evidence here, too, is mainly in the nature of stated opinions by insurance men (who are not completely disinterested parties concerning benefit levels which claimants should receive): One insurance executive (D. F. Grahame, Paul Revere Life Insurance Company) testified before a Congressional committee: "We do not like to insure over 60 per cent to 80 per cent of a man's income, especially considering that disability benefits are not taxable (*Social Security*, 1965, p. 1156)." Other testimony points out that disability insurance is written under a prime rule that to the greatest extent possible the economic incentive to remain disabled, rather than return to useful employment, should be avoided (*Social Security*, 1965, p. 539)'. The American Medical Association also held that disability payments may lessen an individual's incentive to return to work. One writer says:

> It has been repeatedly demonstrated that disability tends to be unduly prolonged when overinsurance exists, particularly if such benefits are payable as a matter of contractual right. If those benefits approach the level of what might be earned in active employment, the incentive to work is lost. . . . The economic incentive to return to work or to seek rehabilitation if necessary depends upon the margin between earnings . . . over the tax-free and expense-free amount of disability benefits available [Social Security, 1965, p. 140].

This belief concerning incentives has been built into the Social Security system: "In our program, impaired persons are encouraged to return to some kind of work. This is accomplished by the economic fact that disability compensation is on the average 59 per cent of earnings in the lowest and 32 per cent in the highest

earning brackets [Roemmich, 1961, p. 60]." The emphasis placed
upon incentive to work is evident in the above statement, in which
payments are, on the average, at least 40 per cent less than previous earnings, despite the fact that only 3.1 per cent of applicants
for rehabilitation are accepted. The result is that 97 per cent of
those applying for rehabilitation, and all of those not so applying,
are relegated to standards of living considerably below those previously experienced, as a result of accidents or illnesses for which
they are not responsible, and against which they are supposedly
insured, lest some persons who should be included in the 3.1 per
cent not apply.

The final piece of evidence that such lack of incentive
would indeed occur was offered by the International Association
of Health Underwriters (*Social Security,* 1965):

> Lowered disability requirements will decrease individual initia-
> tive and increase malingering among the less responsible segment
> of our population. The experience of our life insurance com-
> panies with total disability income during the 1930's when
> many people were unable to find suitable work automatically
> became disabled proves that this statement is true [p. 814].

The question of double benefits, or benefits from two sources,
came into focus in the following manner: In 1956 Aid to the
Permanently and Totally Disabled was added to the Social Security
Program. This law provided that when the same person received
both Workmen's Compensation and Social Security for disability,
there would be an "offset"—the amount received from Workmen's
Compensation would be deducted from the Social Security payment.
In order to protect the rights of veterans to other types of compensation, however, the "offset" provision, which had been written
in general terms and therefore affected veterans, was removed
from the law in 1958. Although this made possible double payments, the people affected seemed to be few and the amounts
minute, so little attention was focused on the provisions. In 1965,
however, the federal government moved to broaden the definition
of permanent disability from one of long continued duration or one
expected to result in death, to a continuous period of six months.
Both Workmen's Compensation officials and private insurance
companies contended that this would give double benefits to large

numbers of the disabled, and thus affect their incentive for rehabilitation and/or work.

Congressional hearings around this issue were voluminous
and replete with testimony concerning both the extent and the
result of the expected double coverage. Thus, the American Insurance Association (*Social Security*, 1965, p. 814) testified as to
the "catastrophic effect that this duplication was having and will
have on Workmen's Compensation insurance [p. 814]." The
Journal of American Insurance held that there were probably some
63,000 persons receiving duplicate benefits (*Social Security*, 1965,
p. 261). Senator Curtis said (*Social Security*, 1965), "State Workmen's Compensation administrators tell us that since the repeal of
the offset provision from the Social Security law, they have en-
countered a great deal of resistance to rehabilitation from injured
employees who are receiving both Workmen's Compensation and
Social Security Benefits [p. 219]." Similar testimony was presented
by a large number of insurance companies and Workmen's Compensation officials.

The search for the actual number of people who were
receiving double benefits, however, proved frustrating, and the
number eluded the Congressional committee until and after the
end of the hearings. Similarly, the amounts that would theoretically
be paid to such double beneficiaries and whether those amounts
would equal their earning capacities proved equally elusive. Thus,
in 1958 it was estimated from one source that 3 per cent of those
getting Social Security disability benefits were also getting Workmen's Compensation (*The Disability Insurance Program Under
Social Security*, 1963), whereas in 1965 the then-Secretary of
Health, Education, and Welfare testified that about 2 per cent
of those *receiving* disability benefits under the Social Security program were also *entitled* to receive Workmen's Compensation (*Social
Security*, 1965; emphasis added). Although some figures were
quoted from the National Council on Compensation Insurance, the
sources of these figures were not given, and an estimate that between
42,000 and 47,000 persons would be entitled to double benefits
under the proposed broadened provisions was not substantiated by
any evidence. Even the question as to whether double payments
had been or would be greater than recipients' earning power was

not clarified, with insurance companies presenting tables to indicate that they would, and the government presenting tables based upon other assumed salaries, differences in life conditions, possible income increases from continued work, and so on—which indicated that the danger that duplication of disability benefits might produce undesirable results is not of sufficient importance to justify reduction of the social security disability benefit (*Social Security*, 1965).

The final result was a decision to undertake an investigation into the effect of such double benefits on incentive to work, a decision that never came to fruition as Congress decided both to reinsert the offset provision and to broaden the base of eligibility. Consequently, the entire controversy and the testimony which it evoked clarified little concerning work incentives nor, in the opinion of at least one observer, was this the real issue. Instead, the latent issue was whether Workmen's Compensation or Social Security would be the basic compensation program, with the other as supplement (Somers, 1965).

The third area of disability compensation which has some relevance for work incentives is that of lump-sum vis-à-vis weekly or monthly payments. Although the evidence in this instance is purely on logical grounds, some facts concerning lump-sum settlements should be noted. There appears to be pressure from some insurance sources on the disabled to accept lump-sum settlements, which are considerably cheaper for the companies. There is also the pressure that, regardless of the lump-sum settlement, the injured feels that he must accept it because he simply cannot live on the weekly payments (Morgan et al., 1959). As a matter of fact, "70 per cent of lump-sum and 71 per cent of weekly payments people are *not back to the financial position* (in terms of the weekly earnings of the injured person) that they were in before their accident [p. 92]." Nevertheless, the lump-sum payments seem more disadvantageous: "*In more than half of the cases, in fact, the lump-sum compensation amounted to less than five per cent of the expected income loss* [p. 99]."

With these factors in mind, the logic of lump-sum payments would be that such payments (like severance payments to fired workers) are quickly spent, and that need would force recipients of such payments back to work, while those receiving regular benefits would be disinclined to seek work. Morgan and associates found that this was not the case: "Some critics of Workmen's Compensation argue that weekly payments discourage injured workers from returning to the job. If these claims are well founded, more of the lump sum settlement cases should have been back at work than weekly payment cases. The data . . . do not support this expectation [p. 105]." In fact, even the stereotype of recipients is confounded by the finding that, when race is considered, many more Negroes on weekly payments are back at work than Negroes receiving lump-sum settlements (62 per cent versus 31 per cent) (Morgan et al., 1959).

The case for no incentive effects arising from compensation payments, or for positive effects, is no stronger than the reverse. It was found helpful to the blind that they receive their compensation whether they work or not, because it gives them an opportunity to experiment with various vocations without the risk of losing benefits should they fail in one endeavor and find it necessary to try another (*Social Security*, 1965). This factor has been accepted by the Social Security Administration to the point that:

> The 1960 amendments to the Social Security Act provided that disabled beneficiaries who go to work despite a severe impairment may continue to be paid benefits during 12 months. . . . Not until 9 months of work will a decision be made as to whether the beneficiary has shown that he has regained his ability to work. If the decision is that he is able to engage in substantial work and is therefore no longer disabled within the meaning of the law, he will still be paid his benefits for three months longer, making a total of twelve months of trial work and adjustment [*Continuing Disability Experience*, 1961, pp. 1–2].

In addition, the logic of the International Association of Health Underwriters, quoted above to the effect that the rise in disability during the 1930s proved that people unable to find work became disabled to qualify for compensation, can and perhaps should be reversed: If people became disabled because they could not find work, this means that they did *not* become disabled when they *could* find work; ergo, people prefer work to disability compensation. Only if disability were positively related to full employment would rise in disability rolls indicate lack of work incentive. Rather than disability benefits being preferred to employment, or even to under- and unemployment, Nagi (1967) found that applicants reach a distress threshold before applying for disability benefits.

There appears to be only one empirical study of the effect of disability payments on work patterns, and this is the study, mentioned previously, done by Salzberger and Shapira (1966) on disabled Israeli army veterans. Veterans rated as 20 per cent disabled, and therefore compensated, were compared with veterans 19 per cent disabled, and therefore not compensated. The type of disability was matched for two groups, as well as demographic variables deemed important, and their work records were compared. The findings suggested that the monetary grants acted as social equalizers insofar as they seemed to enable veterans with less farovable socioeconomic endowments to achieve employment behavior ratings similar to those with better endowment. Unfortunately, the data do not indicate the size of the payments, but there is reason to believe that they were quite small. However, the receipt of payments, no matter how small, did not seem to create a disincentive effect, but on the contrary, seemed to have a positive effect on those who might otherwise have been more disinclined to work due to lack of endowment.

Again, as in other areas, there appear to be several factors which are associated with application for disability benefits and which might be mistaken for, or mask, incentive to work. One study found that the lower the socioeconomic status, the greater the disability inclination, which might mean that dissatisfaction with living conditions generally spills over into the work situation. However, insofar as financial incentives are concerned, "It is important to note that the levels of income before and after disability showed no consistent relationships to disability inclination [Nagi, 1967, Ch. VII, p. 10]." The same study found that although the highest rate of disability allowances was for nonwhite males, these workers were also more frequently judged by the clinical teams as incapable of competitive work; that is, not work incentive but work ability and opportunities were the important factors.

The likelihood of cessation of disability compensation payments varied with age, with the youngest most likely to recover and return to work. Contrary to other beliefs, one study (*Continuing Disability Experience,* 1961) found that the length of time that one stayed on compensation did not affect the chances of returning to work; that is, recipients did not become "dependent" and stop trying to work. In fact, the employment "failures" among the disabled have been found to resemble the unemployed men in the entire United States. They tend to the older, less-well-educated, semiskilled and unskilled Negro and Puerto Rican (Jaffe et al., 1964).

Finally, the difficulty of drawing cause and effect conclusions from such statistical relationships is evidenced by the findings of one study that marital instability is related to high disability inclinations, which should be guidance to insurance carriers to pressure workers to stay single or obtain divorces, as they now press for low compensation (Nagi, 1967).

In summary, it can be said that there is a widespread belief, especially among rehabilitation workers and insurance personnel, that disability payments—and especially regular, as opposed to lump-sum payments—inhibit work incentives, or the desire and willingness to undertake rehabilitation. The evidence that this is true is mostly "proof negative" rather than "proof positive." Compensation which continues throughout and beyond rehabilitation efforts, and is paid—at least for a long period—whether the effort is successful or not, seems to encourage rehabilitation and work experimentation on the part of clients. The implication is that compensation not paid in this way and through such conditions inhibits rehabilitation and work applications.

However, studies which find that noncancellable grants may result in efforts to earn more money, while grants which are reduced as money is earned have no such effect, may be considered *non sequiturs* which prove only that human wants are insatiable, and that people, even the disabled, will work to obtain more than they have, even if they will not work for the same amount as they can receive without working.

10

Unemployment Insurance

$\mathcal{L}$ike other forms of income maintenance, the effect of unemployment compensation on incentive to work is hard to assess, due to conceptual questions, lack of comparability of data, and a dearth of evidence. A short description of the program, and a look at the conceptual problems, must therefore precede such evidence as exists.

Unemployment insurance is a state/federal program established under the original Social Security Act. It is intended to replace a portion of the income lost through unemployment, for limited periods. It is paid for by employer contributions in all but three states, which require comparatively small employee contributions. The payments are thus linked to length of previous employment and earnings.

Achieving wide coverage under unemployment insurance has always been a problem. One authority (M. S. Gordon, 1965) estimates that approximately two-fifths of the labor force, and more than one-fifth of all wage and salary workers, are excluded from the federal/state unemployment insurance service. Another source (Fernbach, 1965) holds that only about half of the jobless draw any benefits at all because of limitations of program coverage, disqualifications, and maximums on length of time benefits.

Adequacy of benefits is another difficulty. From 1948 to 1960, for example, it has been estimated that unemployed benefits compensated for about 20 per cent of the wage and salary loss from total unemployment. If partial unemployment is included, the rate of compensation is reduced to 15 per cent (M. S. Gordon, 1963). In part, this is true because unemployment benefits are deliberately pegged at a percentage of the wage level.[1] The justification for this earnings-benefit link has been given as:

> In a democratic society it is undesirable that the workers who happen to become unemployed should have to change their standard of living drastically each time they become unemployed. The payment of benefits in proportion to wages helps the unemployed person to maintain something approximating his usual standards of living until he regains employment—his normal status [J. M. Becker, 1961, pp. 14–15].

The low level of compensation payments also arises because the unemployed tend to be the lower-paid workers: "Those in lower-paid occupations are more likely to experience unemployment and to be unemployed for longer periods than those in more highly paid occupations. For many workers, therefore, low incomes are a product of low levels of pay when working, and also of the loss of income when not working [Wilcock, 1965, p. 37]." In addition, unemployment insurance is not usually geared to the number of dependents, and many poor families are at marginal levels even when the breadwinner is working.

---

[1] In 1963, payments as high as average weekly salaries were possible in only one state (Mangum, 1965).

The factors which make for a high proportion of poor people among the unemployed, and which may be mistaken for lack of incentive, include the inability to hold many types of jobs. One study tested 680 able-bodied people in a large city, and found that more than one-half were functionally illiterate because they could not read well enough to do fifth-grade work (May, 1964). Lest it be assumed that such illiteracy is also caused by lack of incentive, it should be noted that a study of 131 cities found that illiteracy is a function of differences in levels of poverty, occupational mix, economic opportunity, and social mobility; in short, that the context of economic and social opportunities is the important element (Dentler and Warshauer, 1965).

In a test of job aptitudes, 68 per cent of clients tested had very limited ability for the occupations tested for (Wickersham, 1963). In 1959, Armour and Company tested 170 laid-off workers for vocational training, and 65 per cent of the total were simply told that the best chance of employment would be in casual manual labor (May, 1964). The lack of actual skill is not the only problem, even among more skilled people, that is, managerial and professional workers. One study indicates that more than nine out of ten workers who lost their jobs did so for reasons that do not even remotely pertain to know-how. These people got fired because they had poor health, poor personalities, and poor dispositions; because they talked too much, were careless, untidy, intemperate, and unreliable (McFarland, 1957).

Another area of difficulty involves the very definition of unemployment. Not only must the person be not working to be so defined, but he must be able to work, be available for work, want to work, and have no place to work. Each of these factors, in turn, is subject to definition, such as being able to do only certain kinds of work, being available for more work than he is presently doing, indicating availability by checking-in regularly at an employment agency, and being able and willing to travel the necessary distance to the open job. The definition of unemployed may, or may not, include those who are waiting to be called back to a job, waiting to start a new job, and the temporarily ill. A subjective element enters into the definition when the job offered must be considered "suitable"—or, more often, when the worker is allowed to refuse an "unsuitable" job and continue to draw his compensation.

Also, a difference exists between employability and placement, which becomes important in those instances in which other forms of welfare are not payable to a person who is considered "employable," even though he is not, in terms of jobs available, "placeable," and even if he is not, or is no longer, eligible for unemployment compensation. Consequently, the term and concept "present unemployability" have come into being (Miller and Harrison, 1964).

Then there is the problem, insofar as comparability of data is concerned, of "recurrent unemployability." One study indicates that during a one-year period, 13 per cent of the compensation claimants had been unemployed three or more times; and 15 per cent twice (Mueller and Schmiedeskamp, 1962). Another study indicates that turnover rates of 200 per cent per year are not uncommon in heavy industry (Caplow, 1954). Thus, for the six-year period 1957 through 1962, there was an annual average of almost 13.7 million individuals who were unemployed some of the time, although the annual unemployment level was approximately four million persons (Wilcock, 1965).

Finally, there is the problem of measuring and including in incentive studies those people who are out of the labor market, not because of age, disability, young children, or studies, but because they have despaired of finding jobs, or, for whatever reason, do not report themselves as actively seeking work, even though they would go to work if they could find jobs, or suitable jobs. It has been estimated that official unemployment figures must be doubled to account for such people. Similarly, if people who are partially employed but want full employment are considered, the unemployment rate would increase to between 7 and 9 per cent of the potential labor force. Further, additional unemployment is believed to exist among those in industries such as agriculture, who would move to more productive employment if it were available. It has also been estimated that another 800,000 to 1,500,000 persons would enter the labor force if job opportunities were more readily available (Mangum, 1965).

From such problems of definition and counting has come

the need for more precise operational definitions. Although it may be true, as Murray (1965) says, that "Unemployment, to a certain extent, is a state of mind; that is, to be genuinely unemployed, a person must want to work and be able to work [p. 69]," this is not amenable to measurement. Consequently, the Bureau of Labor has recently begun to make use of another term—"subemployment" —in order to reflect the magnitude of the problem correctly. Sub-employed people are defined as those who are employed part-time but desire full-time employment; those not looking for work because they have despaired of finding it; and those making less than the legal minimum wage. This category has been applied to slum areas of ten cities, and the results in Cleveland are typical.

The reported unemployment rate in the United States today is 3.7 per cent. For the Cleveland metropolitan area as a whole it is 2.4 per cent, one of the lowest rates in the country. However, in slum areas of Cleveland, where 144,826 people live, the unemployment rate is not 3.7 per cent or 2.4 per cent, but four times the U.S. rate and six times the Cleveland rate—15.5 per cent, and this percentage includes only those making active efforts to find work. The unemployment rate for out of school youth is 58 per cent. When the subemployment criterion is used, it is estimated that half the people living in such slums who are working or who should be working are subemployed (Sub-Employment in the Slums of Cleveland, n. d.).

The official rate of unemployment in February 1966 was listed as 3.7 per cent, or 3,150,000 people. This consisted of 1.5 million adult men (2.6 per cent); 750,000 adult women (3.6 per cent); and 700,000 teen-agers (10.9 per cent) (Unemployment Insurance Review, 1966). A Boston study indicated that one-half of the "officially" unemployed were Negro women, and one-half of them were in the sixteen to twenty-four age group (Unemployment in the Boston Urban Employment Survey of 1966, 1966). To the extent that this can be extrapolated, one-quarter of the unemployment would be relieved by measures which found and gave suitable jobs to the Negro women between the ages of sixteen and twenty-four. Concerning the unskilled among such groups, and among the unemployed generally, Secretary Wirtz has no optimism (Seminars on Private Adjustments . . . , 1964): "The truth of the matter is that there is no longer any substantial amount of un-skilled work in the labor market for these people to take [p. 33]."

There are implications for incentive research in a number of the questions raised above. For example, since so few of the un-employed are covered by unemployment insurance, care must be exercised in generalizing from the covered unemployed to the poor generally. In addition, the statistics do not indicate the differences between the unemployed. They cannot be treated as a group of people who all act and think alike. They show no evidence of being "A group set apart from their fellows in thought, ideas, or actions [Langer, 1965, p. 43]." Similarly, because unemployment compen-sation is generally inadequate, not only in terms of replacing salaries, but as income generally, even at a subsistence level, the desire of most people to work (as evidenced by the data below) rather than to receive unemployment compensation, can be seen in terms of pressing need, or insatiability, rather than an equal choice between compensation or salaries.

Again, there are problems in assessing the effect of unem-ployment compensation, since it might be supplemented by private pensions, second jobs, or public assistance.[2]

Finally, there is the question of the extent to which unem-ployment compensation is seen as unearned income by those re-ceiving it. Although employee contributions are required in only three states, the underlying assumption of the work-benefits link is that workers have "earned" their compensation, or have a right to it, through their previous work. That is, their work not only produced income, but some of the income, or the result of the work, was put aside for them in the form of unemployment com-pensation. Thus, the phenomenon of people exhausting their un-employment compensation rights before withdrawing from the labor force—by retirement, for example—might be linked to a desire to make full use of their rights, rather than have the employer or someone else benefit from funds which are rightfully the worker's.

[2] Although some states make virtually no provision for public as-sistance to the employable unemployed—in 1959 seventeen states had no such provisions—it is at least theoretically possible in other states to receive both unemployment insurance and public assistance. (See Wickenden, in J. M. Becker, 1965).

Such complications make it difficult to discern the effect of unemployment compensation on incentive to work, and yet the assumption of a disincentive effect is an important part of policy-making regarding this program. Breul (1965) points out that, historically, "Whenever proposals have been made for providing . . . adequate financial assistance, two insistent questions have been raised: Does not the very availability of relief encourage indolence? And does not the provision of adequate maintenance to those out of work tend to distort the level of wages in the community [p. 6]?" The unemployed poor have always been considered a special problem, and it has traditionally been felt that relief to those able to work should be provided with care, and in small amounts. Proposals to strengthen the unemployment insurance system are hampered by continuing fear that higher benefit levels will enhance work disincentives.

In assessing the evidence of the extent to which this fear is justified, it should be pointed out again that in many cases unemployment compensation is only a percentage of what had been essentially inadequate wages, and its effect cannot be applied directly to that of an income guarantee which would, presumably, be more adequate than either the unemployment compensation or the salary. Even so, the evidence that unemployment compensation has a disincentive effect is very sparse. A Hawaiian study of those drawing both pensions and unemployment compensation indicated that they remained jobless longer than other unemployed persons— 21.5 weeks as compared to 13.8 weeks (*Hawaii's Unemployed Pensioners,* 1964). In another study, 5,000 workers laid off by an automobile factory were studied, with the result that 82 per cent of those obtaining new jobs were found to have used up all of their unemployment compensation before doing so (Buckingham, 1961), which might be taken as an indication of lack of work incentive while unearned income was being received. However, the study also noted that the jobs which were eventually taken paid less than the original jobs, so that the effect of unemployment compensation seemed to be to allow the workers to resist a change in their status and standards of living as long as possible, which, as noted above, was one of the rationales for the unemployment insurance program being structured as it is.

A logical case for disincentives can be based upon Cunningham's comment (1964) that in general the benefits of increased productivity in the past twenty-five years have been taken 60 per cent in higher wages and 40 per cent in leisure, and there is no reason to believe that poor people, or the unemployed, want or take less leisure than the rest of the population.

A somewhat stronger case can be deduced from the fact that, in a series of six studies, family heads were back at work after a period of unemployment in greater proportions than single persons (*Unemployment Insurance and the Family Finances of the Unemployed*, 1961). If the operative factor in these cases was the greater needs of family heads, as compared to single workers, then need is an incentive, and lack of need—that is, higher income—is a disincentive.

Finally, a number of researchers have been careful to point out that the unemployed do not differ from the rest of the population, in that they differ from each other. A Utah study (*Workers Who Exhaust Their Unemployment Benefits*, 1965) commented, "Individual initiative and perseverance . . . are not the exclusive property of any particular group, whether it be derived by occupation, education, age, or what not [p. 25]"; and Langer (1965) found that his study "Gives some indication that there is little difference between the people who were able to get work and those that were not [p. 41]." One might conclude from this that there is little difference between the incentives of the compensated unemployed and the rest of the population; or, if incentive is considered the variable, one might conclude that there being no other appreciable differences, those who were able to get work were those who had more incentive. As usual, the data do not specify.

The evidence that unemployment compensation does not affect incentive ranges from the logical to the statistical. Logically, there is an inherent contradiction in the assertion of humiliation and anxiety, the loss of dignity and status, and the other changes in self-image which are said to be associated with unemployment, and particularly with long-term unemployment; and in the assumption that people would nevertheless prefer such a situation, with unemployment compensation, to working for the same or a greater amount. Langer (1965) concluded, from his study, that "Most of those out of work are desperate for more work and more money, but they cannot find jobs [p. 46]"; and that "Most people when given some temporary help and a reasonable opportunity to find a job, will take care of themselves [p. 55]." Wilcock and Franke (1963) also found that neither unemployment insurance nor severance pay had any particular influence on the extent or timing of the job search.

Barlow and associates (1966) found that household heads with very little education and with low incomes reported a desire for more work than did those better off, whereas Wickersham (1963) reports a study in which

> Over one-quarter of the claimants said they were seeking "any kind of work whatsoever." 48 per cent of the claimants said they would move out of Detroit to get a job. 80 per cent of the claimants said they were willing to attend a school for forty hours per week if they received their unemployment compensation for the period they attended school [p. 7].

M. S. Gordon (1963) points out that the fact that in prosperous years only about a fifth of all beneficiaries exhaust their benefits, as compared with an appreciably higher ratio in recession years, provides evidence that if jobs are available, relatively few jobless workers are content to receive benefits as long as they are eligible, instead of going back to work. J. M. Becker (1965), discussing the extension of unemployment benefits, finds that the demand factor is more controlling than that of supply: "The mere provision of longer duration does not automatically result in its being used and . . . the major factor determining benefit use is the general condition of the nation's economy [p. 103]."

Another study, by Stein (1964), found that 87 per cent of the unemployed in the 9.6 million workers surveyed used two or more methods of looking for work; that is, the state employment service, private employment services, checking with employers, writing or answering ads, and so on. This is a situation which does not bespeak satisfaction with the unemployed condition. J. M. Becker (1953) also studied abuses in unemployment benefits, and found that not more than 1 to 2 per cent of the benefits went to persons who abused the system.

In this connection, it is of interest that the State of North

Dakota studied overpayments and fraud, and found that in a three-year period, only 2.2 per cent of the claimants received an overpayment, four out of five of which resulted from improper reporting of earnings, and almost one half of which amounted to less than $25. The general run of overpayments seems to have occurred when a construction worker or domestic service worker began or left work in the middle of the week and did not report the few days' earnings. This occurs because claimants usually do not receive their first benefit checks until about three weeks after the initial claim is filed. Because of this, many claimants get the impression that they do not have to report their earnings for the week in which they return to work, especially when they only work during part of that week [*Study of Overpayment and Fraud,* 1966].

Insofar as fraud was concerned, there were only 0.27 per cent (2.7 per thousand) cases charged, and of 89 cases, the court dismissed or refused to prosecute 76. The assumption that unemployment compensation offers an alternative to work to the point of inviting deception and fraud to obtain it does not seem borne out. Murray (1965) studied the reasons why claimants were ruled ineligible for compensation and found that in only 0.1 per cent of the cases (one per thousand) was there a refusal of what the employment service considered suitable work.

Perhaps the most valid area of investigation is that of the experience of compensation exhaustees. If the heroic assumption can be made that all other things are equal, and that persons tend not to go back to work as long as they receive unemployment compensation, then a study of exhaustees and nonexhaustees should prove fruitful. Again, little such comparative information seems available, and hence only the result of some scattered studies can be presented.

A Utah study of exhaustees found that two months after exhaustion, 29.8 per cent were working full-time and 20.2 per cent were working part-time. Thus, exactly 50 per cent of those who exhausted their benefits found work within two months afterwards; 7.6 per cent had withdrawn from the labor force, and 42.4 per cent were still unemployed. At the end of four months, 56.5 per cent were working full or part-time, 15.4 per cent had withdrawn from the labor force, and 28.1 per cent were still unemployed (*Workers*

Who Exhaust Their Employment Benefits, 1965)'. One might conclude from this that 50 per cent to 56.5 per cent were deterred from working by receipt of compensation. However, the changes which might have taken place in the labor market are not known, not do these figures indicate what percentage of workers went back to work before exhaustion, so the proportion of those who were deterred from working by compensation, as compared to those who were not, is not obtainable.

A survey of sixteen state studies of exhaustees (which does not include the previously mentioned Utah study) found that two months after exhaustion, from 13 per cent to 41 per cent of the claimants had found work; 50 per cent to 71 per cent were still unemployed; and 4 per cent to 18 per cent had withdrawn from the labor force. Four months after exhaustion, 16 per cent to 53 per cent were working; 35 per cent to 73 per cent were unemployed; and 7 per cent to 20 per cent had withdrawn from the labor force (*Major Findings of 16 State Studies of Claimants Exhausting Unemployment Benefit Rights, 1956–1959,* 1961). Again, the number of persons going to work before exhaustion is not given, so that the same assumptions, with the same limitations, can be made. A Washington study, also not included in the studies above, indicated that half of the exhaustees found work within three months of exhaustion (*Benefit Exhaustion: Benefit Year 1962,* 1964)'.

The evidence from unemployment-compensation studies as listed above is inconclusive, since the assumption of all other things being equal is hardly tenable; for one thing, the relationship between persistent unemployment and the labor market area in which the unemployed live has been clearly shown (*Mueller and Schmiedeskamp,* 1962)'. In addition, in order to draw conclusions from evidence concerning exhaustees, one must, as J. M. Becker (1965)' holds, know the relevant characteristics of the exhaustees, their feelings, motives, and behaviors.

One piece of evidence, although somewhat dated, concerns exhaustees and nonexhaustees on a large scale. At the end of World War II, as mentioned previously, returning veterans were guaranteed $20 per week unemployment compensation for a maximum of 52 weeks. This was jocularly referred to among veterans as the

"52-20 Club." Among those who participated in these benefits, and those who were aware of them, there grew up a bit of American folklore concerning the veterans, who refused to work and enjoyed their membership in the "club" until exhaustion of benefits forced them to rejoin the majority of Americans as workers. As is true of most folklore, however, the memory of the experience is exaggerated. For one thing, only 9.5 million of the 15.1 million World War II veterans filed claims for such benefits at all. Second, their unemployment was ordinarily not of long duration. For example, the number of weeks of benefits paid to these claimants averaged 29; only 11.1 per cent of those receiving first payments drew their full 52 weeks' benefits (*Employment Security Review,* 1955)'. Another survey of veterans of both World War II and the Korean War indicated that 70 per cent obtained a job within six months of discharge; 9 per cent obtained a job before the end of the first year; and another 9 per cent before the end of the second year (*House Committee Print Number 291,* 1956)'. Consequently, the disincentive effect of payments which were granted practically without eligibility requirements—discharge papers were the major documents needed—and which had about them an aura of having been earned through military service and therefore had little stigma attached, seem to have been negligible in the total context of over 15 million eligible persons.

Investigation of the employment situation in a search for clues concerning work incentives would not be complete without a closer look at the entire area of employment and unemployment among youth. In this connection, youth seems to be variously defined, sometimes meaning those from fourteen to eighteen who are out of school; from fourteen to twenty-one; or from eighteen to twenty-one. Nevertheless, regardless of definition, unemployed youth and particularly urban youth, and more particularly nonwhite urban youth, seem to constitute an especially difficult employment problem.

Secretary Wirtz testified in 1966 that 690,000 boys and girls out of work should be recognized as one of the largest remaining unemployment problems in the country (*Washington Bulletin,* 1966). In the same year, a workshop on the employment problems of "disadvantaged" youth held that one million persons

under twenty-one years of age were unemployed at that time
(*Summary of Proceedings,* 1966). Official Labor Department
figures in 1966 placed the rate of unemployment among teen-agers
in the labor force across the country at 16 per cent, with teen-agers
making up about a quarter of all unemployment. Within the
Negro group, the situation has been described (Weiss and Riessman,
1966) as "dramatically worse," with 23 per cent af the Negro
teen-age boys and 31 per cent of the girls who are in the labor
force unemployed, and this includes only those who are defined
as "actively looking for work [p. 607]." When those who are not
in the labor force but who are out of school and unemployed are
considered, the unemployment rate for male youth between the
ages of sixteen and twenty is 22.7 per cent. Among Negro males,
35.6 per cent are either unemployed or not in the labor force; and
urban males who are unemployed, out of school, and not in the
labor force make up 59.5 per cent of the total (Kane, 1966).

Of those who are employed, it has been estimated that 90
per cent of the under-nineteen group earn less than $3,000, and
86 per cent earn less then $2,000. In the next older group, who are
likely to be married and starting a family, 58 per cent earn less
than $3,000 (Kane, 1966).

Regardless of the numbers involved, the prospect of giving
an income guarantee to nonworking youngsters, many of whom are
visualized as hanging around the streets of urban ghettos in any
case, seems to be hard for the opponents of an income guarantee to
accept and harder for proponents to defend. Such feelings do not
seem to be changed by the fact that their incentive to work under
present circumstances may be irrelevant, due to their difficulty in
getting the kinds of jobs they want; or that their lack of incentive
already exists to the point where it can hardly be adversely affected.
A fear exists that an income guarantee will cause those who are
outside the labor market to remain out; cause those who are unemployed to cease looking for work; and cause those who are
employed to quit working.

The testimony of those who work with youth and particularly with disadvantaged youth (and the poor are, by definition,
disadvantaged), seems to offer evidence that there is an incentive

problem. However, financial motives do not appear to predominate or even to play a large part in this situation. Thus, in referring to Project HELP and NYC of the Housing Authority of the City of New York, Weinberg (1966) says: "Incentives, particularly payment for time spent in education or related work skills, while debatable, do not pay dividends in sustaining effort and motivation [p. 15]." Moed (1966) emphasizes the same fact:

> It is felt by some that money will motivate young people to work, and due to the need for money they will cope with bad supervision, routine work, or a job that teaches them nothing. . . . Such is not the case for most young people in the NYC. Money motivates youth to enter the corps; it will not motivate them to continue in attendance unless they enjoy the experience and get a sense that someone is interested in them [p. 8].

Five factors seem to operate in connection with the work incentives of such youth: Their abilities and skills (or lack of them); the types of job open to them; the example of parents; the desire for security; and the effects of discrimination.

The workshop on the employability of disadvantaged youth, held in 1966 (*Summary of Proceedings,* 1966), found that the larger number of jobs available in a tight labor market had not noticeably increased the motivation of many of these unemployed youth to seek employment; they possess limitations which include— along with poor motivation—functional illiteracy, few job skills and poor work habits, and unrealistic expectations concerning wages, status, and promotion possibilities.

Insofar as available jobs are concerned, the same workshop said, "We have to recognize that these so-called entry-level jobs are the least attractive, usually the dirtiest, the toughest, and the lower paid, and there is a lot of resistance to them. You just can't get young people interested in taking them [p. 16]." And again, "Almost all participants agreed that the alienation of many youth from the working world in large measure reflected the numerous negative characteristics of jobs available to them. The boredom and monotony of inherently dull jobs accounted for much of the reported turn-over, poor attendance, and recruiting difficulties [p. 15]." Not salary, then, but the jobs themselves keep many youths from working, and, as one participant put it, "It is necessary to 'change the image of the bed pan' to give workers a sense of importance; to heighten the status of the job [p. 16]."

Parental example also seems to play a part in the desire to work or its lack (*Summary of Proceedings,* 1966):

> Feelings of occupational alienation among disadvantaged youth were said to be derived from their parents, and often their grandparents. Considering that their parents don't have jobs, and if they do, the kinds of jobs they have are awful, the youngster, looking around, doesn't want to follow in their footsteps. He may well become discouraged, cynical or embittered about his prospects in the job market [p. 28].

Further, "A youth's negative attitude toward work appears to be associated with a form of security consciousness. Such feelings are manifested in the acceptability of the status of welfare recipient. This, too, probably derives from parental attitudes and behavior [p. 28]." One informant comments, "When you mention welfare, I have come to recognize this as a form of real social security. It is the only secure thing that many of them have had in their lives. The idea of a job is, you get hired but you can be fired; it offers no real sense of security [p. 28]."

That such limited job opportunities are not evoked solely by the physical appearance of the individuals involved, or their motivation or its lack, is indicated by the analogy of education, in which studies have demonstrated that by holding education as a constant among the variables which determine occupational success, achievement corresponds to the families' social class level. This factor is said to seriously and objectively damage the educational aspiration level of many youth from low-income families [Purcell, 1966]. The same might be said for job achievement and aspiration also.

The same point is more dramatically demonstrated when put into the context of racial discrimination. Levenson and McDill (1966) found that graduates of a Negro vocational school could expect to earn after 4½ years on the labor market what the graduates of a predominantly white vocational school earn after a few months; specifically, the former began at salaries of $15–$20 per week, compared with the latter's $35–$40, and increased their earnings by approximately $6 per week, compared to $12 for the latter.

Consequently, the type of job available is important, and not just for youth. Mauch and Denenmark (1966) hold that *"Decent* employment [secure, well-paying, yielding feelings of status and self-respect, and providing chances for upward mobility] of the male population is a critical factor in the whole picture of the life-style of the poor [p. 7]."

Despite these difficulties, there have been reports of teen-agers participating in training courses and actively seeking work, to the point that there have been communities embarrassed by their inability to cope with unexpected numbers of youth seeking work and training opportunities (Lagey, 1966).

In summary, receipt of income or prospects of unearned income might play a part in work incentives of youth, and particularly of poor youth, but much larger parts seem to be played by the types of jobs which are available, the way youths see themselves fitting into such jobs, and the way that the jobs and those who hold them are regarded by society. It seems questionable as to whether lack of income, short of sheer starvation, would induce youth to take some of the jobs offered; and whether salaries, short of princely, would be sufficient. For the great mass of unemployed and unemployable youth, an income guarantee might change their styles of life, but under present circumstances seems irrelevant to their work incentives.

11

Work Disincentives

*S*ince the primary purpose of this study is to examine the incentive effect of unearned income, the contingent results of large-scale work disincentives which, it is feared, would flow from a guaranteed minimum, are not properly part of the subject. Yet, since so little firm knowledge seems to exist concerning what the effect on work incentives *would* be, it seems useful to try to project what such results *might* be.

If an income guarantee were to have little or no effect upon work incentives, then a projection into the possible future is meaningless. Hence, this chapter will assume that large numbers of the employed poor would leave their jobs for an income guarantee which pays as much or more than their salaries, but would take jobs paying more than such a guarantee. Using the Social Security Administra-

196

tion's definition of poverty; locating the employed poor according to the information in Chapter Three; and considering only those who are working for salaries below the poverty line—that is, leaving out of consideration those who make slightly more and might prefer less income and less work, and those who are outside the labor force due to disability, lack of opportunity, or public policy—the effect of an income guarantee can be sought in the effect on the economy, the effect on the poor, the effect on employment, and the effect on social policy.

Insofar as the total economy is concerned, farmers and farm owners might find that under an income guarantee, it would be more possible and desirable to stay on their farms, rather than migrating to the cities. On the other hand, a guarantee of income in the city might make it possible for those who would like to abandon the farm to do so. The present pattern of farm out-migration would hint that younger people would be more likely to go to the cities, while older people would be enabled to stay on the farms. It might be anticipated, however, that Negro farmers, almost all of whom are in the South and most of whom are not farm owners, might be more likely to leave the farms to seek an environment which they assume to be less discriminatory. In view of the price supports and food gluts which exist in the American agricultural economy, abandonment of marginal farms and reduction of agricultural production should result in at least some reduction in acreage-control payments and farm subsidies of various sorts.

Further, it might be assumed that most of the one million migratory farm laborers, and a number of those who are not migratory, would no longer be content to accept the near-starvation wages and subhuman living conditions which are often theirs. This would result in a rise in the cost of those fruits and vegetables and other farm products which require much human labor, and particularly that which is called "stoop labor." One estimate, obviously somewhat exaggerated, of the amount of this rise, comes from the Congressional testimony of the head of the Lewis Food Company (*Social Security*, 1965):

> The difference between relief payments and gainful employment payments . . . does not provide sufficient spread to encourage workers to get off of relief. This is now being clearly

demonstrated in California where our growers are in desperate need of help—where we have thousands of workers capable of doing farm work, but refusing to take the job of stoop laborer instead of charity checks. . . . Of course, our farm problem was brought about by the fact that the AFL-CIO failed to organize the farm workers and proceeded to lobby through a bill that eliminated the *braceros* and have left the farmers without stoop labor, and the citizens will probably be paying 100 per cent more for vegetables than they have in the past [p. 1085].

Despite the lack of disinterestedness of the witness quoted above, the result of an income guarantee which would require higher wages to farm workers probably would be an increase in the price of some agricultural products, just as minimum wage laws applied to farm laborers and migratory farm workers would do the same. Since, however, the cost of labor is only a part of the price to the consumer, which includes shipping, warehousing, retailing, and the profits of growers and various middlemen, the net increase to consumers would be considerably below the 100 per cent figure.

Restaurant workers, hotel employees, and laundry operatives make up another large section of the employed poor for whom larger salaries might become necessary under a guaranteed income plan. Raising their salaries to only $1.25 per hour, resulting in an annual income of $2,600, would increase the costs of such services from 4 to 8 per cent—again based on the total cost of labor in the sales price (*The Low-Paid Worker*, 1965).

The cost of domestic servants would rise directly in proportion to the amount that the income guarantee would be larger than present salaries, since salaries amount to practically 100 per cent of the cost of such services. This, and other direct-service labor costs, would constitute the largest proportionate increase in costs due to an income guarantee, and in view of the salaries paid to most domestic help, would affect almost all such servants.

There would be some comparatively small increases in the cost of entertainment. Retail clerks would also get somewhat more, and the price of processed food would rise a little.

Looking at the total effect on the economy, Levitan (1967) points out that "Ten million workers in the United States earn less than $1.50 an hour—that is, $3,000 a year or less even if they work full time throughout the year [p. 13]." He assumes that all of these people would stop working. However, the figure must be reduced by those for whom $3,000 is not the poverty level—single persons, farm families, and the aged—as well as by an unknown number of workers who would continue to work because of the status involved, their commitment to the work ethic, their satisfactions at work or with the work group, their expectations of future income by continuing in their present endeavors, and lack of knowledge about or faith in the guarantee.

The total economic impact would also be affected by the number of persons offered salaries higher than the income guarantee, who would then leave the "poor" stratum; by offsets in various income maintenance programs which now exist; by the increased buying power produced by the guarantee and the tax income thus created; and by decreased costs of various civic services now disproportionately needed and used by the poor.

In addition to its effect on the economy as a whole, an income guarantee might have an immediate effect on the poor, increasing their bargaining power insofar as jobs and salaries are concerned. The difficult and dirty jobs, which have traditionally paid the least, might have to offer salaries commensurate with their disadvantages to induce people to undertake them. Galbraith has pointed out that if unemployment is a financially attractive alternative to employment, the bargaining position, both of the individual and of unions, will be increased (Galbraith, 1958). Lester (1955) has made the same point: "Insofar as the benefit level does restrict the available labor supply for low-paying or low-grade work, it is a force exerting pressure for improvement in the wages, work conditions, or promotion prospects for such jobs [p. 305]." Nathan (1966) has attacked the present system by pointing out that there is an ethical and social question involved of whether individuals *should* work at wage rates that yield only substandard means of livelihood.

If, then, an income guarantee were to make necessary higher wages in some areas of the economy, this might result in additional pressure to automate in those areas. In other words, machines might prove cheaper in the long run than decently paid labor. Although the entire question of the imminence of automation is one on which great divisions of opinion have been registered, there seems to be little disagreement that lack of available labor in the past—as, for example, for cotton picking—has led to the invention of machines such as the mechanical cotton picker.

A Rand study by 81 experts (Bell, 1965) indicated that by 1984, a 40 per cent increase in the world population will require automation in agriculture, and by the year 2000, the need will be for sophisticated machines with high I.Q.'s. The area of agriculture has been further demarcated by Hirsch (1965): "One hundred years ago the output of each farm worker could feed four other persons. Today one worker produces for 28 other persons, and farm output is increasing at the rate of one additional person a year [p. 10]." Consequently, one of the results of increased wages to farm workers might be the invention of machines to replace such laborers. It is inconceivable that a technology which has already put a man on the moon could not, if necessary, devise machines to do everything that human stoop-labor now does, and for twenty-four hours a day, rain or shine. In fact, only the availability of cheap labor and the ideology of a work-based economy prevent the widespread use of those machines that already exist.

Similarly, automated restaurants, with cooking, dish-washing, and serving done by machines; new types of machines in laundries to control and perform every operation; vents in the baseboards of homes and offices which suck in dust; the growth of central home-cleaning agencies; replaceable floor coverings; and many other labor-saving devices would undoubtedly be one result of the unavailability of cheap labor; and the manufacture of such machines would, in turn, create new industries and jobs. Secretary Wirtz has summed up the present relationship of the employed poor to automation: "Most work which has been done by people with less than a high school education can now be done more cheaply by machines [Hirsch, 1965, p. 61]." If such people are in a position to ask for higher salaries than they are now receiving, even more work will pass over to machines.

One further aspect concerning the impact of an income guarantee on employment leaves automation out of consideration. The definitional aspects of unemployment are such that if an income guarantee caused the 4 per cent or more of those presently seeking jobs to cease doing so—that is, to move from the category of "unemployed" to that of "out of the labor force"—the ostensible result of the income guarantee would be completely to wipe out unemployment.

Another result of a guaranteed income might be changes in the social welfare system. The justification of some programs and policies might be called into question. Krosney (1966) holds that "The current welfare system . . . was a casualty program for an immediate emergency. It is not a long-term strategy for an attack on poverty. Tragically, a short-term program which develops its own bureaucracy and its own impetus, also begins to help create its own false justifications [p. 146]." Among these justifications seems to be some fear that a guaranteed income would reduce the need for social welfare services (*Social Work*, 1965). Steiner (1966), however, points out that even a fairly good income guarantee would not obviate the need for social work services. In the facilities operated by the Lutherans for emotionally disturbed children, per-case costs run as high as $15,000 per year. On the other hand, the engagement of social welfare services with work-linked programs— OASDHI and Unemployment Insurance, for instance—as well as programs designed to increase employability—vocational rehabilitation, child-care facilities to enable AFDC mothers to work, and the like—may be training clients for incapacity, in Veblen's terms.

Further, although the linking of welfare payments to premiums, coverage, or salaries is supposed to establish a feeling of "rights" to benefits, there is no empirical evidence that recipients feel more entitled to Social Security retirement benefits, for which they have supposedly paid, than to unemployment benefits, for which they have paid nothing. In fact, there seems to be increasing feeling—evidenced by the organizing of welfare recipients into pressure groups—that such payments are rights, and this has been the attitude taken by the new legal services. Indeed, there is no more reason why AFDC recipients who give up or do not take jobs in order to stay with their children *should* view their compensation as less of a right than that of the farmer who gives up or does not undertake to cultivate certain land or crops. However, the establishment of "rights" seems to serve as a limitation to benefits; that is, clients are seen as, and see themselves as, entitled only to the amount "due" them under the provisions of the various programs, rather than entitled to a decent life. In the United States, average and maximum benefits under insurance programs seem to constitute the informal norm against which other types of welfare payments are judged.

There is no immutable reason why payments to allow persons to remain alive, mentally healthy, and with hope for the future need to be linked to work records. It is not so in other countries—for instance, France, which has generous family allowances, or even Iran, where:

> Payments to workers who do not work is the normal and economic equivalent . . . for the more complex form of transfer payments which are common in the more developed societies—old-age and survivors insurance, unemployment compensation, veterans payments, agricultural price supports and many, many others. It is true that the recipients of some of these more sophisticated payments usually have a past record of having performed services for the government—bearing arms in a foreign war, for example, or plowing under a specified acreage of surplus cotton. But the same could probably be said for many of Iran's surplus employees, even if it was only parading in the streets of Teheran, shouting loyalty to the Shah in moments of crisis [Cleveland et al., 1960, p. 164].

The effect of automation, whether stimulated by the unavailability of cheap labor because of an income guarantee, or not, would also affect social welfare services and thinking. Cunningham (1964) poses the question thus: "Once we become aware that perhaps 10 per cent of the population will shortly be able to produce all the goods and services needed by the nation, shall we continue to regard the other 90 per cent in the same light in which we viewed yesterday's 4 per cent or 5 per cent unemployed? The question answers itself [p. 3]." He goes on to say, "To retain our present definitions of 'work,' 'leisure,' 'play,' and 'affluence' is as mistaken as it would be to retain Newtonian definitions of key terms in physics or pre-Darwinian definitions of key terms in biology [p. 3]."

Consequently, if automation—which Kreps (1963) says has already made it possible for many workers to graduate from the drudgery of dull, repetitive jobs into the ranks of the unemployed—continues to increase (and a guaranteed minimum income might encourage such increase), programs which continue or strengthen the link between work and benefits inevitably store up trouble for the future, when the link will have to be broken. A guaranteed minimum income at this time might begin the breaking of the linkage with relatively little upset. It the link is truly broken, then the activities of social workers will have to be directed toward helping people accept and enjoy their nearly workless future, rather than preparing them for reentry into the labor market.

Of course, mass automation may never come, and the presently poor and jobless might be absorbed into the economy through other means and because of other circumstances. Yet, in view of the uncertainty which surrounds the question of disincentive effect from income guarantees, Nagi's argument (1967) concerning individuals seems germane to society as a whole:

> It seems that consciousness of "public funds" and the "tax payers" money which is attached to expenditures of programs such as those of social security influence decision more toward "denial when in doubt." Available evidence points in that direction. . . . An argument can be made that the decision rule . . . should be: "When in doubt allow the benefits." It is much more difficult for an individual, as compared to society, to sustain the economic consequences of an erroneous decision. . . . Also, indications are that people do return to work in significant numbers after being allowed benefits [pp. ix–3].

By analogy, since the effects of an income guarantee are unknown, but lack of such a guarantee has resulted and continues to result in widespread suffering and social dislocation, it would seem advisable to make the experiment, especially since the most likely results would be slightly higher costs for some goods and services and stimulation of automation, which will, in turn, be cushioned by the income guarantee and may result in even greater production at lower costs, and therefore a higher standard of living for everyone.

12

Needed Research

$\mathscr{A}$s the foregoing chapters will indicate, valid and reliable research is sparse concerning the incentive of poor people to work in the face of unearned income, and that which exists is fragmentary, peripheral, and not easily comparable. Not only is there a dearth of basic demographic data, but attitudinal aspects have hardly been touched, neither through studies of verbal responses nor through examinations of actual behavior. Burns (1965) points out that even in regard to the unemployed, we do not know "What specifically . . . people find acceptable or degrading in different forms of aid. . . . How valid is the assumption that if an adequate income is otherwise available people will not work steadily? Is this assumption more valid for some types of worker or societies than for others? Does the validity of the assumption vary with degrees of education or family responsibility or income levels or expectations [p. 287]?"

Chapter Six was devoted to general problems of research as applied to incentive studies, and dealt with value judgments, definitions, cause and effect relationships, and choices of area for study. The present chapter is devoted to the specific research which seems needed concerning the incentive to work of the poor; some problems in carrying it out; and some suggestions of possibilities.

One method of examining the assumed work motivations of the employed poor is to determine exactly where and who they are. Although the census data indicate the location of those who are poor according to the Social Security Administration (SSA) criteria by occupations and by industries for 1964, further information is needed to make assumptions about work incentive. Using available data, the Bureau of the Census is capable of determining the location of the employed poor—using SSA criteria—by sex, color, as family heads or as unrelated individuals, and as full-time year-round workers or not, in somewhat more detail than the occupational listings used by Orshansky (1965a); but, unfortunately, not according to the specific jobs (in the detail listed in the *Classified Index of Occupations and Industries*) which the poor hold. That is, medical and health workers can be designated as salaried or self-employed, but the number of the former who are ward orderlies, practical nurses, case aides, interns, or student nurses, for example, is not available. Conversely, although it is theoretically possible to determine the number of ward orderlies in the United States, it is not possible to determine, using presently available data, how many of them are poor according to the SSA classification. In addition, it would be desirable to know the salaries paid in the jobs, the length of time that people have held such jobs, and the normal turnover time in these jobs. From this, one might be able to begin to deduce the number who are "on the way up" or who might see a future where they are, and the number who would be presumed to abandon their jobs for any other legitimate source of income.

Similarly, it would be helpful to know the types of businesses owned by the "proprietors" among the employed poor, how long they have owned their businesses, and the normal income expectation from such businesses. Again, one might then have a clearer idea as to how many might abandon their businesses for a poverty-level income guarantee. In short, given the resources, it should not be impossible, through the census procedure and machinery, to use the SSA criteria for determining—in greater detail than is presently available—where the poor people work. Although the complexity of motivations which enter into work incentives would not be ascertainable from such demographic data, detailed information on the employed poor would give a much better idea than now exists of the possible magnitude of work disincentives which an income guarantee might cause, and the effect on the economy of such disincentives as might be expected.

There is also a dearth of studies of past experiences with unearned income and its effect upon recipients. From examining such experiences, not only might information be obtainable, but the record-keeping necessary for examining ongoing programs might be clarified.

For example, if the number of persons going back to work immediately after exhaustion of their unemployment compensation rights is assumed to be the number or proportion who did not go back to work because of the compensation, it should be possible to examine the number of claimants who went back to work, by weeks, until exhaustion of their benefits, and whether they then remained in the labor force or withdrew from it; and, if remaining in it, whether they then went back to work; and to correlate this with types of jobs found and with demographic information concerning the participants. Conversely, the number of people remaining in the labor force after exhaustion of their benefits, even though they cannot find suitable work, might be used as a measure of those who were and are interested in work rather than in compensation, and their numbers and proportions can then be measured against those who left the labor force and those who found suitable work during comparable periods.

Such examination of employment experiences would need to be correlated to the employment-opportunities situation, not just on a global basis of national unemployment rates or the number of the covered unemployed, but also in terms of the specific jobs available within a reasonable distance of the unemployed, their abilities to do the job required, and other factors such as employment discrimination based on color, age, or sex.

Another area which offers promise in terms of incentive research is that of early retirees whose pensions are either enough for a subsistence-plus living, or substantially close to what their salaries had been. Their postretirement patterns concerning employment, although not conclusive for incentive research because of their ability to earn more money and to receive the "unearned" income simultaneously, might throw some light on the insatiability aspect of incentives.

In addition to demographic facts and past experiences, there are a number of existing situations which lend themselves to investigation for purposes of incentive research, although each of them has certain weaknesses. For example, it should be possible to study the situations, attitudes, and behaviors of persons who have retired, or been retired, because of disability in one situation, but who have nevertheless found it possible to make a living, or at least to acquire income, in another situation. Within the civil service alone, for example, there are a number of cases of persons who retired because of disability, who are receiving full retirement pensions, but who are actually working full-time in nongovernmental jobs. The same is probably true of persons whose disability makes them useless in one industry and entitles them to pension, but who manage to make a place for themselves doing something else; for example, the victim of Parkinson's disease who can no longer handle merchandise, but who can sell by phone.

Similarly, one could compare employment patterns between disabled veterans with a high degree of compensation and disabled citizens of the same type who receive no compensation. A study of the deaf, whose condition is greatly remedied by hearing aids, but who receive military compensation nevertheless, suggests itself. A weakness in this type of study is the fact that although the amounts are sufficient to make a difference in behavior, the individual is not faced with a choice of work versus unearned income; he continues to receive his unearned income whether he works or not, and the analogy to an income guarantee is thus weakened.

A stronger study might investigate those cases in which

Social Security family benefits amount to over $300 or $400 per month, tax-free, and the effect of this income on the work patterns of family members. In a similar vein, it should be possible to study AFDC families, in those states where the grant is relatively high, in terms of their work patterns before and after coming onto AFDC, although there might be some difficulty holding constant the various clients' and workers' views of the purposes of this program, and therefore encouragement or discouragement concerning work efforts. These studies would contain the unearned versus earned choice factor.

An interesting, although inconclusive, study might deal with those persons whose incomes are assured for life through trusts or similar arrangements, from the time they are youngsters. Their work patterns, and reasons for working, should shed light on the motivations to work which exist in America generally, and these could be contrasted with the work patterns of formerly nonwealthy persons who accumulate, or come into, large sums of money later in life.

Further, although the attitude toward work and leisure may be different in other countries from that in America, the experience of family allowances, children's allowances, and comparatively generous (by American standards) welfare payments in other countries should be examined for the evidence of a work incentive effect. Family allowances in France are a substantial portion of many workers' incomes and may be larger than earned salary; children's allowances are used in Canada and Israel, among other countries; the Scandinavian countries have social welfare arangements which are usually considered lavish by American observers—each of these needs examination concerning work incentive results, on a basis other than simply logic, impressions, or measurement of the GNP.

In addition, despite the methodological difficulties of the survey method insofar as attitudes are concerned, and particularly in an area as sensitive as that concerning work incentives, it should nevertheless be possible to determine: at least what recipients of unearned income say they would do if offered jobs which pay the same or more; how much more than the guarantee would be necessary to induce people who would not work for the same amount of an income guarantee to go to work, and if this differs for the kinds of jobs; and at how much less than they are now making the presently employed say they would stop work for unearned income. Also, much more information is necessary as to why farmers leave the farm, and the effect upon these reasons than an income guarantee would have. The same insights need to be sought concerning the migration from south to north, and from rural areas to cities.

Determining the effect that an income guarantee would have on unemployed and/or poor youth might present more problems of validity, but it might be possible to gain some ideas concerning setting up separate households, contributing to family income, undertaking educational, training, or petty business ventures. Similarly, the effect of guaranteed income on the disabled, in terms of rehabilitation plans and work possibilities, might be revealing.

In a number of studies mentioned previously, there were certain, almost aberrant, cases who showed traits counter to the general trend of the respondents in the studies. An examination of these deviant cases might indicate the similarities or situations which would offer clues to further incentive research. For example, what were the characteristics of the 18 per cent of Burgess and Price's unemployed mothers who *increased* their employment on receipt of AFDC payments? Were there similarities among Hausman's respondents who indicated that they would not refuse employment even for income less than their AFDC grants? It might also be revealing to study the $7\frac{1}{2}$ per cent of civil service employees who are eligible for nondisability pensions, but who have not retired—what are their motivations for wanting to continue working, especially those in the lower income levels whose pensions would be almost as great as their salaries?

Finally, it should be possible to experiment with an income guarantee by giving people unearned income and measuring their responses in terms of employment patterns. In this way, it might be possible to guarantee subsistence income to one-half the case load on GAP or AFDC, in a given area, using the other half as a control. Or it might be possible to do the reverse—to offer jobs paying the same as their relief payments to all of those defined as poor and employable in a given area; or to offer jobs at graduated rates of income to determine the gap, if any, necessary to overcome the lack of work incentive caused by relief payments. Again, it is theoretically possible to withdraw all forms of income maintenance payments to determine who goes to work under such circumstances.

Each of the suggestions contained above contains massive problems of implementation—ethical problems of paying some of the needy more than others, or less than others, or nothing at all; practical problems of finding real jobs which recipients could fill, and paying salaries greater than the going rate; and theoretical problems of holding certain variables constant. However, in the event that some sort of experimental situation could be constructed to measure work incentives of the poor, the following cautions or conditions seem indicated.

Like the results of most societal changes, unearned income will probably have a differential effect upon various individuals and categories of individuals. These differences will involve the dimensions of psychological characteristics (or personality traits); physical characteristics such as health or illness, age, and perhaps appearance; demographic differences such as sex, race, marital status; employment situations, records, and skills; sociological factors, including group memberships and family situations; and others. Consequently, one requirement of meaningful research on incentives is that it indicate who is differentially affected by unearned income, rather than that it result in either-or conclusions concerning the work incentives of the poor. This, then, necessitates a sample large enough to include many variables to a point where differences may be considered statistically significant. The scale of needed experiments is therefore quite large.

Then there is the question of the time span of the experiment. As Dahl and Lindblom (1953) have pointed out, that which has an effect at one time may cease to have the same effect if it is continued or repeated. The law of diminishing utility comes into play, as does expectation, and taking for granted that which was once unexpected. An income guarantee which seems generous at first may appear niggardly once it is taken for granted, and the desire to work to obtain larger income may show up in the long run, though it may be absent at the beginning. Even in an experimental situation, in which people are offered payment in lieu of work, their reactions may be different when the payment is to continue for a long time—thus making future situations more remote and less threatening—than when payments are anticipated only for a limited period, involving the recipient in considerations of loss of job seniority, possible interim promotions and pay raises, and even the problem of reentering a set of social relationships at work which have been voluntarily renounced in favor of money.

The strength of the attraction of future security, even though modest, over immediate but short-term cash gains is a factor to be considered in an experimental situation. Some people may prefer the security, and others the cash, but larger outside considerations weigh heavily in the choice. During the Depression, for example, many bright young people sought to enter civil service, with its comparatively modest salaries but great security, rather than taking jobs in commerce or industry, which offered chances of ultimately attaining better financial rewards, but at greater risk.

Thus, as noted previously, Hausman (1967) says that the recipient who feels that an available job is not secure may choose welfare over work, and Katona (1967) and associates' respondents ranked steadiness of income ahead of the amount. Only at incomes over $10,000 was security not the first choice of the largest group of respondents, and even then it was outranked by "achievement," and not "high income." In addition, Katona and associates point out that these answers have remained stable for more than ten years. Irelan and Besner (n. d.) also state flatly that "Probably the most basic value held by the poor is that of security [p. 6]." Consequently, the time period for which unearned income is offered, or might reasonably be anticipated, might be a factor in determining the effect which such an offer has. Conlisk (1968) attacks the "static theory" in just these terms—that the supposed decrease in work effort which the theory predicts might reverse itself with the addition of a dynamic factor, namely, the passage of time.

The method of payment used might be another important variable affecting the choice of a guaranteed income vis-à-vis lesser, or the same, or even somewhat larger, income from employment. One aspect of this is the ease or difficulty of making application. The distance and ease of access of the agency at which application is to be made, the waiting time involved, the pleasantness or unpleasantness of the physical surroundings and the atmosphere, the length and complexity of the necessary forms, the amount of help in filling out the forms and the attitude of the person helping —all these aspects of making application for help are felt to have an influence on the number and types of people seeking such help, and have been known to be manipulated to encourage or to discourage such help-seeking behavior. It is for this reason, among others such as efficiency, that the New York City Department of Welfare has been experimenting with simple affidavits, in an effort to manipulate the "complexity of application" variable.

Another factor which might affect applications for unearned income, even on an experimental basis, is the amount of documentary proof that must be submitted. Birth certificates, disability determinations, Social Security cards, income tax forms, rent receipts, and the like add up to a "documents safe-guarding" complex which some respondents might not be capable of carrying out.

Further, the method of payment includes the factor of stigma which might attach to such payments—whether real or imagined—and might be a factor in acceptance or nonacceptance of such payments. Similarly, recipients might feel that they are required to accept or to undergo certain services such as counseling, job training, group discussions, or home economics courses in order to receive payments. Gilbert (1966) has pointed out, for example, that the 1962 federal welfare amendments absolutely required that services be offered in AFDC cases, although this was probably not the intent of Congress. Krosney (1966) quotes a youth work-program director as saying, "You hook the kids into counseling through offering to pay and train them [p. 173]," and Kahn (1965), as quoted above, refers to the check as the bait for services. The feeling that income being offered implicitly commits the recipient to accept service is a factor which needs attention in any experiment.

The amount of confidentiality inherent in application, investigation, and payment is another "method of payment" factor. Which people know that one is receiving payment in lieu of working might be connected not only to the factor of stigma, but to potential job offers, requests for participation in social action efforts, research approaches, and perhaps envy and jealousy, on one hand,

and approbation and approval on the other. As Elman (1966) puts it, "Although all the information he (the client) gives is to be regarded by regulation as confidential, . . . this is usually used as a device to insure the privacy of the functionary and to conceal his activities [p. 14]."

If the receipt of unearned income is connected with a prohibition or limitation on earning income, the matter of surveillance, or the feeling of being under surveillance, or the assumption that there will be surveillance, might act as a deterrent to acceptance. Certainly those recipients who have at some time been the subjects of "midnight raids" to detect "welfare chiseling," or even subjected to suspicious questioning, might have hesitations about placing themselves in such positions again.

Finally, the actual point of contact at which payment is made—whether by mail, by a visitor, in an office—and the aura which surrounds such payment might affect the desire or agreement to accept payments. The literature on unconscious, nonverbal, latent, and metacommunication is voluminous, as is that on role-playing and role-taking. All of this adds up to the fact that the total *gestalt* in which one is offered payment may have a powerful effect on the attitudes and even the physiological responses and behaviors of the recipient. Halm (1967), in an experiment involving placebos, concluded that the total configuration of the situation in which the placebo was offered, rather than any sociological situation or individual trait of the recipient, determined whether the placebo had or did not have a psychological and physiological effect. Kronick (1965) also found that the way in which the client views the agency—as coercive, remunerative, or moral—determines whether his response is alienated, calculative, or moral. On a more pragmatic level, a recent riot in Boston was touched off because recipients of welfare payments (MAW—Mothers for Adequate Welfare) objected to the attitudes of those dealing with their problems.

Another crucial factor in designs to measure work incentives is the extent to which other income is allowed, encouraged/discouraged, or prohibited. If guaranteed income were to be paid, as has been suggested, as a demogrant received by everyone, or as family or children's allowances, then continuation of employment would presumably not be limited or prohibited, since the grant would be paid without reference to need. Whether a subject continued or ceased working, in such a case, might be a measure of factors like need, ease of finding employment, enjoyment on the job, and the insatiability of respondent's wants, rather than whether incentive to work was stronger than desire not to work, for the same amount. Consequently, research designed to measure the incentive factor alone would need to prohibit income-producing activities and to enforce the prohibition; or make a direct deduction from the guaranteed income for income earned, which requires adequate supervisory facilities.

Finally, the question of amount of income, as related to work incentives, is relevant. To learn that people who receive less than subsistence income continue to work when in receipt of such income, is to learn about the strength of needs, rather than about incentive as such. Even if the criterion is individually perceived needs or wants, rather than subsistence, evidence that people tend to pursue these goals, rather than settling for less, reflects the strength of the need or want rather than the incentive to work. Research investigating incentives under this arrangement would have to measure and balance the strength of respondents' needs in order to compare the amount of incentive. There is therefore some merit in the approach, despite the weighting of results which it presents, which offers subjects as much money as they want or feel they need in order to stop working—rather than as much as they are earning, or presumably could earn if they could find a job. In any event, research which offers respondents small sums of money, in addition to their present income or in place of it, is not really measuring the strength of the desire to replace unearned income by work, or vice versa.

To summarize, experimental studies should ideally deal with populations large enough to contain a great number of variables, continue for a long time, control different methods of payment, not allow for any other income to be earned, and be in amounts sufficient to test the effect of a "poverty level" income guarantee, or to test for the amount necessary to create a disincentive effect,

13

Conclusions

*M*inimization or eradication of poverty in the United States has become the stated goal of social policy in this country, and a number of proposals have been advanced to achieve this end. Among them are plans to guarantee to everyone who needs it a minimum annual income, either through expansion of existing social welfare and income-maintenance programs, or through the introduction of new programs, such as demogrants, children's allowances, family allowances, or a reverse income tax.

Through all of these proposals, as well as through existing income-maintenance programs, there runs the thread of fear that a work disincentive will result, to the disadvantage of the recipients, the economy, and the society. Although not often so delineated, the

215

fear seems to contain two separable aspects: That recipients will refuse to work for the same or less than they can receive while not working; and that they will refuse to work under any circumstances, even for income greater than that of the guarantee.

In order to examine the evidence concerning impact of unearned income on recipients, it was found necessary to determine the level at which such a guarantee might be set. For this purpose, some of the conceptual problems and value judgments inherent in drawing the poverty line have been explored, and poverty has been projected as based upon relative, normative, or absolute criteria. For purposes of this study, the Social Security Administration's "economy" budget has been adopted as the operational definition of poverty.

Using this definition, the people identified as possibly affected by an income guarantee in terms of their work incentives were classified as the employed poor, other economic strata, those outside the labor force, and the unemployed. The employed poor totaled 5,097,000 individuals and were identified according to occupations, industries, heads of families or unrelated individuals, color, sex, age, and farm or nonfarm residence. Eighteen per cent of the employed poor were found to be laborers, including farm laborers and migrant agriculture workers; 18 per cent are operatives and kindred workers, including laundry workers; 12 per cent are farm owners and managers, including share-croppers; and 11 per cent are in service occupations or industries, including restaurant, hotel, and hospital employees. Somewhat surprisingly, only 9 per cent of the employed poor are private household workers.

Other economic strata include the "near poor," defined as those who are above the Social Security Administration's economy line, but below the low-cost line. This stratum consists of 2,680,000 employed individuals whose work incentives might be affected by an income guarantee at the economy line to the point of giving up their somewhat larger earned salaries for the lesser income without work. Another stratum that might be affected by an income guarantee was identified as the wealthy, for whom the added taxes made necessary by such a program might prove a work disincentive. Those outside the labor force were found to include the disabled, the unemployable, and mothers receiving Aid to Families of Dependent Children.

An examination of work motivations generally and the American attitude toward work indicated that contradictory views exist and are held simultaneously. Thus, there is held to be an instinct to work, and a natural inclination to avoid work; a desire to work to acquire material satisfiers, and a desire to acquire material satisfiers to avoid work; a need to work for the psychological social satisfactions inherent therein, and a need to escape work for leisure, with the greater satisfactions which it provides.

Some possible explanations of these paradoxical views were offered, including ambivalence, goal displacement, dissonance, cultural lag, the difference between norms and behavior, and the assumption of differing majority and minority attitudes. The possibility of the latter led to an examination of various ways of viewing the possibility of a culture of poverty, ranging from the assumption of a completely separate culture, at least insofar as work attitudes are concerned, to the denial of any different reactions to poverty based upon a group or class identity.

Since no guarantee of subsistence income for all who need it exists anywhere in the world, it was impossible to examine directly the effect that such a guarantee would have on work incentives, under either of the definitions given above. Instead, clues were sought in the programs and experiences in which people were given unearned incomes under circumstances and in amounts other than those of the proposed income guarantee. The general evidence was divided into the logical, the qualitative and impressionistic, and the quantitative; applied to incentives to work for the same or less than an income guarantee, and to work for more than that amount; and examined in terms of disincentive, no effects or mixed effects, and positive incentives.

In addition to the more general findings, experiences with AFDC and General Assistance Payments, disability compensation, and unemployment insurance were presented, with special attention paid to youth employment.

Since the evidence, in most cases, was inconclusive, the probable results of a large-scale work disincentive were projected, with the conclusion that the prices of some goods—mostly agricultural products—and some services would rise somewhat, with domestic household help becoming considerably more expensive. It was felt that one direct effect of this situation might be increased automation in some areas, with temporary job opportunities arising in the manufacture of such machinery, but resulting in a long-term lessening of employment opportunities, thus making even more necessary some type of income maintenance program not linked to work.

Methods for testing the probable reaction of the poor to income guarantees were suggested, including demographic analyses, post hoc experiences, surveys, analysis of deviance, and experiments. Problems to be taken into consideration in devising experiments were seen as those of ethics, scale, duration, method, controls, and amounts.

Among the findings of this study is the fact that, of almost 190 million persons in the United States in 1964, 34 million were poor by the SSA criteria. Of these, approximately 3.5 million heads of families and 1.5 million unrelated individuals—a total of 5 million—were employed. About one-half of these (2.5 million)' worked full-time and year-round. Despite this employment record, these people were poor according to criteria which considered 22 cents per meal as not poor, with other necessities on the same scale. The nonemployed were poor despite more than thirty years of Old-Age, Survivors, and Disability Insurance, and current Health Insurance; Unemployment Insurance; Old Age Assistance; Aid to Families with Dependent Children (including need caused by unemployment); General Assistance; and other such programs designed to relieve poverty.

It is no wonder, then, that new methods of relieving poverty are being discussed; but in such discussions, each proposal runs into the expressed fear that incentive to work will be affected. In particular, the proposal to guarantee a minimum income to everyone who needs it seems to raise great fears of a general refusal to work, or the creation of a large permanently dependent class. However, the empirical evidence which bears on the effect that an income guarantee would have on the work incentive of recipients is fragmentary, noncomparable, and peripheral. Little of it is derived under conditions resembling those of an income guarantee, and that which exists can be interpreted in a number of ways. Consequently, the conclusions of this study rest more upon historical analysis, theories of human behavior, and the logic of the situation than upon the individual studies cited.

Using this framework, it seems likely that in the event of an income guarantee which pays more than their salaries, most recipients would choose the guarantee rather than work. It is true that there would be an undetermined number among the five million employed poor who would continue their present work because of future prospects, present commitments, satisfactions derived from and at work, and the desire to retain the status or designation of worker. The bulk, however, getting little or no satisfactions derived from and at work itself, seeing no possibility of advancement, held in low esteem by society for the type of work which they do, and getting their social satisfactions elsewhere, would be caught in the paradox between two normative American attitudes: work as a good in itself of the Protestant Ethic, and laissez-faire's compulsion toward economic maximization. Using Maslow's formulation, the presently potent needs of the poor can be seen as still connected with the physiological—that is, the need for material satisfiers as such—and have not yet been appeased to the point of being replaced by those of status or improved self-image. Consequently, it can be expected that the material items available as a result of the income guarantee would outweigh the psychic satisfactions of work for its own sake. Bernard's findings are in the same direction: the AFDC mothers whom he studied were too anxious about getting money—some money, enough money, any money—to worry about the supposed stigma of its source. Both Herzberg and Dubin's findings also support this view: Herzberg concluded that money is a "motivator" at the lower levels, and becomes a "hygiene factor" only at higher amounts. Dubin found that other satisfactions replaced money only when the amount of money reached at least a subsistence level.

Consequently, it seems theoretically probable and actually logical that most working people below the poverty line would choose to give up their present work, if necessary, to acquire the guaranteed income, unless the conditions under which the guar-

antee was made available were even more distasteful than their
present jobs. Since this view agrees with the conventional wisdom,
there seems little point in documenting it further, except to point
out that in this view, the poor are acting in consonance with one
of the threads of the traditional American ideological fabric—
that of the desirability of economic maximization by each person.

Were such an income guarantee to be made, and shifts
from employment to unearned income to come about, the result
would be two-fold: In some degree, an increase in automation to
replace manpower, and simultaneously, a raising of salaries to at-
tract workers back to the jobs which had been spurned. It is concerning the latter event that the most bitter and emotion-laden
arguments concerning the effect of a guaranteed income revolve.
The effect on the total American economy, and thereby prosperity,
security, and world peace; the effect on the income recipient, including his moral fiber, self-image, living conditions, and descend-
ents; and the effect on the rest of the American people, given this
socially approved model of a nonworker—all are invoked in the
operative question: Would the recipients of an income guarantee
go to work for higher salaries than the guarantee, or would they be
so content with the unearned income and the life which it assures
them that they would refuse to work under almost any conditions,
and remain a parasitic, subsidized underclass in American society?

Again, the conclusions are derivative, rather than direct.
Using Maslow's formulation for guidance, it can be expected that
all of those who can work, and are offered suitable conditions, will
choose to do so, for as the needs which were formerly potent are
met—basically the physiological ones—other needs will come to
the fore with equal force. The insatiability of human needs, on
which the American economy is based, has never been seen as
ending at the acquisition of subsistence but, on the contrary, as
beginning there. An important part of the resocialization of former
immigrants, former poor people, and the former young into the
culture of the American majority consists of their acquiring new
tastes, indulging in new activities, and developing further desires.
Indeed, in no other instance is the waning of the Protestant Ethic
more evident than in the obliteration of that portion of the belief-

system which holds that wealth is not to be spent; that leisure is not to be enjoyed; and that tastes are not to be indulged.

Newly acquired needs are not only for material things. As the reference group with whom the poor compare themselves and toward whom they aspire shifts from people with not enough money on which to live, to people with enough or more than enough for daily necessities, their need for status, respectability, prestige, and power may be expected to rise, and these, in great part, can only be satisfied by or through work activities. As a number of the studies cited above have indicated, such rewards are found in comparative salaries, the status of working without supervision, the number of people being supervised, the very designation of "worker," or "good worker," and so on.

Perhaps it should be emphasized here, at the risk of being gratuitous, that the acquisition of new desires, or the development of new needs, is in no wise a conscious, deliberate process, but one which proceeds whether or not the individual is conscious of it, and it cannot be simply denied or resisted by an act of will, nor can the material and the social needs be separated. Consequently, the poor can be expected inevitably to develop new potent needs and thereby to find themselves in a new social situation. This situation would create new dilemmas for the individual poor if working for need-satisfiers were a minority or deviant pattern in America, and if he had to choose between satisfying his newly potent needs or being like the majority. However, since both economic maximization and productive labor are normative values, and even complement each other, the individual can expect further support, in terms of general approbation, in his need to work. Again, the poor would be within the mainstream of American values in not only maximizing their economic position, but also in doing it through work.

In addition to such theoretical conclusions, daily observation indicates that there seems little question but that most people receiving the income guarantee would thereby be relieved of some of the most pressing of human anxieties—the insecurity which freezes capabilities; the causes of much family disorganization; one of the roots of mental illness; and a cause of general debility which might make it impossible for them to seek work or even to visualize them-

selves as workers. That even a minimum of security results in higher
employment rates and better employment records is supported by the
findings of Salzberger and Shapira that compensated veterans
achieved employment patterns similar to those of the uncompensated, despite lesser endowments; Hausman's findings that labor
force participation among AFDC mothers is a function of the
effective wage rate; the experience of incentive budgeting plans
that greater income results in more work; and the experience of
New Zealand, as reported by Green, and of France, as reported by
Friedlander, that transfer payments do not seem to have hurt
labor force participation. Historically, additional support for these
findings arises from the experience of mass employment under the
pressure of World War II, and the lack of undue exploitation of
veterans' unemployment compensation at the end of that period.

Here the findings of this study diverge from what seems to
be the popular view. It seems to be a firm part of the American
belief system that if people—especially poor people—are given
enough money on which to live, they will refuse to work to achieve
more, no matter what the inducement. This view is based upon no
empirical evidence, aside from isolated anecdotes; is consonant
with no theory of human behavior; and is inconsistent in its logic.
It says, in effect, that the poor are, or have, a different culture,
and although they will be guided by normative American values
in opting for an income guarantee in place of their present, lesser-
paid, work, they will reject normative American values by refusing
income higher than the guarantee. This logic, when examined
closely, holds that the poor are like all other Americans in wanting
more income when they are poor (that is, when they are economically different from other Americans); but that as they acquire more
income (that is, become economically more like other Americans),
they become different from other Americans in rejecting more income. Thus, the more economically different they are, the more
morally similar; and the more economically similar, the more
morally different. This Alice-in-Wonderland logic, on which the postulation of a culture of poverty is based, indicates a widespread need
to believe in the existence of such a culture without regard for either
facts or logic; and it is this need which seems to be more important

in the entire area of poverty discussions and programs than the actual situations, attitudes, and behaviors of the poor.

In seeking an explanation for this need to believe that the poor would react differently than would the nonpoor toward job offers which paid more than their guarantee, the paradoxes and contradictions noted earlier seem important. Changes have been taking place in the American economy since the early days of industrialization. Men are constantly working shorter hours, fewer days per week, taking longer vacations, and retiring earlier. This, coupled with longer life expectancy, has resulted in more leisure than ever before for most people. In addition, partly due to automation, a greater proportion of people are working in the newer "service" areas than in the traditional, and more highly respected, "productive" pursuits. Despite these changes in work behavior, however, the norm that work is good in and of itself, that men should want to work, that work is ennobling, that men should work as hard as they can, that they should enjoy working, and that the well-being of the country depends upon the efficiency and amount of human labor, has not changed. The result is that many men feel guilty because they do not really want to work, do not work as hard as they can, do not enjoy working, know that they do not work as hard as their fathers and grandfathers are said to have worked, and secretly wish that they did not have to work. These self-doubts are reinforced by questions concerning the social usefulness of their work, its necessity, and fears concerning its continuance in view of its uselessness.

The worker handles these doubts by being ambivalent: holding a belief in work intellectually, and doubting emotionally; by goal displacement, in seeing maintenance of the present structure as more important than the outcome; by dissonance, in denying the doubts in face of the activities; by cultural lag, in continuing traditional patterns and institutions regardless of their loss of usefulness; and in paying obeisance to the norm while engaging in variant behavior. All of these devices, however, add up to and result in a widespread scapegoating of the poor.

The erosion of the Protestant Ethic in fact has not yet been accompanied by its erosion in ideology. Despite the fact that Gurin found that only about one-quarter of all workers are satisfied with their jobs; Kornhauser's findings of widespread low self-esteem, low morale, and general dissatisfaction with life among industrial workers; and Dubin's report that only 9 per cent of workers find their preferred associations in their work places, America continues to be ostensibly a work-oriented society, and consequently doubts about work and fantasies concerning not working must be repressed. Since the doubts exist, they are projected onto those who are fantasized as not only holding such doubts, but acting upon them. Thus, the elements of scapegoating are all present: desires, guilt, repression or denial, and projection.

The great American scapegoat thus becomes the mythical figure of the happy, conniving poor who live without work, enjoying guiltless leisure, sexual freedom, immunity from laws and morals, exemption from obligations, and total lack of anxieties or fears for the future. The fact that this picture of the culture of poverty resembles no poor people who have been found or studied —and, indeed, is a travesty on the tense, bitter, anxious, humiliated people who make up the majority of the poor—does not affect the process of scapegoating. Once assigned these desired/reprehensible characteristics, the poor can be punished, changed, charged, victimized, and isolated—exactly what society has proceeded to do. There seems to be no other comprehensible explanation for the spectacle of members of Congress laughing, jeering, making bad puns, and shouting down a minor bill to help control rats in ghettos, other than as a ritual to exorcise their own guilt feelings concerning the treatment of the poor. On a more sedate level, the amendment to the Social Security bill passed by the 1967 Congress which undertook to deprive children of support due to the presumed immorality of their mothers (the basic and latent issue involved) was another example of projecting attitudes and behaviors onto the poor, and then penalizing them as a result. Similarly, many of the proposals for income maintenance programs, including a guaranteed minimum income, suggest amounts insufficient to make up the individual's poverty gap in order to ensure work incentives. In effect, such programs propose to ensure that five million people will continue to work for salaries below the subsistence level (even if they work full-time and year-round). Nor is this semislavery enough to punish the scapegoats—another thirty million poor will be deprived of full subsistence, defined as twenty-two cents per meal.

Scapegoating obviously says more about those who indulge in the activity than it does about their helpless victims, for it is central to this phenomenon that the things of which the victims are accused are the denied feelings of the accusers. The widespread accusation that the poor will not work if guaranteed their subsistence otherwise, indicates an equally widespread doubt about the necessity, justice, and efficacy of our present economic system, in which income is tied to work, and the only value which a human being has is as a means of production. The adoption of some sort of income distribution system based upon man's existence, rather than his productivity, may be closer than it seems, not in spite of the vociferous opposition which it invokes, but because of it.

If the tendency to scapegoat the poor is overcome, and a full-subsistence income guarantee were to be adopted, then it would be important that its philosophic basis and implications be recognized and accepted, in order to avoid even more turbulence as the behavior conflicts with the norm. Consequently, it would seem that the guarantee of a decent level of living would have to be promulgated as the social right of every American, tied to no condition other than need, and specifically not linked to previous or present work record. This right might have to be written into the law in a way that would be enforceable in the courts.

In addition, overt and covert pressures to induce people to work, rather than accept the guarantee, would have to be replaced by a public and announced determination to pursue automation with all possible vigor, in order to free as many people as possible from the burden of unnecessary work. The utilization of the income tax mechanism, as has been suggested, might place the guarantee on a par with tax payments, not only avoiding some of the problems of application, investigation, and stigmatization, but reducing the amount of contact with administrators and clerical personnel who might indicate that accepting an income guarantee, rather than working for subsubsistence wages, is reprehensible. Further, a major part of the activities of social workers and other guidance personnel would have to include helping people to adjust to nonwork, to accept it with equanimity, and to learn not only to enjoy, but to cherish, this new freedom.

For long enough now, we have scapegoated the poor due to our own unacknowledged doubts about the need for human physical labor in America. It is time that we admitted that the Protestant Ethic does not fit the age of cybernation, space probes, and ultimate weapons, and got on with the task enunciated by Harry Hopkins (Sherwood, 1948, p. 21) almost thirty years ago:

> We have got to find a way of living in America in which every person in it shares in the national income, in such a way that poverty in America is abolished. There is no reason why the people of America should dwell in poverty. A way must be found, and a way will be found.

References

AMORY, C. *The Proper Bostonians*. New York: Dutton, 1947.

ARENDT, H. *The Human Condition*. Chicago: University of Chicago Press, 1958.

BAILEY, D. H. "Benefits of Corruption in India." *Western Political Quarterly*, 1966.

BARLOW, R., BRAZER, H. E., AND MORGAN, J. N. *Economic Behavior of the Affluent*. Washington: Brookings Institution, 1966.

BATES, M. "On Being Mean." *The American Scholar*, 1966/67, *36*, 66.

BECKER, H. S. *Outsiders: Studies in the Sociology of Deviance*. New York: Fress Press, 1963.

BECKER, J. M. *The Problem of Abuse in Unemployment Benefits*. New York: Columbia University Press, 1953.

BECKER, J. M. *The Adequacy of the Benefit Amount in Unemployment Insurance*. Kalamazoo, Mich.: Upjohn Institute, 1961.

BECKER, J. M. "The Adequacy of Benefits in Unemployment Insurance." In J. M. Becker (Ed.), *In Aid of the Unemployed*. Baltimore: Johns Hopkins Press, 1965.

227

BELL, D. "The Study of the Future." *The Public Interest,* 1965, *1,* 128.

Benefit Exhaustion: Benefit Year 1962. Olympia, Wash.: Employment Security Department, State of Washington, 1964.

BENNETT, F. "The Condition of Farm Workers." In L. A. Ferman, J. L. Kornbluh, and A. Haber (Eds.), *Poverty in America.* Ann Arbor: University of Michigan Press, 1965.

BERLINER, J. S. *Some Aspects of Poverty in the United States: Dependency and Poverty.* Waltham, Mass.: Brandeis University, 1965.

BERNARD, S. E. *Fatherless Families: Their Economic and Social Adjustment.* Waltham, Mass.: Brandeis University, 1964.

BERNE, E. *Games People Play.* New York: Grove, 1964.

BIDERMAN, H. D. "Sequels to a Military Career: The Retired Military Professional." In M. Janowitz (Ed.), *The New Military.* New York: Wiley, 1967.

BIRD, C. *The Invisible Scar.* New York: Pocket Books, 1967.

BOOKBINDER, H. "Work Histories of Men Leaving a Short Life Span Occupation." *Personnel and Guidance Journal,* 1955, *34,* 169.

BREHM, C. "The Demand for General Assistance Payments: Reply." *The American Economic Review,* 1967, *58,* 585.

BREHM, C. T., AND SAVING, T. R. "The Demand for General Assistance Payments." *The American Economic Review,* 1964, *54,* 1002.

BREUL, F. R. "Early History of Aid to the Unemployed in the United States." In J. M. Becker (Ed.), *In Aid of the Unemployed.* Baltimore: Johns Hopkins Press, 1965.

BROWN, S. D. "The American Philosophy of Social Insurance." *Social Service Review,* 1956, *30,* 268.

BUCKINGHAM, W. *Automation.* New York: Mentor, 1961.

BURGESS, M. E., AND PRICE, D. O. *An American Dependency Challenge.* Chicago: American Public Welfare Association, 1963.

BURKE, K. *Permanence and Change.* New York: Bobbs-Merrill, 1965.

BURNS, E. M. "The Determinants of Policy." In J. M. Becker (Ed.), *In Aid of the Unemployed.* Baltimore: Johns Hopkins Press, 1965.

BURNS, E. M. "Tomorrow's Social Needs and Social Work Education." *Journal of Education for Social Work,* 1966, *2,* 11.

BURNS, E. M. *Needed Changes in Welfare Programs.* Los Angeles: University of California Institute of Government and Public Affairs, 1967.

BUSSE, E. W. "Psychoneurotic Reactions and Defense Mechanisms in the Aged." In P. H. Hock and J. Zabin (Eds.), *Psychopathology of Aging.* New York: Grune and Stratton, 1961.

CALLAHAN, B. "The Migrant Worker." *Hospital Process*, 1965, 68.

CAPLOVITZ, D. *The Poor Pay More*. New York: Free Press, 1963.

CAPLOW, T. *The Sociology of Work*. New York: McGraw-Hill, 1954.

CAREY, J. B. "Labor's Stake." *The Challenge of Automation*. Washington: Public Affairs Press, 1955.

CAUDILL, H. "Reflections on Poverty in America." In H. B. Shostak and W. Gomberg (Eds.), *New Perspectives on Poverty*. Englewood Cliffs: Prentice-Hall, 1965.

CLEVELAND, H., MANGONE, G. J., AND ADAMS, J. C. *The Overseas Americans*. New York: McGraw-Hill, 1960.

CLOWARD, R. A., AND OHLIN, L. *Delinquency and Opportunity: A Theory of Delinquent Gangs*. New York: Free Press, 1960.

COLLINS, L. S. "Public Assistance Expenditures in the United States." In O. Eckstein (Ed.), *Studies in the Economics of Income Maintenance*. Washington: Brookings Institution, 1967.

CONLISK, J. "Simple Dynamic Effects in Work Leisure Choice: A Skeptical Comment on the Static Theory." *The Journal of Human Resources*, 1968, *3*, 324.

Continuing Disability Experience: Cessation of Disability, 1959. Washington: Bureau of Old Age and Survivors Insurance, Division of Disability Operations, Social Security Administration, United States Department of Health, Education, and Welfare, 1961.

COSER, L. A. "The Sociology of Poverty." *Social Problems*, 1965, *12*, 141.

CUNNINGHAM, R. L. *The Philosophy of Work*. New York: National Association of Manufacturers, 1964.

Current Population Reports, Series P-27. No. 35. Farm Population of the United States, 1964. Washington: Government Printing Office, 1965. (a)

Current Population Reports, Series P-60, No. 47. Income in the United States. Washington: Government Printing Office, 1965. (b)

Current Population Reports, Series P-27. No. 37. Farm Population. Washington: Government Printing Office, 1967.

CYERT, R. M., AND MARCH, J. G. *A Behavioral Theory of the Firm*. Englewood Cliffs: Prentice-Hall, 1963.

DAHL, R. H., AND LINDBLOM, C. E. *Politics, Economics and Social Welfare*. New York: Harper, 1953.

DAVIS, H. "The Motivation of the Underprivileged Worker." In W. F. Whyte (Ed.), *Industry and Society*. New York: McGraw-Hill, 1946.

DAVIS, K. "Some Demographic Aspects of Poverty in the United States." In M. S. Gordon (Ed.), *Poverty in America*. San Francisco: Chandler, 1965.

230 Incentives to Work

DE GRAZIA, S. *Of Time, Work and Leisure.* New York: Twentieth Century Fund, 1962.

DENTLER, R. A., AND WARSHAUER, M. E. *Big City Dropouts and Illiterates.* New York: Center for Urban Education, 1965.

DEUTSCHER, I. "Words and Deeds: Social Science and Social Policy." *Social Problems,* 1966, *8,* 235.

DIRKS, L. E. "The Poor Who Live Among Us." In H. B. Shostak and W. Gomberg (Eds.), *New Perspectives on Poverty.* Englewood Cliffs: Prentice-Hall, 1965.

The Disability Insurance Program under Social Security. Washington: Staff Memo to Advisory Council, 1963.

The Disabled Worker under OASDI. Washington: Social Security Administration, United States Department of Health, Education, and Welfare, 1964.

DREW, E. B. "HEW Grapples with PPBS." *The Public Interest,* 1967, *8,* 11.

DUBIN, R. *The World of Work.* Englewood Cliffs: Prentice-Hall, 1958.

DUBIN, R. "Industrial Workers' Worlds: A Study of the Central Life Interests of Industrial Workers." In A. M. Rose (Ed.), *Human Behavior and Social Processes.* London: Routledge and Kegan Paul, 1962.

DUNMORE, C. J. *Social-Psychological Factors Affecting the Use of an Educational Opportunity Program by Families Living in a Poverty Area.* Waltham, Mass.: Brandeis University, 1967.

ECKSTEIN, O. *Studies in the Economics of Income Maintenance.* Washington: The Brookings Institution, 1967.

ELLIS, R. W. *Is Automation Causing Unemployment?* New York: National Association of Manufacturers, n. d.

ELMAN, R. M. *The Poorhouse State.* New York: Pantheon, 1966.

Employment Incentives and Social Services: A Demonstration Program in Public Welfare. Cleveland: Cuyahoga County Welfare Department, 1966.

Employment Security Review, 1955, *22,* 57–58.

ENGEL, M. H. *A Reconceptualization of Urban Lower Class Subcultures.* New York: Fordham University, 1966.

EPSTEIN, L. A. "Unmet Needs in a Land of Abundance." *Social Security Bulletin,* 1963, *26,* 5.

FERMAN, L. A., KORNBLUH, J. L., AND HABER, A. (Eds.), *Poverty in America.* Ann Arbor: University of Michigan Press, 1965.

FERNBACH, F. L. "Policies Affecting Income Distribution." In M. S. Gordon (Ed.), *Poverty in America.* San Francisco: Chandler, 1965.

FESTINGER, L. *A Theory of Cognitive Dissonance.* Evanston: Row Peterson, 1957.

FIELD, M. G. "Structured Strain in the Role of the Soviet Physician." *American Journal of Sociology*, 1953, *63*, 493.

FOLSOM, M. B. "Measures to Reduce Poverty." In M. S. Gordon (Ed.), *Poverty in America*. San Francisco: Chandler, 1965.

FREUD, S. *Civilization and Its Discontents*. New York: Paperback, 1958.

FRIEDENBERG, E. Z. "Neo-Freudianism and Erich Fromm." *Commentary*, 1962, *34*, 389.

FRIEDLANDER, W. A. *Individualism and Social Welfare*. New York: Free Press, 1962.

FRIEDMAN, M. *Capitalism and Freedom*. Chicago: University of Chicago Press, 1962.

FRIEDMANN, E. A., AND HAVIGHURST, R. J. *The Meaning of Work and Retirement*. Chicago: University of Chicago Press, 1954.

FRIEDMANN, G. *The Anatomy of Work*. New York: Free Press, 1964.

FULLER, V. "Rural Poverty and Rural Area Development." In M. S. Gordon (Ed.), *Poverty in America*. San Francisco: Chandler, 1965.

GALBRAITH, J. R. *The Affluent Society*. New York, Houghton Mifflin, 1958.

GALLOWAY, L. E. "The Aged and the Extent of Poverty in the United States." *The Southern Economic Journal*, 1966, *32*, 212.

GANS, H. H. "Income Grants and 'Dirty Work.' " *The Public Interest*, 1967, *6*, 110.

GEIGER, G. "Values and Social Science." In W. G. Bennis, K. Benne, and R. Chin (Eds.), *The Planning of Change*. New York: Holt, 1964.

GILBERT, C. E. "Policy Making in Public Welfare: The 1962 Amendments." *Political Science Quarterly*, 1966, *81*, 215.

GINZBERG, E. (Ed.) *Technology and Social Change*. New York: Columbia University Press, 1964.

GLAZER, N. "A Sociologist's View of Poverty." In M. S. Gordon (Ed.), *Poverty in America*. San Francisco: Chandler, 1965.

GOFFMAN, E. *The Presentation of Self in Everyday Life*. Garden City: Doubleday, 1959.

GOLDBERG, A. J. "Address by the Secretary of Labor." *Public Welfare*, 1962, *20*, 6.

GOODMAN, L. H. (Ed.) *Economic Progress and Social Welfare*. New York: Columbia University Press, 1966.

GORDON, J. *The Poor of Harlem: Social Functioning in the Underclass*. New York: Office of the Mayor, 1965.

GORDON, M. S. *The Economics of Welfare Policies*. New York: Columbia University Press, 1963.

GORDON, M. S. "Poverty and Income Maintenance for the Unemployed." In M. S. Gordon (Ed.), *Poverty in America*. San Francisco: Chandler, 1965.

GORDON, R. A. "An Economist's View of Poverty." In M. S. Gordon (Ed.), *Poverty in America*. San Francisco: Chandler, 1965.

GRAHAME, D. F. *Social Security Hearings before the Committee on Finance, United States Senate, Eighty-ninth Congress, First Session, on H. R. 6675*. Washington: United States Government Printing Office, 1965.

GREEN, C. *Negative Taxes and the Poverty Problem*. Washington: Brookings Institution, 1967.

GURIN, G., VEROOF, J., AND FELD, S. *Americans View Their Mental Health*. New York: Basic Books, 1960.

HALLECK, S. "The Impact of Professional Dishonesty on Behavior of Disturbed Adolescents." *Social Work*, 1963, *8*, 48.

HALM, J. *The Relationship of Field Articulation and Affective Placebo Reactions.* New York: Yeshiva University, 1967. (Unpublished Ph.D. Dissertation.)

HANSEN, M. H., AND CARTER, G. W. "Assessing Effectiveness of Methods for Meeting Social and Economic Problems." In L. H. Goodman (Ed.), *Economic Progress and Social Welfare*. New York: Columbia University Press, 1966.

HANSEN, M. L. "The Problems of the Third Generation." *Commentary*, 1952, *14*, 493.

HARRINGTON, M. *The Other America*. New York: Macmillan, 1963.

HAUSMAN, L. J. *The 100% Welfare Tax Rate: Its Incidence and Effects*. University of Wisconsin, 1967, Ph.D. Dissertation.

Hawaii's Unemployed Pensioners. Honolulu: Hawaii State Department of Labor and Industrial Relations, 1964.

Health and Welfare Indicators. Washington: United States Department of Health, Education, and Welfare, 1966.

HEAP, K. "The Scapegoat Role in Youth Groups." *Case Conference*, 1966.

HERZBERG, F. *Work and the Nature of Man*. Cleveland: World, 1966.

HERZBERG, F., MAUSNER, B., AND SNYDERMAN, B. B. *The Motivation to Work*. New York: Wiley, 1959.

HILL, W. F. "Activity as an Autonomous Drive." *Journal of Comparative and Physiological Psychology*, 1956, *49*, 15.

HIMES, J. S. "Some Work-Related Cultural Deprivations of Lower Class Negro Youths." In L. A. Ferman, J. L. Kornbluh, and A. Haber (Eds.), *Poverty in America*. Ann Arbor: University of Michigan Press, 1965.

HIRSCH, R. G. *There Shall Be No Poor*. New York: Union of American Hebrew Congregations, 1965.

HOMANS, G. C. *The Human Group*. London: Routledge and Kegan Paul, 1951.

HOROVITZ, S. B. "Rehabilitation of Injured Workers: Its Legal and Administrative Problems." *Rocky Mountain Law Review*, 1959, *31*, 496.

HOROWITZ, I. L. (Ed.) *The Rise and Fall of Project Camelot*. Cambridge: MIT, 1967.

House Committee Print Number 291. Eighty-ninth Congress, Second Session, Part B, September 12, 1956. Washington: Government Printing Office, 1956.

HOWARD, D. S. "Discussion of the Strategy of Social Policy Research." *Social Welfare Forum, 1963*. New York: Columbia University Press, 1963.

HYMAN, H. H. "The Value Systems of Different Classes: A Social Psychological Contribution to the Analysis of Stratification." In R. Bendix and S. M. Lipset (Eds.), *Class, Status, and Power*. Glencoe: Free Press, 1953.

The Incentive Budgeting Demonstration Project. Denver: Denver Department of Welfare, 1961.

IRELAN, L. M., AND BESNER, H. "Low Income Outlook on Life." In L. M. Irelan (Ed.), *Low Income Life Styles*. Washington: Division of Research, Welfare Administration, United States Department of Health, Education, and Welfare, n. d.

IRELAN, L. M., MOLES, O. C., AND O'SHEA, R. *Ethnicity, Poverty and Selected Attitudes: An Exploration of the "Culture of Poverty" Hypothesis*. Atlanta, Georgia: Southern Sociological Society, 1967.

JACOBS, P. *Dead Horse and the Featherbird*. Santa Barbara: Center for the Study of Democratic Institutions, 1962.

JAFFE, A. J. (Ed.) *Research Conference on Workman's Compensation and Vocational Rehabilitation*. New York: Columbia University Press, 1961.

JAFFE, A. J., DAY, L. H., AND ADAMS, W. *Disabled Workers in the Labor Market*. Totowa, N.J.: Bedminster Press, 1964.

KAGAN, J., AND BERKUN, M. "The Reward Value of Running Activity." *Journal of Comparative and Physiological Psychology*, 1954, *47*, 108.

KAHN, A. J. "Social Services in Relation to Income Security: Introductory Notes." *Social Service Review*, 1965, *39*, 388.

KANE, R. D. *The Community Agency's Role in Comprehensive Manpower Programs—Planning and Problems*. New York: New York University, 1966.

KAPLAN, M. *Leisure in America: A Social Inquiry*. New York: Wiley, 1960.

KASPAR, H. *Welfare Payments and Work Incentives: The General*

Assistance Program. Madison, Wisc.: University of Wisconsin Press, 1967.

KATONA, G., MUELLER, E., SCHMIEDESKAMP, J., AND SONQUIST, J. S. *1966 Survey of Consumer Finances.* Ann Arbor: University of Michigan Press, 1967.

KATZ, D. *Group Process and Social Interaction.* Ann Arbor: University of Michigan, n.d., mimeograph.

KERSHAW, J. H. "The Attack on Poverty." In M. S. Gordon, *Poverty in America.* San Francisco: Chandler, 1965.

KIMMEL, P. R. *Identification and Modification of Social-Psychological Correlates of Economic Dependency.* Washington: Welfare Administration, Department of Health, Education, and Welfare, 1966.

KLEIN, W. A. "Some Basic Problems of Negative Income Taxation." *Wisconsin Law Review,* 1966, *3,* 23.

KORNHAUSER, H. *Mental Health of the Industrial Worker.* New York: Wiley, 1965.

KREPS, J. M. "Automation and Unemployment." In *Social Welfare Forum, 1963.* New York: Columbia University Press, 1963.

KROEBER, A. L., AND KLUCKHOLM, C. *Culture: A Critical Review of Concepts and Definitions.* Cambridge: Harvard University Press, 1952.

KRONICK, J. C. *Attitudes toward Dependency: A Study of A.F.D.C. Mothers.* Bryn Mawr, Pa.: Bryn Mawr College, 1963.

KRONICK, J. C. *Family Life and Economic Dependency.* Bryn Mawr, Pa.: Bryn Mawr College, 1965.

KROSNEY, H. *Beyond Welfare: Poverty in the Supercity.* New York: Holt, Rinehart and Winston, 1966.

KWANT, R. C. *Philosophy of Labor.* Pittsburgh: Duquesne University Press, 1960.

LAGEY, J. C. *Population Data and Community Self-Surveys for the Planning and Operating of Youth Work Programs.* New York: New York University Press, 1966.

LAMPMAN, R. J. *Negative Rates Income Taxation.* Washington: Office of Economic Opportunity, 1965.

LANGER, H. C., JR. *The Fight for Work.* New York: Pageant, 1965.

LAWLER, E. E. "How Much Money Do Executives Want?" *Transaction,* 1967, *4,* 23.

LERNER, M. *America as a Civilization.* New York: Simon and Schuster, 1957.

LESTER, R. A. "The Nature and Level of Income Security for a Free Society." In J. E. Russell (Ed.), *National Policies for Education, Health, and Social Services.* Garden City: Doubleday, 1955.

LEVENSON, B., AND MCDILL, M. S. "Vocational Graduates in Auto

Mechanics: A Follow-Up Study of Negro and White Youth."
Phylon, 1966, *27,* 347.

LEVITAN, S. A. *Programs in Aid of the Poor.* Kalamazoo: Upjohn
Institute for Employment Research, 1965.

LEVITAN, S. A. "The Pitfalls of Guaranteed Income." *U.S. News and
World Report,* May 18, 1967.

LEWIS, H. *Child Rearing Among Low Income Families.* Washington:
Center for Metropolitan Studies, 1961.

LEWIS, L. S., AND BRISSETT, D. "Sex as Work: A Study of Avocational
Counseling." *Social Problems,* 1967, *15,* 8.

LEWIS, O. *The Children of Sanchez.* New York: Random House, 1961.

LEWIS, O. "The Culture of Poverty," *Scientific American,* 1966, *215,*
19.

LEWIS, V. S. "Stephen Humphreys Gurteen and the American Origins
of Charity Organization." *Social Service Review,* 1966, *40,* 191.

LICHTMAN, R. *Toward Community.* Santa Barbara: Center for the
Study of Democratic Institutions, 1966.

LIPSET, S. M., AND BENDIX, R. *Social Mobility in Industrial Society.*
Berkeley: University of California Press, 1959.

LONG, N. E. "The Local Community as an Ecology of Games." In R.
L. Warren (Ed.), *Perspectives on the American Community.*
Chicago: Rand McNally, 1966.

The Low Paid Worker. AFL-CIO Department of Research. In L. A.
Ferman, J. L. Kornbluh, and A. Haber (Eds.), *Poverty in
America.* Ann Arbor: University of Michigan Press, 1965.

LYND, R., AND LYND, H. M. *Middletown.* New York: Harcourt Brace,
1929.

LYND, R., AND LYND, H. M. *Middletown in Transition.* New York: Harcourt Brace, 1937.

MACDONALD, D. "Our Invisible Poor." *New Yorker,* January 19, 1963.

MCFARLAND, K. "Why Men and Women Get Fired." *Personnel Journal,*
1957, *25,* 307.

MACHLUP, E. "Strategies in the War on Poverty." In M. S. Gordon
(Ed.), *Poverty in America.* San Francisco: Chandler, 1965.

MAISONPIERRE, H. *Systems in Collision.* Atlanta: Georgia State College,
1965.

*Major Findings of 16 State Studies of Claimants Exhausting Unem-
ployment Benefit Rights: 1956–1959.* Washington: United
States Department of Labor, 1961.

MANGUM, G. L. *The Manpower Revolution.* Garden City: Doubleday,
1965.

MARTIN, J. M. *Lower-Class Delinquency and Work Programs.* New
York: New York University Press, 1966.

MASLOW, A. H. *Motivation and Personality.* New York: Harper, 1954.

MASSIE, W. K. *Social Security Hearings before the Committee on Finance, United States Senate, Eighty-ninth Congress, First Session, on H. R. 6675.* Washington: United States Government Printing Office, 1965.

MAUCH, J. E., AND DENENMARK, F. *Educational Deficiencies of Disadvantaged Youth.* New York: New York University Press, 1966.

MAY, E. *The Wasted Americans.* New York: Harper, 1964.

MERTON, R. K. *Social Theory and Social Structure.* New York: Free Press, 1949.

MERTON, R. K., AND KITT, A. S. "Contributions to the Theory of Reference Group Behavior." In R. K. Merton and P. F. Lazarsfeld, *Continuities in Social Research.* Glencoe: Free Press, 1950.

MESSER, E. A. "Thirty-Eight Years is a Plenty." *Civil Service Journal,* October/December, 1964, 24.

Methods of Adjusting to Automation and Technological Change. Washington: United States Department of Labor, n. d.

MILLER, H. P. *Rich Man, Poor Man.* New York: Crowell, 1964.

MILLER, H. P. "Changes in the Number and Composition of the Poor." In M. S. Gordon (Ed.), *Poverty in America.* San Francisco: Chandler, 1965.

MILLER, H. P. *Income Distribution in the United States.* Washington: United States Department of Commerce, 1966.

MILLER, S. M. "The American Lower Classes: A Typological Approach." In H. B. Shostak and W. Gomberg (Eds.), *New Perspectives on Poverty.* Englewood Cliffs: Prentice-Hall, 1965.

MILLER, S. M., AND HARRISON, I. E. "Types of Dropouts: 'The Unemployables.'" In H. B. Shostak and W. Gomberg (Eds.), *Blue-Collar World.* Englewood Cliffs: Prentice-Hall, 1964.

MINSKY, H. P. "The Role of Employment Policy." In M. S. Gordon (Ed.), *Poverty in America.* San Francisco: Chandler, 1965.

MOED, M. *Increasing the Employability of Youth: The Role of Training.* New York: New York University, 1966.

MOORE, W. E. *Industrialization and Labor.* Ithaca: Cornell University Press, 1951.

MORGAN, J. N., DAVID, M. H., COHEN, W. J., AND BRAZER, H. E. *Income and Welfare in the United States.* New York: McGraw-Hill, 1962.

MORGAN, J. N., SNIDER, M., AND SOBOL, M. G. *Lump-Sum Redemption Settlements and Rehabilitation.* Ann Arbor: University of Michigan Press, 1959.

MUELLER, E., AND SCHMIEDESKAMP, J. *Persistent Unemployment.* Kalamazoo: Upjohn Institute for Employment Research, 1962.

MURRAY, M. G. "Unemployment Insurance: Risks Covered and Their

Financing." In J. H. Becker (Ed.), *In Aid of the Unemployed.* Baltimore: Johns Hopkins Press, 1965.

MUSGRAVE, R. *The Theory of Public Finance.* New York: McGraw-Hill, 1959.

MYRDAL, G. "A Summing Up." In M. S. Gordon (Ed.), *Poverty in America.* San Francisco: Chandler, 1965.

NAGI, S. Z. *Disability and Rehabilitation.* Columbus, Ohio: Ohio State University, 1967, mimeograph.

NATHAN, R. R. "Social Planning for Economic Abundance." In L. H. Goodman (Ed.), *Economic Progress and Social Welfare.* New York: Columbia University Press, 1966.

1960 Census of Population Classified Index of Occupations and Industries. Washington: United States Department of Commerce, 1960.

NOSOW, S., AND FORM, W. H. (Eds.), *Man, Work and Society.* New York: Basic Books, 1962.

Operation Fairplay. Topeka, Kans.: State Department of Social Welfare, 1967.

ORNATI, O. "Affluence and the Risk of Poverty." *Social Research,* 1964, *31,* 334.

ORSHANSKY, M. "Counting the Poor: Another Look at the Poverty Profile." In L. A. Ferman, J. L. Kornbluh, and A. Haber (Eds.), *Poverty in America.* Ann Arbor: University of Michigan Press, 1965. (a)

ORSHANSKY, M. "Who's Who Among the Poor." *Social Security Bulletin,* 1965, *28,* 3. (b)

ORSHANSKY, M. "More About the Poor in 1964." *Social Security Bulletin,* 1966, *29,* 3.

OVERS, R. P. "Domestic Household Worker Problem Needs Research." *Employment Service Review,* 1967, *4,* 1.

PARRINGTON, V. L. *Main Currents in American Thought.* New York: Harcourt Brace, 1927.

PARSONS, T. "General Theory in Sociology." In R. Merton, L. Broom, and L. S. Cottrell (Eds.), *Sociology Today.* New York: Basic Books, 1959.

PARSONS, G., AND SHILS, E. A. *Toward a General Theory of Action.* New York: Harper, 1962.

PERLIS, L. "The Constructive Use of Free Time." *The Shorter Work Week and the Constructive Use of Free Time.* New York: AFL-CIO, 1963.

PERRY, R. B. *Realms of Value: A Critique of Human Civilization.* Cambridge: Harvard University Press, 1954.

PFOUTS, J. H. *Vocational History of 309 Arm, Leg, and Bilateral Amputees of World War II.* Baltimore: Veterans Administration Outpatient Clinic, n. d.

POLIER, H. W. "The Invisible Legal Rights of the Poor." *Children,* 1965, *12,* 215.

Program and Operating Statistics. Welfare in Review, 1967, *5,* 28.

PUMPHREY, R. E. "Social Welfare in the United States." *Encyclopedia of Social Work.* New York: National Association of Social Workers, 1965.

PURCELL, F. P. *Low Income Youth, Unemployment, Vocational Training and the Job Corps.* New York: New York University Press, 1966.

PUSIC, E. *Reappraisal of the United Nations Social Service Programme: Report of the Secretary General.* New York: United Nations, 1965.

RAINWATER, L. *And the Poor Get Children.* Chicago: Quadrangle, 1960.

RAINWATER, L., AND YANCEY, W. L. *The Moynihan Report and the Politics of Controversy.* Cambridge: MIT, 1967.

REISS, A. J., JR. *Occupations and Social Status.* New York: Free Press, 1961.

RHYS WILLIAMS, J. *Something to Look Forward To.* London: Longmans Green, 1943.

RIBICOFF, A. *Testimony before the Appropriations Committee, House of Representatives.* Washington: United States Government Printing Office, 1963.

RICHARDS, L. G. "Consumer Practices of the Poor." In L. M. Irelan (Ed.), *Low Income Life Styles.* Washington: Division of Research, Welfare Administration, United States Department of Health, Education, and Welfare, n. d.

RICHARDSON, J. H. *Economic and Financial Aspects of Social Security.* Toronto: University of Toronto, 1960.

RIMLINGER, G. V. "Social Security, Incentives, and Controls in the U.S. and the U.S.S.R." In M. N. Zald (Ed.), *Social Welfare Institutions.* Wiley: New York, 1965.

RODMAN, H. "On Understanding Lower Class Behavior." *Social and Economic Studies,* 1959, *8,* 441.

RODMAN, H. "The Lower Class Value Stretch." *Social Forces,* 1963, *42,* 205.

RODMAN, H. "Illegitimacy in the Caribbean Social Structure: A Reconsideration." *American Sociological Review,* 1966, *31,* 673.

ROEMMICH, W. "Determination, Evaluation, and Rating of Disabilities under the Social Security System." *Industrial Medicine and Surgery,* 1961, *30,* 60.

ROETHLISBERGER, F. S., AND DICKSON, W. J. *Management and the Worker.* Cambridge: Harvard University Press, 1939.

SALZBERGER, L., AND SHAPIRA, M. *A Study of Two Groups of Rehabilitees in Terms of Selective Factors Influencing Movement*

Towards Gainful Employment and Job Tenure. Jerusalem: Paul Baerwald School of Social Work, The Hebrew University, 1966.

SCHORR, A. L. *Social Security and Social Services in France.* Washington: United States Department of Health, Education, and Welfare, 1965.

SCHORR, A. L. "On Selfish Children and Lonely Parents." *The Public Interest,* 1966, *4,* 8.

SCHOTTLAND, C. I. "Poverty and Income Maintenance for the Aged." In M. S. Gordon (Ed.), *Poverty in America.* San Francisco: Chandler, 1965.

SCHULTZ, T. W. "Our Welfare State and the Welfare of Farm People." *Social Service Review,* 1964, *38,* 123.

SCHUMPETER, J. A. *Capitalism, Socialism and Democracy.* New York: Harper, 1942.

SCHWARTZ, E. E. "A Way to End the Means Test." *Social Work,* 1964, *4,* 3.

SCOTT, J. C. *The Poor as Reporters: Some Problems of Data Gathering Related to Poverty.* Ann Arbor: University of Michigan Press, 1966.

Seminars on Private Adjustments to Automation and Technological Change. Washington: President's Advisory Committee on Labor-Management Policy, 1964.

SHERWOOD, R. E. *Roosevelt and Hopkins.* New York: Harper, 1948.

SHOSTAK, H. B., AND GOMBERG, W. (Eds.), *New Perspectives on Poverty.* Englewood Cliffs: Prentice-Hall, 1965.

SHYNE, A. W. *Comments on Chemung County Study.* Unpublished.

SILLS, D. L. "The Succession of Goals." In A. Etzioni (Ed.), *Complex Organizations.* New York: Holt, Rinehart and Winston, 1965.

SIMMEL, G. "The Poor." (Trans. C. Jacobson.) *Social Problems,* 1965, *13,* 123.

SMITH, A. D. *The Right to Life.* Chapel Hill: University of North Carolina Press, 1955.

SMITH, M. "An Empirical Scale of Prestige Status of Occupations." In S. Nosow and W. H. Form (Eds.), *Man, Work and Society.* New York: Basic Books, 1962.

SMITH, R. E. "In Defense of Public Welfare." *Social Work,* 1966, *11,* 97.

SMOLENSKIN, E. *The Past and Present Poor: The Concept of Poverty.* Washington: United States Chamber of Commerce, 1965.

Social Security in France. Paris: Ministere du Travail, 1964.

Social Security Hearings before the Committee on Finance, United States Senate, Eighty-ninth Congress, First Session, on H. R. 6675. Washington: United States Government Printing Office, 1965.

Social Work, 1965, *4, 2.*

SOMERS, H. M. "Poverty and Income Maintenance for the Disabled."
    In M. S. Gordon (Ed.), *Poverty in America*. San Francisco:
    Chandler, 1965.
A Statement on Adaptation to Free Time: The New Social Frontier.
    New York: National Advisory Committee to the AFL-CIO
    Community Services Committee, 1963.
STEIN, H. D. (Ed.), *Planning for the Needs of Children in Developing
    Countries*. New York: UNICEF, 1964.
STEIN, R., AND ALBIN, P. S. "The Demand for General Assistance Pay-
    ments." *The American Economic Review*, 1967, *57*, 585.
STEIN, R. L. "Work History, Attitudes, and Income of the Unem-
    ployed." In S. Lebergott (Ed.), *Men Without Work*. Engle-
    wood Cliffs: Prentice-Hall, 1964.
STEINER, G. Y. *Social Insecurity: The Politics of Welfare*. Chicago:
    Rand McNally, 1966.
STOUFFER, S. H., LUMSDAINE, A. A., LUMSDAINE, M. H., WILLIAMS, R. M.,
    JR., SMITH, M. B., JANIS, I. L., STAR, S. A., AND COTTRELL, L. S.,
    JR. *The American Soldier*. Princeton: Princeton University
    Press, 1949.
Study of Overpayment and Fraud. Bismarck, N.D.: North Dakota
    Employment Security Bureau, 1966.
Subemployment in the Slums of Cleveland. Washington: United States
    Department of Labor, n. d.
Summary of Court Decision—Disability. Washington: Medical Ad-
    visory Committee, 1960–1961.
*Summary Data on Operation of O.A.S.I. Vocational Rehabilitation
    Referral Program*. Washington: United States Department of
    Health, Education, and Welfare, 1964.
*Summary of Proceedings: Workshops on the Impact of a Tightening
    Labor Market on the Employability and Employment of Dis-
    advantaged Youth*. New York: New York University Press,
    1966.
TAWNEY, R. H. "Economic Virtues and Prescriptions for Poverty."
    In H. D. Stein and R. A. Cloward (Eds.), *Social Perspectives
    on Behavior*. New York: Free Press, 1958.
THELEN, H. A. *Dynamics of Groups at Work*. Chicago: University of
    Chicago Press, 1954.
THEOBALD, R. *Free Men and Free Markets*. New York: Potter, 1963.
THEOBALD, R. *The Guaranteed Income: The Pressing Need and Key
    Issues*. Speech given before a Leadership Conference on the
    Guaranteed Income, Chicago, 1966.
THOMAS, E. J. "Psychological Dependence and Its Relationship to
    Economic Deprivation." In *Social Welfare Forum 1966*. New
    York: Columbia University Press, 1966.

TILGHER, A. "Work Through the Ages." In S. Nosow and W. H. Form (Eds.), *Man, Work and Society.* New York: Basic Books, 1962.

TOBIN, J. "The Case for an Income Guarantee." *The Public Interest,* 1966, *4,* 33.

TRAFTON, G. H. *Employment and Earning of Self-Employed Workers Under Social Security.* Washington: Division of Research and Statistics, Social Security Administration, United States Department of Health, Education, and Welfare, 1964.

ULMAN, L. "Foreword." In M. S. Gordon (Ed.), *Poverty in America.* San Francisco: Chandler, 1965.

Unemployment in the Boston Urban Employment Survey of 1966. Boston: Research Department, Massachusetts Division of Employment Security, 1966.

Unemployment Insurance and the Family Finances of the Unemployed. Washington: United States Department of Labor, 1961.

Unemployment Insurance Review, March, 1966.

VADAKIAN, J. C. *Family Allowances.* Miami, Fla.: University of Miami Press, 1958.

VEBLEN, T. *The Theory of Leisure Class.* New York: Huebsch, 1918.

VROOM, V. H. *Work and Motivation.* New York: Wiley, 1964.

WALINSKY, H. "Keeping the Poor in Their Place: Notes on the Importance of Being One-up." In H. B. Shostak and W. Gomberg (Eds.), *New Perspectives on Poverty.* Englewood Cliffs: Prentice-Hall, 1965.

WARNER, W. L. *Democracy in Jonesville.* New York: Harper, 1949.

Washington Bulletin. Washington: Social Legislation Information Service, 1966, *19,* 194.

WATTS, H. W. "Introduction." *The Journal of Human Resources,* 1968, *3,* 279.

WEBB, S., AND WEBB, B. *The Prevention of Destitution.* London: National Committee for the Prevention of Destitution, 1911.

WEBER, M., *The Protestant Ethic and the Spirit of Capitalism.* (Trans. T. Parsons.) New York: Scribners, 1952.

WEINBERG, S. L. *Supportive Services in Youth-Work Programs.* New York: New York University Press, 1966.

WEISS, R. S., AND RIESSMAN, D. "Work and Automation: Problems and Prospects." In R. K. Merton and R. A. Nisbet (Eds.), *Contemporary Social Problems.* New York: Harcourt Brace and World, 1966.

WICKENDEN, E. "Welfare Services." In J. M. Becker (Ed.), *In Aid of the Unemployed.* Baltimore: Johns Hopkins Press, 1965.

WICKERSHAM, E. D. *Detroit's Insured Unemployed and Employable Welfare Recipients: Their Characteristics, Labor and Market Experience and Attitudes.* Kalamazoo: The Upjohn Institution for Employment Research, 1963.

WILCOCK, R. C. "Who Are the Unemployed?" In J. M. Becker (Ed.), *In Aid of the Unemployed*. Baltimore: Johns Hopkins Press, 1965.

WILCOCK, R. C., AND FRANKE, W. H. *Unwanted Workers*. New York: Free Press, 1963.

WHYTE, W. F. *Money and Motivation*. New York: Harper, 1955.

WILENSKY, H. L., AND LEBEAUX, C. N. *Industrial Society and Social Welfare*. New York: Free Press, 1958.

WINSTON, E. "Social Welfare Problems in a Changing Society." In *Converging Social Trends—Emerging Social Problems*. Washington: Division of Research, United States Department of Health, Education, and Welfare, n. d.

Workers Who Exhaust Their Unemployment Benefits. Salt Lake City: Utah Department of Employment Security, 1965.

Index